Leadership Explained

T0362183

Unfortunately, leadership does not have a one-size-fits-all definition. We all have our own ideas as to what makes a good leader and the types of challenges that will be faced. The author bridges a gap by presenting how modern leadership happens while simultaneously combining a description of leadership and its practical application in today's environments. In this book, Nicholas Harkiolakis integrates the various theoretical perspectives into a unified model that can be understood by both the academic and the practitioner (existing and future leaders). This understanding is necessary to effectively treat and apply leadership to the challenging settings of today's operational environments: virtual, distributed, multicultural and so on. Some of the key topics covered are:

- leadership through the ages
- characteristics of leadership
- modern perspectives
- an integrated leadership framework
- the application of leadership
- the twenty-first-century leadership practices.

Nicholas Harkiolakis is Vice President for Europe and Middle East and Director of Research for Executive Coaching Consultants. He is Editor of the *International Journal of Teaching and Case Studies* and Associate Editor of the *International Journal of Social Entrepreneurship and Innovation*. He also teaches graduate courses and supervises dissertations at various universities in France, the UK and the US.

Leadership Explained

Leading Teams in the 21st Century

Nicholas Harkiolakis

Routledge
Taylor & Francis Group

LONDON AND NEW YORK

First published 2017 by Routledge

2 Park Square, Milton Park, Abingdon, Oxfordshire OX14 4RN
52 Vanderbilt Avenue, New York, NY 10017

Routledge is an imprint of the Taylor & Francis Group, an informa business

First issued in paperback 2020

British Library Cataloguing in Publication Data
A catalogue record for this book is available from the British Library

Library of Congress Cataloging-in-Publication Data
Names: Harkiolakis, Nicholas, author.
Title: Leadership explained : leading teams in the 21st century /
    Nicholas Harkiolakis.
Description: Abingdon, Oxon ; New York, NY : Routledge, 2017. |
    Includes bibliographical references and index.
Identifiers: LCCN 2016026336| ISBN 9781472469533 (hbk) |
    ISBN 9781315591780 (ebk)
Subjects: LCSH: Leadership. | Teams in the workplace—
    Management.
Classification: LCC HD57.7 .H3674 2017 | DDC 658.4/092—dc23
LC record available at https://lccn.loc.gov/2016026336

ISBN: 978-1-4724-6953-3 (hbk)
ISBN: 978-0-367-60598-8 (pbk)

Typeset in New Baskerville Std
by Swales & Willis Ltd, Exeter, Devon, UK

Contents

Figures

1 Why not another book on leadership?

A classic question that spontaneously pops up when a new text appears on the subject of leadership is what is possibly left for anyone to add to the existing plethora of similar publications. Reversing the question here is meant to bring out the lack of a thorough representation of a social behaviour that we either fail to define appropriately or seem to consistently fail to master its application. While the latter might seem evident from the thousands of years of political and economic conflict, the former is not an insignificant realization and deserves proper attention.

Differentiating between the emergence of the phenomenon and its application will provide some clarity and purpose in accepting a suitable explanation. A phenomenon is something that 'appears' and can be described as a clear and identifiable observation. In that sense individuals have been identified as leaders due to their role and privileges among a group of individuals. The privileges (responsibilities in some respect) can be summed up in terms of control and influence on the group members regarding certain aspects of their lives. In some groups these aspects could be specific and include obedience to laws and the command of the leader, while in others they could be general and more in the form of ideological attraction, like in the case of religion and politics. Whatever the reason, leadership will sprout in most groups almost spontaneously, even if that is a fluctuation from the norm that the many established.

This emergence of leadership begs the question as to whether it is a random or a systematic process. To illustrate the difference, let us consider a physical phenomenon like the flow of sand. If we were to observe the sand as it flows through an hourglass (Figure 1.1), we will see a sand-hill forming in its lower part. One grain of sand will almost always claim the top position. Would that make this grain the leader of the pack? It is in a prominent position, but we will undoubtedly claim that it has arrived there by a totally random process. Remove one (with the exception of the 'leader') and an avalanche will form, making someone else the leader of the new formation. Can we thus say there is something special about the leader grains? Is there something they do to be in that position? All other grains would in general have the same probability of ending up at the top either at that turn of the hourglass or at a future one.

We can safely conclude for this physical process that the choice of 'leader' is totally random and circumstantial, and there is nothing that a grain does to reach that position. Although this example might seem far from the realities of leaders we are familiar with in our social structures, it can very well serve as a baseline of what a leader is: *a randomly acquired, widely visible position with some control over others.* In that sense, anyone can be a leader if the conditions and circumstances are appropriate and bring that

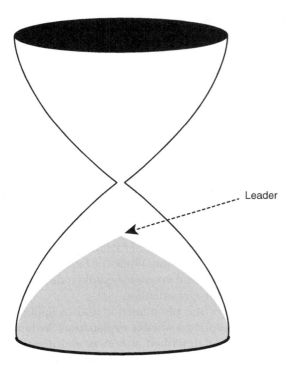

Figure 1.1 The leadership baseline

individual to the top. Imagine now that someone starts heating parts of the sand-hill or blowing air in its direction. The hill will start changing shape because certain grains will have acquired enough energy to move and push other grains around. This dynamic situation will bring new 'leaders' to the top, which in turn will give their place to others and so on as long as there are enough external stimuli to unbalance the stable sand-hill formations. By this analogy, leadership is a role, a statistical possibility that relates to time and place. The place is a group and the time is when an individual becomes the focus of attention.

This mechanistic and seemingly random view of leadership might seem far from the preconceived notions we all have about leaders, but the reality of the phenomenon, as it will hopefully be presented in this book, is not far from this image at certain times. What distinguishes human leaders is the autonomy of their actions, with their constitutions, drives and desires that act to shape their environment and in this way trigger the re-alignment of positions. Eventually, such targeted activity can bring one at the top or, to be fair, at least from a perspective point of view, push others below. The choice of stance, as we will see later on, can make a difference in the type of followers that leaders want to have.

Is leadership, then, a phenomenon or something else? Since it involves visible/observable and identifiable/specific change, by definition it is one. We can also say that it belongs to the class of social phenomena, in distinction to the physical phenomena we observe in nature. Comparing it to a grain of sand might seem contrary to the generally accepted view of leadership as a process with purpose, but it offers a starting baseline for a comparison of the various concepts, theories and frameworks we will discuss. The minimalist definition and description of leadership or, better yet, the lowest form of leadership we will consider is *random leadership*, that is, someone becoming leader through a completely random process. Hereditary leadership could be seen as such a form of leadership as we don't really know 'who' comes out when leaders procreate.

Substituting the position of a grain of sand with social status, and the wind and heat with need, will and qualifications (to name but a few), we can probably end up with a potentially more advanced model for the leadership process. Although this analogy and thinking might signify that this book has already achieved its purpose in explaining leadership, we still have a long way to go, simply because the details and drives of the phenomenon have not yet been understood in a satisfying way that could also be of value to potential and existing leaders. Additionally, our human ability (privilege in some sense) for cognition and meta-cognition can make us arrogant enough to believe that we can easily master an explanation of something that we experience so often like leadership.

1.1 If it was me . . .

It might be hard to find anyone (I personally don't know anyone) who at some time in their life did not say (aloud or in their head) 'if I was the leader, I would have done things differently' (meaning better, of course). This simple recollection proves that we have all been leaders – if not in reality, then at least in our fantasies – and this can be easily explained from our need to be in control in a constantly changing environment. We lead when we raise our children, when we take care of our pets and when we arrange our private space; and in the more extreme sense we lead ourselves when we react to our environment and plan our future actions. The latter might seem counterintuitive, but from the point of view of this book, managing and leading ourselves has all the elements of leadership, as we will see in the following chapters.

One only needs to see leadership from the point of view of arranging our environment to meet our present and future needs. The resources at our disposal can be personal like our wit and strength (both physical and emotional), physical like materials and tools, and natural (different species including humans). Although this formalization of leadership might sound to a professional like management, one can very well say that *leadership is the management of the future*. Of course, any change such as the ascent to leadership doesn't necessarily mean it is a good change. What might initially seem like a solution and a survival practice (having a leader who seems fittest to deliver) might very well end up in *aligning with someone who can promise instead of one who can deliver.*

At this point and before we go into more detail, we need to provide an important clarification. The characteristic of leadership has been interchangeably used with that of pioneer, innovator, revolutionary and influencer among others. Albert Einstein and Vincent van Gogh can easily be classified as such. While the work of these individuals had immense influence on their contemporaries and the future of their field, they cannot be categorized as leaders of a specific group that worked under their command to accomplish their achievement. From the perspective of this book, leadership is a social phenomenon that involves the direct interaction of a designated individual as the authority with control of others in accomplishing a goal.

Contrary to the sand-hill in Figure 1.1, in our societies individual 'grains' can reach the top if fuelled by motivation, persistence, competence and the ability to influence others. By considering leadership as a social activity, we do not in any way exclude the characteristics of pioneer, innovator, revolutionary and influencer (and many others) from those of leaders. In fact, as we will see, many of these attributes are vital for effective leadership and their lack in a number of cases is an indication of inefficient leadership. We simply emphasized here the immediate and social nature of the group as a constituent of leadership.

1.2 The leadership constructs

To understand leadership, we will follow an analytic approach and study the various constituents that synthesize the phenomenon. These need to be autonomous and identifiable elements that, when assembled properly, will reveal the true nature of leadership (like a puzzle that reveals its image when completed). While the dynamics and the internals of leadership might be debated by theorists and practitioners, the physical structures that give rise to leadership are easy to identify. A social setting is obviously the field where leadership emerges. Without a group of people, there will be nothing to lead. For example, groups of one person cannot be counted as groups (although in set theory they can) unless one is considering schizophrenics, where multiple personalities can exist. A social setting from the perspective of this book is any group of people who coexist in some physical (societies) or virtual context (social networks). To distinguish groups from random assemblies (our baseline of the emergence of leadership), we will need to instil a purpose that brought everyone together. Given that humans exist in space and time, it is fair to assume that the purpose is the outcome of environmental pressures that deem the formation of the group a vital necessity. The group allows the members to sustain the environmental pressure in the same way as the bricks and other materials of a building make the whole stronger than its individual elements.

Environmental pressure (both physical and social) is the force that drives humans and other life forms to self-organize into groups for the purpose of countering its effects (Figures 1.2 and 1.3). Bringing people together, like any process that brings entities together, demands organization in order for the various pieces to fit within the confines of the group's activities. While this organization might have initially been achieved by trial and error, after a while, certain individuals must have been privileged to take it upon themselves to coordinate the group. Leadership thus arose (Figure 1.4). The environmental pressures do not have to be in the form of competition over resources from other groups, but could equally be the limited, depleted or destroyed natural resources of their environment. A prolonged period of drought, for example, can have a devastating effect on an ecosystem, draining life from it and forcing its inhabitants to seek other regions for their survival.

Once again, we can claim that a sufficient and rational explanation of the emergence of leadership is found, so our objective has been achieved. Although this conjecture sounds simplistic, it perfectly explains the emergence of leadership. What it fails to explain, though, is why that particular individual became the leader and not someone else, and how leaders exercise their authority. The importance of the individual and their close environment also becomes apparent in any attempt to explain leadership. The environment should not be seen as a static representation of

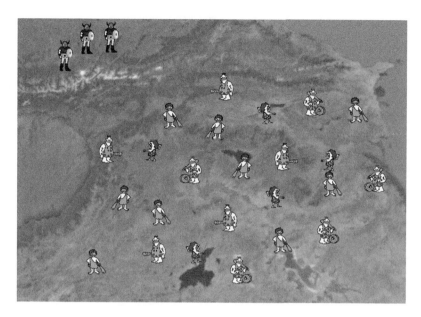

Figure 1.2 Environmental pressure

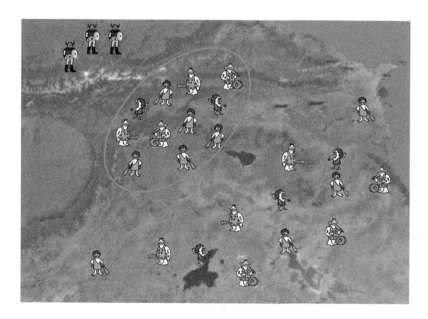

Figure 1.3 Self-organization into a group

surroundings that influences a group and its leader, but instead it should be seen as a dynamic entity that evolves over time. Things always change and this fluidity is important and part of the expression of leadership.

A point of interest here is the common perception that leaders shape their environment. This is absolutely true, but one should avoid a chicken and egg situation where

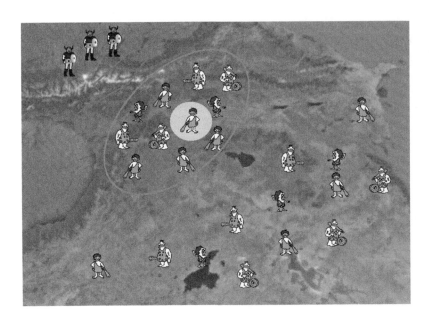

Figure 1.4 Leadership emerges to coordinate the group

Figure 1.5 Who came first?

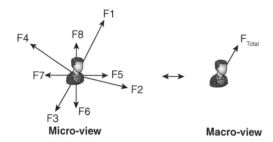

Figure 1.6 The individual perspective

the debate forms around who came first: the leader or the environment (Figure 1.5). This causality dilemma can easily be resolved using a multitude of stances, but here we will use the exclusion principle to answer the question. If we were to remove one or the other, who would be able to exist alone? For sure, there can be no leader without an environment in which to operate, while there is always an environment where living entities can exist.

This position also enforces the emergent aspect of leadership and its classification as a phenomenon. Of course, by accepting this stance, in no way do we minimize the impact of leaders on their environment. We simply consider leadership as part of the dynamic nature of the environment or otherwise an element of the environment that simply interacts with the other entities that make up the environment. A physical analogy (Figure 1.6) is more appropriate to this book's approach and will be further discussed in Chapter 5. The environment will be assumed to exert forces on a leader either in the form of genetic predispositions, upbringing, education and social pressures (among others) that, overall, combine to create a resultant force that drives individuals towards a particular direction in their group.

For a more distinct categorization of the sources of forces, a grouping according to the time that leaders were exposed to them will be considered here. Relating leadership directly to influence (either in the form of motivation or control) requires the consideration of the spread and strength of that influence throughout the group. The influence factor among members of groups is an element of importance in any theory that attempts to explain leadership and in this book we will adopt the concept of areas or circles of influence as they exert their forces on the leader (Figure 1.7). Although these circles will be discussed in Chapter 5, it can easily be seen in Figure 1.7 that the influences of the social groups that an individual gets exposed to as they grow up are included, from inherited genetic traits, to the influence of the immediate carers of the baby, to the extended family of the child and the local close society as they grow up. All these influences/forces are themselves influenced by the world at large nowadays as communication barriers broke down under the pressure of globalization.

If we presume that the same situation exists for the other members of the group, then we can see the dynamic nature of the group (Figure 1.8) where every member interacts with the others as the conditions in the environment and the group change. At the macro-level, when a group can be seen as an entity (like a business organization),

Figure 1.7 Types of influence on individuals

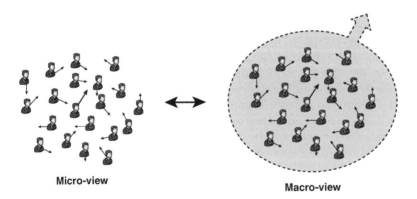

Figure 1.8 The group perspective

we can see that the resultant force of its individual members will move the group in a certain direction. In this case the leader can easily be seen as one of the dominant forces that guide the group towards the direction of movement (ideally growth for organizations).

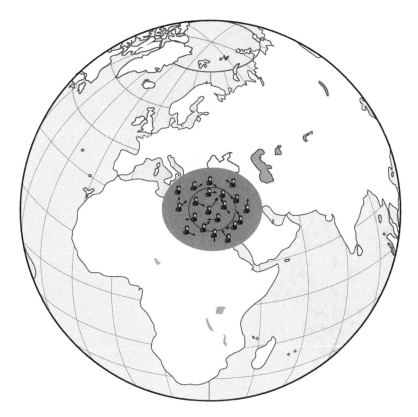

Figure 1.9 Circles of influence of individuals

If one considers the various levels of abstractions on Figures 1.6 and 1.8, we can see in Figure 1.9 that a generic view of the environment needs to include everything from the inherited characteristic of the leaders (the circle), to their close environment (family, friends, acquaintances), to the group influence and finally to the world in general. As we will also see in Chapter 5, the leader is influenced and influencing their environment in a constant and dynamic interaction process that we are abstracting as leadership. One can extend this image to consider the interaction among groups to a worldwide view (Figure 1.10) where groups/organizations compete with each other for resources and dominance.

In the discussions of the various aspects of leadership in this book we will be switching back and forth between the micro-views and the macro-views in order to validate associations between variables and parameters that we adopted as descriptors of one level with their manifestation as observations at the other level. For an observation at the macro-level of the organization, for example, we might observe organizational growth (macro-view) that we can attribute, for example, to a decision to move in a certain direction (e.g. innovate) at the executive level (micro-view). Similarly, when we zoom in on the individual leader, we might observe that the influence of an inherent urge to control (micro-view) forces a leader to impact organizational culture (macro-view) by restraining the free exchange of ideas.

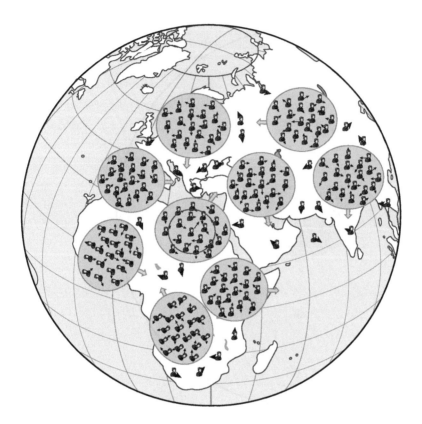

Figure 1.10 World view of organizations

1.3 What this book is and what it isn't

There is a general perception that books on leadership are also guides to effective leadership. Like a to-do list and what-if scenarios, one might expect to find in a leadership book the descriptions of situations and actions one should take to rise up the hierarchy and master a leadership position. Frankly, if any books actually did that, the world would be a better place. However, the reality of today's global affairs points to the opposite, so either these books are not effective in transforming the reader into a leader or they approach the subject from an impossible angle. The latter was the basis for developing this book and so there is no attempt in this book to provide a list of 'magic' steps that will make someone a leader.

Following this brief introduction to leadership, our journey (Chapter 2) will initially take us through an evolutionary account of leadership and some leadership figures who left their mark in history. This pantheon of leaders will be supplemented later on (Chapter 3) with some modern leadership figures from a variety of fields ranging from politics, to military, to religion and business, among others. Having seen some historical and modern cases of leaders, we will then discuss (Chapter 4) some of the most prominent theoretical attempts to explain leadership and will suggest ideal forms of expression. With all these taken into account, we will formulate a framework

(Chapter 5) that explains (adequately, hopefully) the ascent to leadership. Retaining a leadership position is usually a different job altogether, requiring a much different skillset from used in the ascent. For this reason, Chapter 6 has been dedicated to the application of leadership with a special focus on teams. Our journey will end (Chapter 7) with some specifics about leadership that seem to potentially influence the future of the leadership practice.

In closing and in reference to the writing style of this book, it is assumed that the reader is an active participant, accepting and rejecting the positions presented here, and contributing in this way in the development of a mutually worked-out coverage of the topic. Hopefully, 'we' will be able to continue this dialogue to better understand the subject of leadership.

2 Leadership through the ages

While leadership seems to be as old as the human species, its reach in terms of the leader's role seems to expand in the living world and metaphorically speaking in the physical world. One could poetically say that the leader of the solar system is the sun or the leader of the atom is its nucleus and so on. In the natural world, things can get closer to our experience with leadership, so we easily identify the leader of the beehive as the queen bee or the leader of a wolf pack as the alpha male or female and so on. In this chapter we will provide an evolutionary and historical approach to leadership by discussing the emergence of leadership and presenting select cases of well-known historical leadership figures.

2.1 Leadership in the animal world

Long before human societies appeared, there were social animals that formed groups with hierarchical structures. A leader becomes a natural necessity in these social organizations to provide direction and coherence to the group. The characteristics, responsibilities and privileges of those leaders (usually referred to as the *alpha*) have been studied extensively and can range in terms of gender, age and physical strength. Alphas have preferential access to mates and food, and are the first line of defence when it comes to protecting the group from outside threats. They preserve order among the group members and fight any that will challenge their authority. Physical strength in animal societies appears to be the defining characteristic of leaders, although age, gender and descent also appear to play a role in certain species.

Gorilla groups (called troops) exhibit a strong hierarchy where the leading male is the undisputed decision maker, while the predominantly female members of the group are obedient subordinates. These groups are usually formed in the wild from male gorillas that attract emigrating females. In a similar manner, wolf packs are formed when outcast males and females decide to mate and grow their own family away from their natal groups. Outcasts would usually join such groups, but the position of the leader and creator of the group will remain undisputed.

In other cases, like elephant groups, a strong matriarchy is observed, with the leading female passing leadership to her firstborn female and so on. An interesting feature with elephants is that their family groups may come together and form clans, usually during dry seasons. While female elephants are the leaders of groups, their male counterparts are usually at the edge of their groups, occasionally leaving and interacting with other groups. When male elephants form groups, the strongest individual becomes the leader. Like elephants, matrilines exist in killer whales where members of the family (male and female) stick together for their entire life. Another interesting type of leadership can be seen in African wild dogs, where a shared form of leadership is observed, with males and females seemingly forming separate dominance hierarchies within the same group.

The aforementioned examples indicate that leadership in the social animal world can be either inherited or acquired. In some species leadership is usually a prerequisite for a group in the sense that leaders form their own packs mostly through the development of families, while in matriarchal groups leadership tends to be inherited from the leading female to her immediate descendant. What we can take from this is that at least from the point of view of the natural world, these two types of leadership are evolutionarily preferable for the survival of social species. It makes sense to presume that similar group structures have been used by early hominids and, in extended forms (tribes), can even be seen today, especially in isolated indigenous populations.

2.2 Hunter-gatherers/forager tribes

Evolutionary humans didn't follow, initially at least, a separate path with respect to leadership from social animal groups. The first social groups we are aware of were hunter-gatherers, or foragers as most of them are called. These groups would rely on natural resources for their survival and they would move according to the supply of animals and plants that a region provided. This adaptation led to the organization of individuals into family groups initially and tribes later on as more family groups came together to compete against individual threats, either in the form of other human families and groups or in the form of cooperation to maximize their utilization of resources for hunting and gathering. In this way cooperating groups outperformed individuals and smaller groups. Leadership of the strongest or the oldest as they are observed in strong family groups would have been the way to rise to leadership, although external or internal challengers might have occasionally succeeded in establishing their line of leaders.

The leader's job in those days might have been simply to ensure the survival of their group by leading them to prosperous lands and protecting them from outside threats. Along with physical and emotional strength, skill and experience must have been greatly valued in those times. Some of these skills have survived today and are evident in the few remaining hunter-gatherer tribes in the world. The Kalahari bushmen, for example, practise the oldest form of hunting – persistence hunting. By relying mainly on endurance, they will outrun an animal until it drops dead from exhaustion. They are in essence taking advantage of our unique physiology that allows us to sweat and release excess heat while running marathons and outpacing any animal on earth over long distances. Experience also plays a great role as they need to be able to identify a suitable target in a herd and track it down over huge distances until it succumbs to exhaustion. Amazonian tribes and aborigines in Australia are some of the remaining hunter-gatherers, although 'civilization' is catching up with them fast, primarily in terms of destroying their habitat.

There must have been a moment in time when some steady environmental conditions might have led some groups to observe the life-cycle of plants from seeds in the ground to plants. Collecting seeds and replicating the process in fertile lands would have given rise to agriculture. The revolutionary effect of this 'discovery' would be that for the first time, the tribes would be able to control production, saving enough for them to last through to the next season, when they could repeat the process again. This obviously led to the first settlements and a switch in the leader's role from guiding the migration of their tribes to ensuring the safety of production. This was of course in addition to their traditional role of protecting the tribe against outside threats.

Steady settlements allowed for defence structures and storage areas that could sustain populations through hardship. Naturally, the populations in such settlements would have been protected and would have experienced increased survival rates, allowing them to grow and continue the cycle of exploiting resources and growing. As the story went on, overpopulation and inadequate resources must have at some point pressured these groups to expand into other regions, leading to the mass migrations that eventually spread our species throughout the globe.

2.3 From city states to kingdoms and empires

With the advent of agriculture and the formation of stable settlements, boundaries of ownership and influence appeared, forming what would later become city states. These initial boundaries were rather fluid and are better described as frontiers in most cases, but they had defined areas around the settlements where agriculture and, later on, mining would provide resources for the city. Naturally, a lot of these cities would be formed near water, be it a lake, a river or the sea. These positions would offer opportunities for trade with other parts of the world, especially when shipping became an active form of trade with other city states. At this level of concentration of the population, the role of the leader, while more or less similar in function to that in the hunter-gatherer tribes, must have required something other than attention and knowledge of each individual group member. The population, although concentrated, was too large to allow the leader to be able to interact with every member of the group individually in practice. Thus, politics was born. Leading by reputation and influence took a defining turn in the practice of leadership, and oratory and negotiation skills became vital. Leaders at the time had to impress influential people and families to ensure their support when reaching out to individuals otherwise inaccessible to them. In this way, the leaders would influence and be influenced by these centres of influence, leading to alliances and dependencies. Negotiation skills would have been vital in maintaining the balance between the leader's intentions and actions, and the interests of their people. The sheer size of the population also made it impossible for the leader to directly command and control every individual, so they began forming leadership teams that would eventually evolve into a government. From the members' perspective, things may well have looked a little different now, as they would have to communicate indirectly with their leaders through their representatives (either elected or enforced). Remnants of city states still exist today, with Monaco probably being the most famous example.

More populous and economically stronger cities would have expanded their influence and control across other areas and cities, creating nations over time. A common culture would persist in most cases and citizen profiles would be more or else typified and established according to specialization, status and wealth. This expansion had an important influence on leadership with the introduction of representatives (local leaders) who would govern and control on the leader's behalf. This is probably the first time in history that the leader was not in direct contact or had first-hand knowledge of everyone they led.

The dynamics thus changed from direct knowledge of every individual and their relationship and place within the group to knowing only the representatives of various groups. Delegating power and control must have been of primary importance at this stage, so building trust and negotiating responsibilities and obligations would have been valuable skills for leaders. Enforcing their power when challenged would be of equal importance in such cases, so the physical strength of the leader in the first groups was now represented by the military and economic strength of the kingdom.

Up to now, the evolution of leadership closely follows the aggregate nature of human population and the exploitation of larger territories. This is a very important observation as it represents a transformation of influence and control according to the limitations of the leader in reaching, through face-to-face communication, larger and wider distributions of populations. As a last step in the evolution of governance structures, we have the formation of kingdoms and empires under selective visionary leaders who wanted to expand their reach and control beyond the regional domains of their initial group to the very boundaries of the known world. The Roman Empire under Julius Caesar and the Mongol Empire under Genghis Khan are typical examples of a diverse range of groups that were conquered and governed by the same leader. The reason for such excessive spread was now beyond the survival needs of the original group and was motivated by personal ambitions and the lack of strong and cohesive resistance from its neighbours. Leaders were tempted to test the limits of their power and the only obstacle to their ambitions was the limitations of their army in terms of controlling the lands they captured.

The delegation of power to control vast territories required local rulers with a high degree of autonomy in terms of the execution of their power. Maintaining strong armies (physical strength) became of vital importance in sustaining piece in the conquered lands and also in suppressing internal challengers. Forming alliances with neighbours externally and strong individuals internally was also very important in ensuring the obedience of those segments of the population and the army that were not under the leader's direct control. Negotiation skills and strong displays of power were of primary importance in this phase. Very few remnants of such empires exist today – probably the most cohesive of them in terms of population and spread (despite its many transformations) is the People's Republic of China. In modern times the role of the initial leader (Mao Zedong) has been replaced by a strong bureaucracy with an enforced hierarchy of public servants.

In Table 2.1 and Figure 2.1, we can see a summary of the important points made so far, keeping in mind that the adopted classifications are rough representations used to highlight the leadership perspective.

2.4 Historical leaders

Having briefly presented the evolution and application of leadership as a function of group size from a sociological perspective, we will now move on to discuss how leadership has been carried out in the past. We will approach this part by providing a historical account of leadership through the presentation of key leadership figures. In so doing, we will not consider any moral or ethical implications of their leadership, but will focus instead on the effect they had on their followers, the way they ascended to power, and the skills and traits that helped them achieve and sustain that power. While for some of the leaders we have plenty of sources to reliably present an account

Table 2.1 The evolution of leadership

Group	Family	Tribe	State	Nation	Union/empire
Population size	Tens	Hundreds	Thousands	Millions	Billions
Prevalent leadership characteristics	• Inherited	• Inherited • Physical strength • Skill • Experience	• Inherited • Military and economic strength • Influence • Negotiation	• Inherited • Military and economic strength • Influence • Negotiation • Empowerment	• Inherited • Military and economic strength • Influence • Negotiation • Empowerment • Control of bureaucracy
Modern-day example	Families	Amazon tribes	Monaco	UK	China

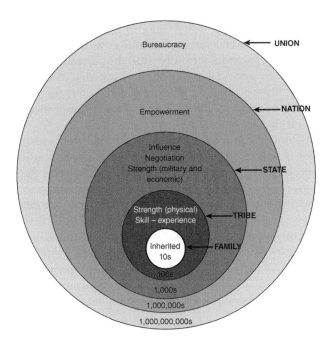

Figure 2.1 The 'growth' of leadership

of their story, for others (especially the older ones) we have to rely on our assertions based on the limited sources available to us. A point of interest here is the distinction between leaders who succeeded in maintaining their leadership status until the end of their career (their death in most cases) and those whose 'career' ended badly for themselves and, in most cases, for their organization/followers.

2.4.1 Alexander the Great

Alexander was born in the fourth century BC. His father Philip II was the ruler of the ancient Greek kingdom of Macedon, while his mother Olympias was the daughter of the king of the nearby kingdom of Epirus. She was a power-hungry and manipulative woman who was bitter about her rejection by Philip for a younger queen and was apparently quite a powerful figure in Alexander's life. Philip had a reputation for being a ruthless leader and a military genius with ambitions to rule the known world of his time. Raised in this environment, from early on Alexander felt the need for his father's approval. It is said that this need was his greatest motivation in campaigning to rule the known world.

As with any offspring, the traits of his parents were also found in Alexander. Although highly intelligent, he was known for a range of contradictory traits, such as being impulsive, emotional, decisive, bold, fearless and reckless. As the king's son, he was privileged in terms of the resources available to him. Having Aristotle (one of the greatest philosophers of all times) as his personal tutor, he was exposed to medicine, philosophy, logic, art and history.

Complementing this education with the best military training that his father and his generals could provide, Alexander had the best the world could offer at his time in terms of preparation for leadership. The culture of the times was strongly influenced by mythology, with religion and history intermixing wars, adventures, love and betrayals among gods and mortals with epic strength. Divinity, right and wrong, and pride were dominant principles among the Greeks of his time and Alexander was ingrained with those principles.

Democracy was in its early stages at the time and was mainly seen as a tool for influential leaders to take control and govern the public. The city states of the time and their colonies would experience fast-paced swings from democracy, to tyranny, to aristocracy and back again. Glorious victories would succeed defeats and enslavement, with monuments signifying victories and the status of leaders and states. On the world stage, there were the barbarians (those with no significant cultural achievements), the Persian Empire, the Egyptians and in the Far East the vague presence of Indians. Among the various smaller kingdoms and city states, Egypt was mainly known for its great pharaohs and as a source of knowledge, while the Persians were known for their wealth and military and economic power. India, on the other hand, was seen as a mystical destination that supplied the West with exotic herbs and spices.

With his early successes, Alexander saw divinity as a naturally bestowed claim that he displayed throughout the remaining of his life. Acting as god, Alexander attempted to unify the nations under his command, in the process spreading the Hellenistic civilization throughout the known world. From a leadership perspective, Alexander is credited for being appreciative and supportive of his men. He loved them and they in return reciprocated this through their love and loyalty. There was nothing that his men wouldn't do for him and he would generously reward them with the spoils of each victory. He was not afraid to get his hands dirty and would always lead from the front, quite visible to both his and the enemy troops. He would regularly get wounded, but he would be up and running in no time, presenting the image of a hard-working and courageous leader. He planned ahead and patiently waited for the time to move before or during the battle. When committed, he would pursue his target until he succeeded.

2.4.2 Justinian I

Born in the fifth century as the son of a farmer, Justinian became the favourite of his childless uncle, who was a high-ranking military commander, on his way to becoming emperor of the East Roman Empire. He moved to Constantinople during his teenage years and received the best education available at the time. This allowed him to become the trusted adviser of his uncle when he became emperor. His loyalty to his uncle paid off and he succeeded him as emperor of the Roman Empire. At this time, the empire had shrunk to its eastern part, with the west having been captured by Ostrogoths and other tribes.

While Justinian's political actions were highly calculated and planned, his personal life was quite rebellious and eventually resulted in him even changing the law to marry the actress Theodora (a lower-class profession at the time; actresses were often considered as prostitutes). This decision eventually proved to be one of his best, as he found in Theodora a dedicated and strong-willed partner in terms of running the affairs of the state. Her support proved vital, especially during a revolt when Justinian was thinking of abandoning the throne. She insisted on facing the rebellion and, with the help of their trusted generals Belisarius and Mundus, the rebels were defeated; about 30,000 of them were slaughtered when he invited them to discuss their demands unarmed in the Hippodrome (the sporting and social centre of the capital). That action alone eliminated any opposition and left Justinian (and Theodora) as the absolute rulers.

Justinian abided by the church and state philosophy, tying the two together. This outlook among others prompted him to pursue the unification of the lost pieces of the Roman Empire under a theocratic regime, with him as the chosen leader as if directly appointed by God. He focused his attention on rebuilding the capital and regaining the lost lands of the empire. He defeated the Vandals in North Africa and the Ostrogoths in Italy, completing the pacification of the Italian peninsula. He fought the Visigoths and took back southern Spain, but he avoided engaging the Franks as they were Christian and in a sense allies by religion. Where he could not afford military might, he achieved his means with diplomacy. One such example is his alliance with the Christian kingdom of Abyssinia in order to bypass the Persian control for commerce with the East. Stretching his military across the Mediterranean did come at a price as Hunnic and other tribes from the north managed to get a foothold in the Balkan peninsula, from where they would pose a constant threat to the empire for centuries afterwards.

Justinian was considered the last of the Roman emperors as drastic changes followed his reign that totally changed the nature of the empire. From then on, it became known as the Byzantine Empire. It was a primarily Christian empire with Greek as its formal language instead of Latin. He reformed and refined the legal code that remained one of the most influential sources of Western legal history. He promoted officials based on merit in an effort to stop corruption, which led him into conflict with the status quo of his time. As a leader, he relied on capable and talented advisers and generals who carried out his wishes. This was particularly crucial for foreign affairs. We have in him a leader who capitalized on a well-built executive team to make things happen. His civil reforms and conquests contributed to the survival of the empire for another eight centuries. While it is not exactly proven historically, it is worth keeping in mind here that his wife Theodora is credited by many as being the motivational force behind many of his actions.

2.4.3 Genghis Khan

Like Alexander the Great, Genghis Khan (12th century) was of noble descent, as his father was the head of a ruling clan (Borjigin) of the Mongols. As was customary, parents would arrange marriages at the time and boys would move to their promised wife's family early on (at the age of nine years old for Genghis). This switch of male role models from father to father-in-law must have had some impact on young boys of the time. This arrangement would end at 12 years old (the marriageable age), at which point the boy and his new wife would return to his family of origin. At that time, Genghis's father was poisoned by his enemies, who refused to accept the young boy as their chieftain. After some harsh times in the wild with his family, Genghis was imprisoned by the enemies of his father. He eventually managed to escape and, with an initial core of trusted friends, he started building his leadership identity and empire.

The Mongol culture where Genghis was born was a typical and simplistic tribal environment with simple rules and principles. Anyone was free to believe what they wanted to believe in terms of religion and spirituality as long as they respected each other's beliefs. Trust was of the utmost importance and breaking the simple laws was mainly punished by execution. The Mongols would fight to vanquish their opponents (win or die) and take ownership of the spoils of war, both material and living.

The political environment during Genghis's ascent to power was formed by scattered Mongol tribes where active infighting kept them disconnected and economically poor. Alliances would be formed by arranged marriages among the tribes, but tribal warfare was a constant reality of the time. Bartering was the main business activity of the time and while the tribes could identify their connection to each other, there was no unity among them in the form of a national identity. However, the global scene featured uniquely identifiable entities like the Tartars, the Keraits, the Uighurs and the Chinese Chin dynasty. These players would rise in strength periodically, with the Chinese aligning with opposing factions to keep them from getting too powerful to threaten China.

In that environment, Genghis managed to ascend to power by breaking traditions and establishing a meritocratic system of delegating authority and a new rule of law that provided its troops and allies shares of the spoils of war. He integrated his opponent's troops into his ranks after his victories and considered them as part of his tribe. This ensured their trust and loyalty and helped in the formation of the nation idea, making Genghis stronger and eventually the ultimate ruler of the Mongols.

In terms of strategy, Genghis was always reliant on intelligence and a thorough understanding of his opponent's mind and intentions. He spent a lot of effort developing an extensive spy and communications network to provide him with reliable information on his opponents and adopted innovations from foreign practices like staging a siege according to Chinese practices and deceiving his opponents by retreating and attacking unpredictably. He would leave no provocation or challenge unanswered. After his delegates were murdered by the Turks, he invaded their territories and burned their cities to the ground, while eliminating any future threats by completely massacring their populations. His tactics were brutal but effective. This can be seen in modern times in the business world, where businesses can drive competition into extinction.

2.4.4 Christopher Columbus

The fifteenth century was a time of exploration and discovery of lands that would allow for new trade routes and colonies. Shipbuilding and navigation technology allowed exploration into unknown seas for those brave and capable enough to take on the challenge and venture following hypothetical estimates of promised lands. Christopher Columbus was a product of those times and although he didn't lead great armies like Alexander the Great and Genghis Khan, he did manage to lead his team to the successful discovery of a continent.

Columbus was born into an Italian family of a middle-class weaver and trader, who he regularly helped from early on. From his teenage years, he started sailing around the Mediterranean, gaining valuable experience and skills as a sailor and entrepreneur. This was a time when the West was actively interacting with the Muslim lands that mediated the trade with the East. This dependency created the need for alternative routes to access the Far East and motivated Columbus to consider the possibility of sailing around the globe in the other direction to reach Asia.

As Columbus grew older, he also got exposed to travel and doing business in the Atlantic. Relocating to different countries and engaging in trade was normal during this time. In that sense, venturing into new territories and reaching out farther into the unknown was not rare. He became skilful in managing a ship and its crew, he learned the waters and weather of the known parts of the ocean, and became comfortable in negotiating with the rulers and merchants of his time. We can safely say that at that point in his life, he was an experienced sailor, navigator and entrepreneur, well aware of his environment and its dynamics. His personal ambitions to explore for profit and the exploitation of natural resources were undeniably motivators for his ventures, as was his persistence to succeed at all costs. Suppressing three mutinies during his journey was an indicator of his strength and determination to achieve his goal.

Having a clear vision of what he wanted to accomplish, Columbus gathered resources and support to enable him to form a team that shared and followed his vision. His persistence and wit helped him overcome innumerable internal and external obstacles to keep his team on track with his mission to discover China in a way that no one else had done before. In Columbus we have a combination of traits that contributed to his success and supported his strong vision. Having a good understanding of his environment (political, economic and operational) and being willing to take risks along with his personal traits of being persistence, resilient and adaptability allowed him to lead his team into the unknown.

Columbus was considered as being a great persuader, politically acute and a skilful negotiator. He operated in the midst of many adversaries who would not hesitate to sabotage him using every opportunity they had. The team he assembled that helped him venture in search of Asia was composed of qualified seafarers and convicts who were given the option to join him and have their criminal records erased. He could engage with his sponsors, the Spanish royal court, and ensure their support and he could talk his way out of difficult situations like encounters with the Portuguese and his own commanders when they would challenge his authority. In short, Columbus can be seen as an entrepreneurial leader who succeeded in building his own ventures.

2.4.5 Catherine I

The reign of Peter the Great in Russia in the seventeenth century is closely associated with his successor and wife Catherine I (not to be confused with Catherine the Great, who followed years later). We have here the extraordinary life (Cinderella-style) of someone who started at the bottom of the social ladder as the daughter of a Lithuanian peasant and climbed up to succeed Peter the Great, one of the great rulers of his time. Of course, Catherine didn't have the goal (as far as we know) of becoming the leader of an empire, but circumstances brought her to a situation that helped her emerge as one.

Catherine's early life was spent as a lowly servant with no exposure to reading and writing (she remained illiterate throughout her life). Her only observable skill at the time was her beauty, which led to her early marriage. She eventually served as a household maid or mistress in some accounts to a Brigadier General and eventually ended up as mistress to Peter the Great. As a person, she was known as very energetic, charming and companionate. Her hard life probably contributed to the latter trait. She followed Peter in his campaigns and, according to some accounts, engaged in diplomacy to avoid a great defeat by the Ottomans.

After Peter's death, Catherine gained the throne in a coup organized by her supporters. Her popularity with the guard's regiment helped in achieving this. She was well received by the majority of her subjects as she related to the commoners and supported those who ascended to positions based on competence. The real power, though, lay with a select few who supported her and formed her council. Despite the fact that she was more like a figurehead leader, she opened up the way for women to ascend to positions of power and managed to reduce the highest expense of the economy, the enormous army of the empire (at that time the largest in Europe). This resulted in the lowering of taxes and increased her popularity as a fair leader.

Although in Catherine we see a leader who appears to have risen to power due to circumstances, we nevertheless have someone who could take the opportunities that appeared before her, despite her deficiencies in education and training, and the biases she faced in relation to her gender and origins. She managed to negotiate her way through the royal courts, forming proper alliances, eliminating her opponents and exercising her power to establish her authority. With the exception of her origins and upbringing, one can see a similar situation in Elizabeth I of England. A more obvious similar case can be found in Theodora, the wife of the Byzantine Emperor Justinian, as she also came from humble origins and went on to become an actress, mistress of the emperor and eventually his wife and empress.

2.4.6 Napoleon Bonaparte

Born in Corsica in the eighteenth century, with origins in the minor Italian nobility, Napoleon was the third son of a lawyer and Corsica's representative to the king's court. Although Italian in origin, his family made every effort to fit into French culture, including changing their original name Buonaparte to Bonaparte. Napoleon's Corsican origins resulted in him speaking French with a slight accent that attracted teases from his peers. The somewhat privileged environment where he was born afforded him a good education and eventually led to his graduation as an artillery officer from the top military academy in France.

Despite his initial support of Corsican separatists, Napoleon made it to the position of captain in the regular French army. The new form of governance that France was trying to establish, and that Napoleon supported, was one of the main reasons for the hostile treatment France received from the other European powers of its time.

They perceived this form of governance as a threat to their own traditional systems. The revolutionary environment of his time was no doubt a great influence on Napoleon, who became quite active in politics and used his military successes to rise to power. He exercised strict censorship and even used the press as part of his propaganda in his attempts to control his troops and the nation in general.

Although Napoleon is viewed as a leader who commanded his troops from afar, this was far from the truth. With his troops under fire, he would be seen loading cannons and exposing himself to the dangers his troops were facing. This gained him the respect of his troops as they saw him as one of them. For Napoleon, the privilege of telling someone what to do meant he knew what he was asking for and wasn't afraid to get his hands dirty to achieve his goals. He was seen as a great motivator for both soldiers and generals, and would make great efforts to ensure their trust. He would also do the same for the territories and cities he conquered, as he would present the conquest as liberation and himself as the representative of the revolution.

On the battlefield, Napoleon was quite resourceful and adaptable in his manoeuvring, allowing for the flexible deployment of his forces and trying to hide his intentions as much as possible. While this provided him with numerous early victories the beginning, his persistence in applying the same tactics again and again, coupled with his loss of confidence after his first exile, led to his final downfall. Among the other traits responsible for his eventual downfall, historians credit his huge ego, which drove his lust for power. Of course, other leaders like Alexander the Great and Genghis Khan also had huge egos, as we saw before, but it was maybe the complexities of Napoleon's time that couldn't support a leadership personality like his.

2.4.7 Abraham Lincoln

Born in a log cabin in the nineteenth century to a family of migrants who arrived in Kentucky, Abraham Lincoln was the second child in his family. Court disputes over land titles forced the family to move to slave-free Indiana, where he was raised in the farms his father bought or leased. The family belonged to the Separate Baptists church, which held strict moral views against alcohol and slavery. His inclination towards reading and writing, and his aversion towards physical work, gave off the impression of laziness initially, but eventually led to him being a self-educated lawyer and politician. His physical presence, being both tall and strong, was regarded as an intimidating factor for his political opponents.

After a mix of failures and successes in business and politics, Lincoln eventually made it to the US House of Representatives and finally to the presidency. It was obvious in his case that failure was a synonym for persistence, eventually allowing him to overcome the many setbacks in his path to becoming President of the United States of America. In his words, 'My great concern is not whether you have failed, but whether you are content with your failure', suggesting that the amount of rejection one receives is not a defining factor until the moment one stops trying. Lincoln was elected in 1861 as the sixteenth President.

As a team leader, Lincoln always strived to have the most competent men around him, even when they would be seen as rivals in his political field. He preferred people who were comfortable questioning his authority and could defend their positions and arguments. The era of his leadership was critical for the nation and his strong belief that only the best should lead resulted many times in him having teams composed of rivals. The downside of these types of teams was that he ended up spending a lot of time talking and arguing with them, even on areas where he was not the authority. This ambiguity required strength to fight for a consensus and he took it upon himself to make the decision when necessary.

Probably due to the influence of his religious beliefs and personal experiences, Lincoln was credited with liking people and being lenient and forgiving, always wanting to give people second and third chances. This in many circumstances was seen as a weakness and a flaw in his leadership although one could attribute it to his lack of knowledge in certain areas like military affairs. His inability to be decisive with his subordinates resulted in many losses during the American Civil War in the hands of not so ideal generals. However, he did try to compensate for his lack of understanding to a great extent by constantly educating himself in the areas where his knowledge was weakest.

Starting from zero with no social and inherited status, he turned himself into an inspirational speaker and communicator who could motivate people. With similar ease, he could destroy his opponents with words when challenged. He matured as a speaker and public figure from a young politician who wouldn't hesitate to deceive in order to make his point, to a compassionate and inclusive leader. He has served since then as an example of a great leader and role model for future presidents and politicians around the world.

2.4.8 Gandhi

Born in the nineteenth century to a deeply religious mother and having the chief minister of Porbandar as a father, Mahatma Gandhi is credited with an elitist background that afforded him the privilege of a good education. Despite his mother's influence of strong Hindu ethics (religious tolerance and non-violence), Gandhi appeared to be a rebellious teenager involved in womanizing, drinking and eating meat, breaking the traditions he was raised with. He got married at the age of 13 and one of his greatest regrets was his father's moment of death because he chose to have sex with his wife instead of being by his side.

While Gandhi was studying in Bombay, he was offered the chance to study law in London and despite the advice of his caste to stay in India, he seized the opportunity and immersed himself in Western culture. Despite the adoption of a Western dress code, he managed to reunite with his Hindu principles and form his ideas about unity of people and religions. After his graduation, he returned to India and after failing and embarrassing himself as a lawyer, he moved to South Africa. This is where he faced the blatant discrimination against his colour and began a movement against segregation through non-violent civil protest. From this point on, he wore the traditional white Indian robe (dhoti) as a symbol of mourning.

The movement evolved to the point of leading a strike again a tax imposed on Indians, which led to Gandhi's arrest. However, the spread of the unrest was strong enough to lead to his release and the withdrawal of the tax. This was his first public victory and made him renowned internationally. Returning to India and shocked by the poverty he observed, he began his protest against British rule. His rising popularity allowed him to transform and raise the Indian National Congress to appeal to the masses. His calls for non-violent protests were embraced by Indians regardless of their class and religious beliefs. His boycott of British goods led to his arrest and imprisonment.

The British were eventually forced to give in and began discussions on India's independence. The lack of unity of the Indian delegation didn't achieve the desired result, so Gandhi withdrew from politics. Following the outbreak of the Second World War, the British looked to India for support. Gandhi opposed participation in the war unless the British would consider the independence of India. Under mounting pressure from calls for freedom, the British agreed to independence, but, to the detriment of Gandhi, they formed the two independent states of India and Pakistan. Standing up to his belief that people of different religions could live in harmony, Gandhi supported the right of Muslims who wanted to stay in India. This move eventually led to his death by Hindu extremists.

Gandhi's leadership triumphs can be attributed to his ability to appeal to the different ethnic and religious groups of India that accepted him as their inspirational leader. He stayed true to his beliefs with unprecedented persistence. He was even determined to die for what he believed (and he actually did so). Beyond his enthusiasm and discipline, he was also credited as a structured and methodical leader who reorganized his party and provided a clear and easy-to-follow ideology. He was recognized as one of the most ethical leaders of all time and as proof of the value of ethics in successful leadership.

2.4.9 Adolf Hitler

Adolf Hitler was born in an Austrian family in the late nineteenth century and early on in his childhood moved to nearby Bavaria in Germany. His father retired soon after he failed in his attempt as a farmer. Hitler had major conflicts with his father as he could not conform to the strict school discipline in place at that time. The death of his younger brother from illness marked a change in Hitler's behaviour as he became more detached and in constant conflict with his father and teachers. This conflict resulted in his father overriding his wish to go to a classical school and become an artist, and instead sending him to a traditional technical school. Whether intentionally or not, he didn't perform well in school and as soon as his father passed away, he left. He eventually managed to finish school at another location by undertaking his repeat final exam with no prospects for further education.

As a young adult, Hitler attempted on many occasions to study art in Vienna, but he was not successful. Following the death of his mother and with no steady source of income, he embraced German nationalist ideas that grew popular under the fear of immigrant influxes from the East (especially Jews). It appears that this period in Vienna is when he embraced antisemitism and other related ideologies that would later on shape his life. Following the outbreak of the First World War, he joined the German army as a dispatch runner and was wounded on many occasions. Like many Germans of his time, he was of the belief that the army's defeat and humiliation was the fault of the civilian leaders.

As a decorated war hero, after the war, Hitler continued to serve in the army as an intelligence agent. During his reconnaissance missions, he became interested in the German's Worker's Party and he formally joined as soon as he was retired from the army. He became effective at speaking and manipulating large audiences, and soon became the leading public figure of his party. Eventually he was made party president and was a key player in German politics. After failed coups and some time in prison, he managed to rise to power after the 1929 stock market crash and the great depression that followed. He eventually managed to rebuild Germany's economy and drastically reduce the unemployment rate. Although this was achieved by printing money and seizing the assets of 'enemies' of the state, he is credited with the large infrastructure project that prepared the economy for war. In defiance of the international treaties that restricted Germany's build-up of a war machine, he managed to develop a formidable army to carry out his expansionist plans. By using a combination of diplomacy, military acts and forming opportunistic alliances, he managed to expand Germany's control of Czechoslovakia and Poland and to commit to a full-out war on multiple fronts. His ambitions to expand and achieve overall control of Europe, along with his extended war frontier across multiple continents, wore down his army and eventually led to his downfall.

As a leader, Hitler didn't demonstrate much trust in his generals and insisted on being personally involved in controlling and commanding his army, although from afar, despite his limited experience in war matters. To many, his illusion as a military leader and strategist, and his authoritative control, prevented his more experienced staff from conducting an effective war campaign. In addition to his mistrustful and controlling nature, he was stubborn and indecisive, putting off difficult decisions that resulted in worse military outcomes for his operations. A case in point is when he delayed his attack to Russia in order to have the latest version of his tanks available, giving the Russians enough time to prepare their defence and successfully defeat him.

2.4.10 Walt Disney

Walt Disney was born into a poor family mainly involved in farming at the beginning of the twentieth century. While his elder brother ran away to avoid the harsh working conditions, Walt went to school. He was interested in drawing and movies from early on and attended Sunday courses at an art institute. Later on in his childhood, his father bought a newspaper delivery route and Walt worked exhausting hours delivering newspapers while attending school. He continued his schooling and arts education in his teenage years, eventually drawing cartoons for his school newspaper. He attempted to join the army during the First World War, but because he was underage, he ended up serving the Red Cross in France as an ambulance driver.

After the war, Disney became a cartoonist for a newspaper and created advertisements for print media and movie theatres. With a colleague from work, he started his first business, which was not successful. He eventually switched to cel animation and started a new business developing cartoons for a local theatre. His success allowed him to acquire his own studio, which he eventually lost to bankruptcy due to the high salaries he had to pay his animators. The failure did not discourage him and, with his brother Roy, he decided to set up a studio in Hollywood, the heart of the movie industry. After some modest successes and plenty of hardships, he managed to build one of the most successful companies of all times. In addition to the motion pictures studios, television networks and media segments, the Disney empire now includes other areas of the entertainment industry such as holiday resorts, theme parks and hotels.

Disney's vision was clear: to provide continuous entertainment for families around the world. This meant being creative and innovating in an industry (cartoon movies) he created. He was like the explorers of the past where he would continuously risk everything to conquer new territory. The difference was that he was creating something that hadn't existed before. New land, oceans and continents of creation formed his territory, which led to one of the most successful enterprises of all time. He was known as a charismatic personality, always treating his employees as part of his family. He was quite approachable and he would regularly entertain his employees at his house on Sundays, giving them the sense that they were part of his extended family. This ensured their trust in him (calling him Walt or Uncle Walt occasionally) and their buy-in to his vision. They would commit themselves to long hours of work without pay simply because they felt part of something worthy and far bigger than themselves.

As the company grew, Disney had to adopt a more hierarchical structure and the studios lost their family atmosphere and became more segregated and impersonal. This level of command and control brought out a more autocratic Disney, who would expect everyone to be aligned with his final decision; before that point, though, he would still be asking their opinion before making a decision. Another aspect of his leadership that went against modern practices is that he would take all the credit for his productions (including signing the animations of his employees). The growing size of Disney's enterprise proved quite challenging for him as he could not handle employee demands like better conditions and unionizing. He was lucky at that point that his brother and partner Roy was able to take over certain aspects of the operation and bring harmony between management and employees, thus allowing the enterprise to grow and thrive.

2.4.11 Leonard Bernstein

While conducting as a form of leadership has being undeniably acknowledged, it has hardly been studied or associated with the image of leaders as, historically, we are aware of them. However, Leonard Bernstein was an acclaimed twentieth-century musician who deserves credit as a role model of a leader. He was born in Massachusetts to Jewish immigrants who came to the US from Ukraine. His father was a hair product businessman and, despite his objections to letting his son explore his musical interests, he would regularly take him to concerts and piano recitals. Eventually, he ceased his objections to Leonard becoming a musician and young Leonard managed to learn piano. His talent and ambition took him to Harvard University, where he studied music theory and counterpoint. He continued studying conducting under the strict disciplinarian Fritz Reiner, who believed in mastering every detail of every piece.

Despite his talent and passion, Bernstein found himself unemployed after his studies. After some odd jobs, he found a position as assistant conductor of the New York Philharmonic Orchestra. Due to a stroke of luck, he was called one afternoon to replace a senior conductor who was ill. His performance astonished everyone and overnight he became famous, and a regular conductor of the Philharmonic. As his career blossomed, he performed in several international tours and television shows, wrote melodies like those for *West Side Story* and taught and mentored countless musicians of his time.

As a leader, Bernstein was well known for his ability to encourage discipline while allowing for creative freedom in his orchestras. He kept true to his principle that everyone's voice should be heard as he believed that freedom of expression was not just an ethical but also an organizational necessity. He would even get to the point of expecting his orchestra members to take the initiative to perform to his expectations without telling them what to do, like asking a soloist that he wanted a certain feeling, which it would be up to them to deliver. This would force someone into a dialogue even if they didn't want to engage. The end result would be a highly effective partnership between the leader and his team.

Being an effective member of the team and being successful were synonyms for the success of a project and, for Bernstein, the job of the leader was to create opportunities for individuals to shine. Another of his characteristics, which might seem counterintuitive to today's leaders, was his complete immersion into his role. He strongly believed that compartmentalizing the emotional, intellectual and other aspects of our lives would only impair the experience the audience would get from his work. This is in great contrast to the work-life balance many promote in the workplace, but oddly enough makes sense for people working online and in virtual teams.

2.4.12 Nelson Mandela

Nelson Mandela, the first black South African president, was born in the twentieth century to a branch of the Thembu royal family. Tending herds and playing with other boys, his childhood was influenced by the customs, rituals and taboos of his culture. Despite these traditions and under the influence of Christianity, he became the first person in his family to attend school. He moved away from his mother to continue schooling near the palace under the care of a Thembu regent. His privileged background allowed him to continue to high school and get the best education available at that time. Eventually he studied law and was exposed to anti-colonial movements. His engagement in a boycott at university led to his expulsion before completion of his degree. Trying to avoid an arranged marriage, he ran away to Johannesburg, where he ended up working as a clerk at a law firm. He was quite poor at the time, but he managed to continue his education through a correspondence course with the University of South Africa.

After the establishment of apartheid by the white minority, Mandela rose to a leadership position in the movement against it. While the oppressive forces mounted more opposition, his initial non-violent involvement transformed into militant activities against the government. He was eventually arrested and convicted to life imprisonment. After twenty-seven years in prison, mounting an international campaign that associated his name with the fight against apartheid led to his release. In prison he remained active, even with the limited privileges he had, in communicating and meeting with his family and supporters, while at the same time advancing his education. His time in prison helped in building his profile as a political leader who succeeded without the exercise of formal authority. He became an inspiration for black South Africans and a role model throughout his life, regardless of whether he was in or out of prison.

Upon Mandela's release from prison, he cooperated with the government in abolishing apartheid and establishing multiracial elections. He led his party to victory and became the first black president of his country. More than his victory and the collapse of apartheid, he became known for his efforts to integrate South Africa into a coherent state where the various African tribes, the whites and other migrants from Asia could live and prosper in peace. He managed to control the natural tendency of someone who had experienced suffering to retaliate, and instead he collaborated, making his authority appreciated and widely respected worldwide. His ability to unite different cultural and political perspectives and his perseverance in sustaining momentum towards a cause, even in the most difficult circumstances, allowed him to change the face and position of South Africa in the global economy.

2.5 Characteristics of historical leaders

The leaders that we have briefly presented here are a select few that were lucky enough to have their reign accompanied by enough historical records to allow us to understand their life in some detail. Not many were privileged with such records, so people who study leadership need to be reserved in their conclusions and generalizations about the traits and characteristics (of some of the older ones at least) that contributed to their success. As we come closer to our own time, we can be fairly confident that the historical records become more accurate in detailing the leaders' personalities and actions. The purpose of this chapter was to present leaders from different eras in an attempt to identify common traits and characteristics indicative of leadership. With that aim in mind, it was necessary to minimize biases that could come from gender, social status, education and other demographics we usually consider in social science research in order to allow for a more representative sampling of the leadership population.

A summary of some of the characteristics of the leaders we have discussed above is presented in Table 2.2. While the information listed is minimal, a simple comparison of the leaders' characteristics might show their diversity and the lack of an identifiable pattern. It is left to the reader to include additional columns like who died in action (Gandhi, Lincoln and maybe Hitler), who spent time in prison (Napoleon, Hitler and Mandela), who had siblings, who was their close support (Alexander had his generals, some of whom were also his childhood friends, Justinian had Theodora, Catherine had her court, Disney had his brother, etc.), who were megalomaniacs (probably all

Table 2.2 Demographics of historical leadership figures

Leader	Century	Area	Initial social status	Leadership style	End result
Alexander the Great	4th BC	Military	Privileged	Inclusive and autocratic	Successful
Justinian I	6th	Politics	Privileged	Inclusive	Successful
Genghis Khan	12th	Military	Privileged	Autocratic	Successful
Christopher Columbus	15th	Business	Not privileged	Inclusive	Partially successful
Catherine I	17th–18th	Politics	Not privileged	Inclusive	Successful
Napoleon Bonaparte	18th–19th	Military/ politics	Privileged	Autocratic	Failure
Abraham Lincoln	19th	Politics	Not privileged	Inclusive	Successful
Gandhi	19th–20th	Politics	Privileged	Inclusive	Partially successful
Adolf Hitler	19th–20th	Politics/military	Not privileged	Autocratic	Failure
Walt Disney	20th	Entertainment	Not privileged	Dictatorship	Successful
Leonard Bernstein	20th	Music	Privileged		Successful
Nelson Mandela	20th	Politics	Privileged	Inclusive	Successful

of them in a way), among others. This aforementioned list could go on forever and would possibly increase the diversity of characteristics, making it almost impossible to deduce common themes among them.

Given that not all information about a leader can be available and that the list of known or unknown leaders can go well beyond the 12 we presented here, it is unlikely that we will ever be able to have a statistically strong and unbiased sample to conclusively decide whether there is a prevailing characteristic or environment that allows someone to rise to the position of leadership and remain there for as long as they did. Whether the leaders we included here would still have become leaders if the circumstances were different is another great challenge that leadership research faces. What would Genghis Khan or Alexander the Great have been if they were both in the midst and the aftermath of the French Revolution? Was Napoleon the best Alexander the Great of his time? Was he the best among his contemporaries in dynastic Europe? Would the privileged education and training that a lot of the leaders received at their time have made a difference to what they became?

It will be difficult for anyone to tell whether the fraction of the populace that we have included here are more like the exception than the norm. The chances of someone becoming a leader in the form of a historical celebrity are minimal to almost infinitesimally small. Unless we accept historical leadership figures as exceptions, our research and knowledge of modern societies tells us that leadership is apparent in many levels and forms of social groups.

3   Leadership in the twenty-first century

Considering the past as we did in the previous chapter is probably a good start in terms of understanding leadership. One could argue that the environment in which leaders operated in the past is different from the environment we live in today, and extrapolating our findings from the past to today and the future might result in uncertainties. Fortunately, we can attempt an extrapolation to today with leaders from the twenty-first century. Understanding the present can be a challenge in itself as 'present' and 'environment' change faster than we are accustomed to as human beings, mainly due to the impact of information and communication technologies that have shaped today's world. It could be said, for example, that our memories are overloaded with the amount of information we get and our senses cannot process the stimulus we receive from the environment fast enough, deeming us unable to function in a fully informed way. In addition, living standards and social influences seem to affect our emotions. If leadership is affected by the environment and today's environment is drastically different from that of the past, then our discussion here should take these differences into consideration, at least when we make comparisons with the leaders of the past.

3.1 The early twenty-first-century environment

Roughly defined, the environment of 'something' includes everything that is not part of 'something' and can interact with it. The environment in which human beings operate includes the physical world of objects and forces, and the social world of humans and their societies. While the physical world can be more or less clearly defined and accounted for (gravity pulls you down, friction inhibits movement, and collisions with other objects can be unpleasant), the social world can be elusive at times and especially nowadays. The world experiences today a globalization that works towards an integration (albeit slow) of values due to the dominance of Western entertainment and lifestyles, urbanization and the great migrations from underdeveloped and war-torn regions to developed countries. Cities have grown into entities with the characteristics of nations, having citizens with multiple nationalities, fighting to attract talent, and valuing diversity and growth above any commitment to national and historical ties.

Another reason why our social world can be difficult to define is that the social world has experienced a radical expansion into the virtual world of the World Wide Web. A change in one 'place' can be almost immediately be transmitted to everyone in the world, so even if something is not happening in our immediate surroundings,

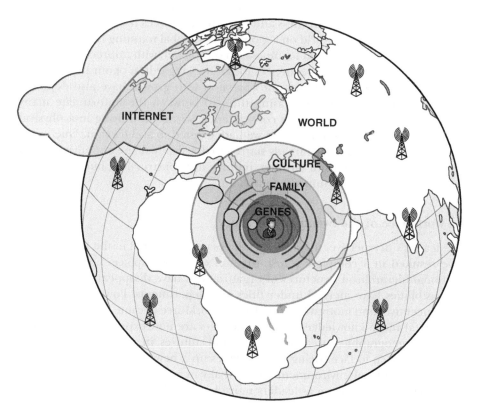

Figure 3.1 The twenty-first-century world

we are well aware of it happening in all its live and vivid detail. What is happening, though, and what is presented as happening might be quite different, making believing an issue of faith, critical thinking and experience. The advances in information and communication technologies enable the influence factor to expand its reach on a global scale. An event such as the Arab Spring can spread with unprecedented speed. If we could consider the spread of religions in the past, they would take centuries to spread, whereas nowadays such dramatic influences usually take weeks to do so. The world in which we live is dramatically different from the world in which our children will live and probably unrecognizable from the one in which our grandchildren will live.

As if the physical world were not big enough, we managed to delve into inhabiting another dimension: the virtual world. Our advances in information and communications technologies have enabled direct and immediate access to information and other organizations on a global scale. The boundaries of the physical and natural world have been redrawn in the virtual world and now we have 'countries' like Facebook and Google that we can easily cross and join as their citizens. The corporate world embraced the virtual and even set up totally virtual enterprises like eBay and Amazon that, with a minimal physical footprint, can reach millions of consumers regardless of their physical location.

Despite the expansion of the world we experience with the introduction of the virtual dimension, our competitiveness and thirst for resources has intensified to the point of altering our physical world on a global scale. Global warming is the most profound alteration we have managed to impose on our planet, with unprecedented and unpredictable (to an extent) consequences to our lives regardless of our location and social norms. Overconsumption and our obsession with growth have also depleted our planet's natural resources, increasing the gap between the unfortunate many (poor) and the select few (rich). As a consequence, we are now living in a physical world that is drifting away from the ideal we had adapted to and lived in. One could argue here that in reality, we had already started to drastically shape our environment from even the ancient times with farming, mining and construction, but the scale at which we affect it nowadays is unprecedented.

3.2 The workplace of the twenty-first century

From the leader's perspective, the drastic changes we mentioned in the previous section have resulted in a complete transformation of the workplace. For one thing, the traditional hierarchical structures of organizations have disappeared and duties and responsibilities have merged under titles and departments. Power and control, along with incentives and motivators, faded as the workforce became (at least in developed countries) more knowledge-oriented. Leaders are now expected to command teams that span geographical areas, time zones and cultures, in addition to managing their local teams face to face. Being present takes up a new reality as it could mean both physically in a local environment and virtually in a global scene. Even physical presence takes a tentative form as leaders move between branches, subsidiaries and organizations. Traditional business practices often interchange with modern practices in the leader's life faster than the brain can adapt. Not only are leaders nowadays expected to intellectually switch between cultural and operational norms, they are expected to do so at an emotional level in order to engage the diverse teams they lead. They need to do all this while balancing between long-term goals and short-term, results-oriented behaviours. The leaders of the past could spend decades in a job, while the leaders of today usually jump from one organization to another after a few years. Time traveling a leader of past centuries to lead today would probably cause them a psychotic split without a very long adaptation period.

This 'confusion' also spreads to team members as they now have an upgraded role in acting as leaders of themselves and their domain. Acting more as freelancers, moving from one job to another, it seems like they work for organization Earth and simply move from project to project among different organizations. In that sense, they are exposed to international, national, organizational and personal influences in parallel. You might have a nice romantic dinner one moment and the next the phone rings and you have to respond to colleagues or your team leader on the other side of the globe. For Europeans and Americans, it becomes even more challenging as their markets have been invaded by lower-wage and same-quality individuals from all over the world. Physical labour has been replaced by intelligence and creativity, which comes not only from a variety of cultures but also from educational and professional backgrounds. Growth is no longer associated with more people working to produce more of something, but instead efficient use of technology and innovation are used to increase productivity and sustain growth.

In the global competitive environment in which we live nowadays, both leaders and team members are becoming players. Switching roles between leader and follower, and eventually transcending into the player role is easier said than done. Players live for the game, and the rules of the game obey certain realities that everyone needs to comply with. Common rules take the form of a common language and, for better or worse, English has become the acceptable medium of communication. As with any choice, some are privileged by this, in this case those who are native English speakers, and some are disadvantaged as they will be forced to become bilingual at a master's level. Switching from English at work to one's native language at home can have a dichotomous effect and can be challenging when abstract concepts are involved that cannot be semantically matched. For example, switching frequently between reading from left to right to reading from right to left and even from top to bottom can be more challenging than it seems. Similarly, conducting a meeting in a room at 1 p.m. with everyone physically present can be quite a different experience from conducting a meeting in front of a screen at 1 a.m. with everyone virtually present and in different time zones. The skills required for such performances as well as their impact on the individual and organization are to a great extent still unknown.

No leader is expected to know many of the details of their organization. In fact, employees (or players as we stated above) will definitely know more in their area of expertise than any leader could possibly know. For a leader, this is like being the smart guy amongst geniuses. How are leaders supposed to lead teams where most members are smarter than themselves? Being the 'dumbest' person in the room with all the authority might look like a toddler being in control of the missile launch button. In such cases, specialists have direct control over their domains and the only connecting fibre between the leader and their teams can be trust and respect of each other's domain expertise. Individuals now have the power to bring whole projects down and leaders need to be extra careful when choosing team members. After the selection point, to a great extent, teams of capable and mature experts will self-assemble into fluid structures to efficiently and effectively achieve their goals.

3.3 Leaders of the new millennium

Following the presentation of historical leaders from the beginning of recorded history to the twentieth century in the previous chapter, we will present here some leadership figures who impacted their fields and organizations in the early years of the twenty-first century. The choice of leaders is in no way exhaustive, but is hopefully diverse enough in terms of their fields and expertise. Since all of them at the time of writing are alive and in most cases active, it will be difficult to reach a final conclusion about their cases, but at least in terms of their rise to power, they have all had a pretty impressive career.

3.3.1 Alex Ferguson

Manchester United is considered one of the best football (soccer) teams in the world. In addition to being a great team in the field, it has become one of the most successful and valuable franchises in sports with a team value of over $3 billion. The team achieved such a status over the past few decades with hard work and under the leadership of Sir Alex Ferguson. Ferguson remained as a coach for a record 26 seasons and during his tenure, the team accumulated 13 English titles and a number of local and international trophies.

Ferguson started his professional career as a player by playing for small Scottish clubs, initially in the position of striker. After some challenging times, he managed to land a full-time position with some of the top Scottish teams of his time. As a result of falling out with managers, he turned his career to coaching. He became known for imposing strict discipline and using young talent while pursuing attacking strategies. His coaching proved very successful for the teams he managed and eventually led him to take charge of Manchester United.

The factor that distinguishes Ferguson from other managers is that he dared to plan for the future, while the great majority of his colleagues would focus on winning and surviving. This is in most cases a requirement for coaches as the owners and fans have gone through a series of failures and expect new managers to solve the problems as soon as possible. In such a demanding environment, managers can be sacked even after three consecutive losses. This pressure naturally impacts the practices a manager tries to adopt, leading most of them to focus on winning the next game instead of working to ensure the team's long-term sustainability. Ferguson managed to avoid succumbing to this type of pressure and continued to experiment with his team's core players even after successive wins.

One of Ferguson's first moves when he took over the management of Manchester United was to plan for the long term. By modernizing the club's youth programme with promising players from the age of nine to hiring talent scouts, he managed to enlist players like David Beckham and Ryan Giggs (the most decorated footballer in England). These investments in the early acquisition of yet unknown talent, while unusual at the time, formed the core of the team that in the following decades led Manchester United to victories and shaped its identity. Investing in youth afforded Ferguson a steady supply of enthusiasm and talent for the main team. Managing talent became one of his prime activities. In doing so, he ensured the stability, consistency and continuity of the club, which offered him the additional satisfaction and pride of watching young players develop their skills and become professionals. Trust helped build loyalty and in return ensured that his players would follow his lead and give the best of themselves.

One important lesson from Ferguson's style of leadership practice is the absolute control of the leader over the team. In his case, this was not a small issue, as most of the team members were well-established and strong-minded professionals (all of them millionaires). Ferguson wouldn't hesitate in letting players go regardless of their position and importance if they failed to be a supporting member of the team. Quick and forceful responses allowed him to resolve problems in their infancy and before their influence affected the core of the team. Projecting a personality bigger than the individual team members allowed him to assume a position of dominance in decision making that preserved the unity of the team. At the same time, he would ensure that his players got the respect they deserved, especially from him, by communicating his concerns and decisions privately, and making clear that these were guided by the collective good.

As a manager, Ferguson was keen to delegate responsibilities, trusting that the job would be done. This allowed him to observe behaviour and pick up details that might be missed by someone focused exclusively on the task. This ability afforded him the luxury of intervening early on critical issues. Combined with his willingness to adapt his recruiting, training and field tactics, this allowed him to ensure the sustainability of his club.

3.3.2 Elon Musk

Born in South Africa, Elon Musk is probably the 'geekiest' of modern entrepreneurs, to use the slang term for technology entrepreneurs. The son of an engineer father and a nutritionist and author mother, he taught himself computer programming early on and developed a computer program that he sold for $500. He moved to Canada when he was 17 in an attempt to avoid serving in the South African army. He then moved to the US to seek his fortune in the most entrepreneurial market in the world. He pursued his education and was awarded degrees in physics and business. Following this, he pursued a PhD in applied physics and material sciences at Stanford University, but his entrepreneurial aspirations had another path planned for his future.

Musk soon dropped out of school to create with his brother his first start-up business, Zip2. This was a website that provided content publishing software for various news organizations. Their customers included some well-known organizations like *The New York Times* and the HEARST Corporation, among others. Working up to 100 hours per week, he managed to ensure the success of his business, which he later sold for over $300 million, making him a millionaire at the age of 28.

With the profits he made, Musk created PayPal, offering online financial services and email payments. After an initial public offering, the company was bought out by eBay (rather unwillingly). Following some of his childhood fantasies, he decided to move into the space industry and literally compete with NASA in space technology by forming the SpaceX company. He started the venture on his own, investing almost his full net worth at the time.

The risk paid off and in 2009 the company became the first to launch a privately funded, liquid-fuelled rocket into space and put a satellite into orbit. This was followed by the 2012 launch of the SpaceX Dragon vehicle that successfully docked with the International Space Station. This was another first for a commercial company and established SpaceX as a mature space company. Musk's software knowledge came into play when he led a team in his company to develop software for designing rocket parts by hand movements through the air.

In parallel with his space venture, Musk invested in building the first fully electric production sports car with the creation of Tesla Motors. The company produced the Tesla Roadster and it proved to be a great success. This allowed the company to produce a more affordable model for the public with a hybrid option for gas engines. However, this success was not easy, as the company ran into financial difficulties due to the high cost of the end products, leading Musk to personally take over as CEO. The company's comeback was outstanding, resulting in $70 million in profits.

Musk was also involved in another venture at the time, SolarCity, which developed solar power systems. With all three ventures growing and trying to reach maturity at the same time, he can probably be conceived as the top start-up entrepreneur. This situation was far from easy, as capital issues that many start-ups face hit him. The fact that neither one of his companies at the time was mature enough to support the others forced him to lay off staff and shrink his operations. To the surprise of most observers and the public, he managed to pull through and even negotiated a $1.6 billion contract with NASA. SolarCity also became the largest provider of solar power systems in the US.

As an entrepreneur, Musk is quite ruthless when taking risks, in the sense that he doesn't mind throwing everything he has (both materially and emotionally) into something that excites him and he believes has the potential for success. He is more of the renaissance type of personality, engaging in many of the arts and crafts of his time. He faced a lot of suspicion and doubt as he challenged traditional industries like the automobile industry, but it could be said that he literally took them by surprise, as most were rather inactive to his threat to react, seriously betting heavily on his failure. His career is a clear case of the will and wit of the individual challenging a sluggish establishment and changing it.

Musk seems like he came out of science fiction (a technological wizard of some sort), as if he fell of a spaceship now pushing humanity to reach the levels that technology nowadays permits. It is a rare case of a young life with big dreams and ambitions that came true so fast. However, this is by no means an accident – it is a testament to his vision, passion, dedication, hard work and a great dose of good old talent.

3.3.3 Vladimir Putin

Vladimir Putin was born in the Soviet Union to a mother who worked as a factory worker and a father who worked for the 'secret' police of the time. His lower social status and his exposure to death and loss in the post-Second World War era make him aware of his humble beginnings. As a young boy, he didn't make it into the youth party organization of his time due to his rebellious behaviour. Instead, he modelled his behaviour on the Soviet intelligence officer role models of his time that he would see in films. He engaged in martial arts, learned German and graduated with a degree in international law from Leningrad State University, allegedly by plagiarizing his thesis. He joined the KGB after graduating and was stationed in East Germany. After the fall of the Berlin Wall, he returned to Russia, where he completed his 16 years at the KGB and retired to become a politician in his native St Petersburg in 1991. Five years later, he moved to Moscow to join President Boris Yeltsin's administration, eventually becoming Acting President in 1999 and assuming the presidency in the 2000 elections. During his presidency, the country experienced unprecedented growth, with unemployment dropping and wages rising. This growth is credited to an extent to the concurrent worldwide economic growth and his prudent economic and fiscal policies. After serving the maximum period allowed by law (two consecutive terms), he ensured that the new president would appoint him as the Prime Minister. Upon the end of his term and after ensuring a change in the law to allow for six-year terms for presidents, he sought re-election and won the presidency for a third time in 2012.

Putin ascended to the leadership of the largest (geographically) country in the world, the Russian Federation, in 2000. He immediately established what is known as the 'dictatorship of the law' as his primary goal in an attempt to overcome the legal fragmentation of the country in the federal system. In reality, though, it appeared that he used the law to enforce his will, promote party loyalty and unify the country. While his motives might not be seen as altruistic, it is important to consider the situations in which he found himself that challenged the internal peace of his country and exposed it to outside threats. Russia has been a country of contradictions that has seen more transformations than probably any other country in the last century.

Some of the challenges that Putin faced included the Chechen insurgency, terrorist threats like the sieges at the Dubrovka theatre in Moscow and the school in Beslan, where hundreds of people died. More recent challenges included the crisis in the

Ukraine, with the annexation of the Crimea and the intervention to support President Assad in Syria. While in the eyes of the West these actions might seem aggressive, authoritarian and in violation of international laws, in the eyes of the Russian people, they reflected a revived patriotism and pride in their country.

The contradictions of Putin's leadership can easily be reflected in the contradictions of his country and the world at the time of his presidency. With strong historic ties to the Soviet era and the complexity perestroika added to the mix, Russia struggled to establish an institutional framework that would allow the country to develop into a capitalist democracy. Putin was viewed as an heir of the Yeltsin tradition, which used democratic terminology to establish an 'aristocracy' of a powerful elite that ruled the country and was insulated from popular accountability. For the Russian people, the strong roots and role of the state are reflected in the country's historical achievements, the most prominent of all being the victory over Nazi Germany in the Second World War.

It is necessary to consider here that the state in Russian minds raises contradictory feelings. On the one hand, it enabled great achievements like the victory over Nazi Germany, but on the other hand, it relates to persecution and suppression like that which occurred in the Stalin and Brezhnev eras. This contradictory role of the state is still reflected nowadays in the Russian society and government. Putin had first-hand experience of both expressions of the state and while he in no way wished to revert to the practices of the communist era, he was careful and sensitive in relation to the traditional Russian values of patriotism, solidarity and a powerful state.

Putin followed a technocratic approach to the management of public affairs and promoted a persona of grandeur and problem solver that allowed him to maintain high levels of popularity. While the solutions he provided might not have always been democratic in nature, they gave Russians a sense of pride and accomplishment, and also ensured the stabilization of the political order.

Putin is attributed to using 'surgical hits' to eliminate his opponents (a change from the infamous massacres of past Russian leaders), while taking measures to please the people (low taxation, keep the price of vodka low, allowing 'unhappy' citizens to leave the country, etc.). He managed to ensure the acceptance and support of the majority of his constituents by establishing an authoritarian stability on the pretext of democratic principles – something that many ambitious leaders tried, but very few managed to achieve for such a long time in modern globalized societies.

3.3.4 Pope Francis

Religious organizations are probably the longest-lasting entities in modern human history. The Catholic Church has a long history of famous and infamous acts that influenced the way in which modern Western societies evolved. Being the leader of such an organization is a challenge for any individual and the current leader of the Church seem to be working 'miracles' in terms of putting things in order.

Francis was the first-born child of Italian immigrants in Buenos Aires. His father moved from Italy to escape the dictatorship of Benito Mussolini. Francis finished his education with a technical degree in chemistry and, before joining the Jesuits, he worked as a support technician in a chemistry lab, as a janitor and as a bar bouncer. Early on in his adulthood, he suffered from a life-threatening disease that cost him part of a lung. He joined the priesthood after being inspired by a priest. In addition to his religious studies, he also studied humanities and philosophy, eventually teaching literature and psychology in various posts. At the age of 33, he was eventually ordained to the priesthood. He continued as professor of philosophy at a local seminary and completed his final stage of spiritual training as a Jesuit in Spain. He continued his academic career in the Church by serving as rector up until his removal by the Jesuit leadership due to his disagreement with the philosophical and educational roots of the Jesuits. Tensions and friction led to his eventual dissent and expulsion from the Jesuit order. He eventually became Archbishop of Buenos Aires and took initiatives to modernize the administration of the Church and bring it closer to those in need.

Francis assumed the pontificate in 2013 and projected the popular image of a transformational leader who reflects the changing image of the Catholic Church as available and open to the public. In his first day as Pope, he invited the people to bless him instead of him blessing the crowds, as was traditionally done. He followed this by washing the feet of prisoners, women and Muslims instead of only priests, and expected his bishops to engage in pastoral activities.

He personalized his engagement with his public by using multiple mediums like handwritten communication, Twitter (7.3 million followers) and riding a bus instead of the bulletproof limousine used by the predecessors. His tweets are especially popular not because they represent the Church, but because they are inviting, humble and companionate.

In order the reduce the bureaucratic heritage of the Church administration, Pope Francis innovated by restructuring the papacy into a flatter and sustainable organization. He transformed the Synod of Bishops into a decision-making body rather than a ceremonial group and adopted what others would consider radical positions on subjects like evolution and the Big Bang theory. His active engagement in environmental and political conflicts and his continuous support for the marginalized and less fortunate in society, as well as his efforts to crack down on corruption have enhanced his appeal as a leader of an institution like the Catholic Church. He even went so far as to allow priests a 'year of mercy' to forgive the 'sin of abortion', a radical and unprecedented idea for a man of God. As a man who sticks not only to the letter of his religion but also to its spirit, he continued engaging everyone he could reach by travelling around the world, improving the image and popularity of the Catholic Church while addressing the realities and the needs of the world we live in.

3.3.5 Carlos Ghosn

Born in Brazil to Lebanese immigrants, Carlos Ghosn moved to Lebanon with his mother when he was six due to health issues. He completed his secondary studies at the local Jesuit school and moved to Paris, where he completed his university studies with degrees in engineering. After graduating, he worked for a long time for the tyre manufacturer Michelin and managed to advance to the position of plant manager, head of research and development and Chief Operating Officer (COO) of the company's South American operations in Brazil. One of his achievements there was the establishment of cross-functional management teams that capitalized on best practices among the multicultural workforce of the organization, eventually returning the company to profitability. He then became CEO of Michelin North America, where he initiated and organized the restructuring of the company after the acquisition of Uniroyal.

At the age of 42, Ghosn was recruited by ailing Renault as Executive Vice President and, through restructuring, he managed to make the company profitable within a year. At that time, the company purchased a stake in Nissan and formed an alliance with it, having Ghosn as the COO. Nissan at the time was a sinking proposition both domestically and internationally, but under his leadership, drastic actions (like cutting jobs and closing plants) led to the eventual return of the company to profitability. His interventions were not only structural: he defied Japanese tradition to a great extent in multiple ways. From establishing a meritocracy (against seniority and age), tying tenure with company success and performance, and eliminating the company's complicated web of suppliers, he managed to consolidate Nissan's presence as a profitable key player in the automobile industry and raised himself to the position of CEO of both Renault and Nissan. His successes led him to extend the alliance he led with the inclusion of the largest Russian automaker AVTOVAZ. Together the companies he managed sold almost 8.5 million vehicles in 2014 and are considered to be among the industry giants.

Ghosn has a reputation as a hard-working leader (leading the life of a monk, as he said in an interview) with transnational success in some of the most diverse cultures. Inspired by the ingenuity of Indian engineers, who could innovate with the very limited resources available to them, he coined the term 'frugal engineering' to reflect the realities of today's market, where there is growing demand to deliver more value with less. This is reflected in development that does not seek to produce the best in the market, but to create something good enough for customers to buy. To showcase this philosophy, he had teams from France, Japan and India come up with a solution to a technical challenge. While all teams produced quality solutions, the Indian team produced something at a fraction of the cost of the other teams.

Expanding the partnerships of his companies with the Indian manufacturer Ashok Layland, Ghosn managed to ensure the development of one of the most successful pick-up trucks in South-East Asia and the Middle East. Focusing and spreading the best engineering practices of various cultures, Ghosn managed to develop teams that can innovate in adverse and competitive market environments. This allowed his organizations to grow in periods of economic crisis and form alliances to capitalize on talent and skill wherever in the world this was available.

3.3.6 James Cameron

Considering a film director as a leader might seem unusual, but if one considers that a team of 3,000 people developed a film like *Avatar*, which grossed more than $2.7 billion worldwide, the connection with effective and efficient leadership should become apparent. If we also consider that *Avatar* was not the exception but the norm, as it followed *Titanic*, which grossed $2.1 billion, and a preceding series of box-office hits like *The Terminator* and *Aliens* to name but a few, we have a person with exceptional leadership skills comparable to those of most well-known leaders, both past and present.

The son of an artist and a nurse, James Cameron was born in Ontario, but moved to California with his family when he was 17. He attempted to study physics at a community college, but he soon switched to English and eventually dropped out to work at different places, including becoming a truck driver. He became fascinated by film technology and would constantly study the latest developments in the industry.

Inspired by *Star Wars* in 1977, he got involved in filmmaking as an amateur first and later on as a professional in small productions. He taught himself to use the technology involved in filmmaking and became resourceful and efficient while working on small projects.

Growing as special effects director, Cameron eventually made his debut as a film director for *The Terminator*, the screenplay for which he himself developed. As a new and untested director, he sold the screenplay for one dollar just to get the opportunity to direct it. The movie was his first hit, earning ten times more than it cost and establishing him as a successful film director. He is credited for much of the innovation and success of 3D film technology and action films. He is also well known for his interest in science and engineering, and he is credited as the first man to perform a solo deep-sea dive at the deepest part of the Mariana Trench.

As a film director, Cameron gained the reputation of being very demanding, selfish and even cruel at times. His leadership style seemed dictatorial as he would expect absolute dedication and professionalism from those working for him. However, his temper seemed to have subsided after his experience leading teams on the open sea during his deep-sea dive explorations.

Of course, breaking new ground all the time is not something that standard leadership practice can guarantee, so the sense of exploration for motivating and building teams became an absolute necessity for Cameron. The rewards following the successes more than compensated for the effort expended and the criticism endured by his team in developing his masterpieces. Another aspect of his leadership style is his engagement with frontline tasks (something other directors consider unworthy of their time), which sets an example for collaboration amongst his team. He also makes sure he is surrounded by department heads that can be supportive and engaging with their teams in fulfilling his demanding requests. By placing enormous effort and emphasis on every detail of his products and surrounding himself with a leadership team that was supportive and complemented his demanding leadership style, he ensured that the films they produced offered the best movie experiences of his time with the highest grossing movies ever.

3.3.7 Indra Nooyi

Despite having been born to a conservative Tamil-speaking Indian family in Madras who valued kindness and the good in every person, Indra Nooyi was an avid cricket player and played guitar in an all-girl rock band. After completing her secondary education at a private Catholic school in Chennai, she was awarded an undergraduate degree in the sciences from the Madras Christian College in 1974 and an MBA in Calcutta. She started her professional career as product manager in India and moved to Yale University in the US to complete a master's degree in management. She began her career in the US by holding strategy positions at Motorola and Asea Brown Boveri until 1994, when she joined PepsiCo. She rose to the position of President and CFO of PepsiCo in 2001, where she directed the restructuring, divestiture and strategy of the company until she became CEO in 2006. Since then, she has featured in the list of the most powerful women in *Forbes*, *Fortune*, *TIME* and the *Wall Street Journal* almost continually.

Nooyi's philosophy is summed up as performance with purpose and reflects the modern trend to fight obesity by improving the content of the company's products while making the company environmentally friendly. This practice allowed her to establish a clear vision for PepsiCo and herself as an inspirational leader. To support this vision, she worked on acquiring companies with healthy product lines and, ahead of the competition, she reduced the sugar and fat content of the beverages produced by the company while developing biodegradable packaging solutions. While this affected short-term earnings, it has proven successful in terms of the long-term growth of the company. In addition, she became instrumental in streamlining the company by selling its fast food chains (Pizza Hut, KFC and Taco Bell) and its bottling division, which financially, and in terms of image, were dragging the company down.

Regarding her team's performance, Nooyi expects nothing but excellence from herself and those who work for her. She is quite persistent in getting her people to come up with solutions and she is comfortable providing negative feedback, occasionally with a dose of humour. She listens to her team even though she might disagree with them, but she is quite focused and direct when she makes up her mind. She does not hesitate to ask for help (ex-CEOs of the company serve as her trusted advisors) and remains highly collaborative at all times.

Nooyi brings with her to work many of the principles of her Indian background. She appreciates diversity and ensures that it is appreciated and that everyone who works for her brings the values of their heritage with them. Assuming that people have good intentions, as she was raised to believe, allows her to show empathy and avoid misunderstandings. Her spontaneity, empathy and respect for diversity allow her to relate to anyone from the bottom line and all the way up to the boardroom. These traits, complemented by her great analytical skills, make her one of the most efficient business leaders of her time.

3.3.8 Mark Zuckerberg

Born into a well-educated family of doctors in 1984 right outside New York City, Mark Zuckerberg had a privileged life and an inclination for both science and classical studies. He could read and write French, Hebrew, Latin and Ancient Greek, and excelled at fencing. He was quite a fan of the Greek *Iliad* and *Odyssey*, while obeying the 'healthy mind, healthy body' Greek philosophy. Early on, his father taught him programming and even went so far as to hire a software developer to tutor him privately. He got to the point of taking graduate courses while still in high school and developed a communication network among the computers in his home and his father's business. He was the kind of 'geek' who not only played computer games, but actually created them. While still in high school, he developed a music player capable of learning the user's listening habits, which received recognition from the software community.

Zuckerberg studied psychology and computer studies at Harvard University. While there, he developed software that brought students together in deciding about class selection and forming study groups. This served as the precursor of what would become Facebook. He dropped out of college in his sophomore year to officially launch Facebook and has worked on that venture since then. Something that started as a Harvard initiative spread to other schools and eventually took over the world, with over 1.5 billion active users in 2015. With a clear focus on its mission to connect people and opening up the world, Facebook managed to combine profit from a free product that allowed users to comfortably connect with each other across physical and national boundaries.

Facebook was organized as a flat hierarchy, with Zuckerberg at the top and in absolute control of the company. This reduced hierarchy allows for more collaboration and creativity among the workforce, while creating an inviting atmosphere that makes it attractive for talent to join and move up the ranks fast. Facebook's flat organizational structure also resulted in cost reductions, improved communication efficiency for messages and ideas, flexibility in organizing units arounds products and sustainable innovation.

As a leader, Zuckerberg is flexible in accepting his mistakes and learning from them. He is confident in his beliefs and decisions, even to the point of disregarding or ignoring his board. His dominant personality and technical expertise seem to portray him as a stereotypical success model of the millennial generation. Raised by supportive parents, he projects the image that things come easy to him, but his commitment and hard work might suggest that success is more an issue of persistence and effort than upbringing and luck. He is one of the few leaders who advance to the position of CEO at a young age, and through a product and company he developed with his team. One would expect that his limited experience of organizational structures and politics would impede his ability to lead his company, but he made sure that the company evolved to fit his style as it matured and grew through the fast learning curve he established for himself.

Zuckerberg has been named many times as one of the leading and most influential business leaders of his era. His ambition remained to connect everyone on planet Earth and beyond when this became possible. He strongly held the belief that a connected world can more efficiently communicate issues and develop solutions that will effectively resolve conflict and suffering. His decision to donate 99 per cent of his Facebook shares (roughly $45 billion at the time of the announcement) to charity is a testimony to his belief that a better world can be created when people share and work together.

3.3.9 David Petraeus

As a career officer, David Petraeus was considered one of the most successful military leaders of his time. He was born 50 miles from New York City into the family of a librarian mother and an immigrant sea captain father from the Netherlands. His father used to captain merchant vessels in convoys in the Atlantic under the U-boat threat during the Second World War. He picked up a lot of his father's traits, especially the drive to take on hard challenges and excel. This led him to become a star cadet when he entered the US Military Academy at West Point, from where he eventually graduated at the top of his class.

Petraeus joined the infantry and managed to steadily grow in the ranks while devoting a lot of his time to education. Always excelling in his studies, he managed to earn a master's degree and eventually a PhD in international relations. His thesis on counterinsurgency in Vietnam helped him to form his military philosophy, which later guided his command. After a brief career as a professor at West Point, he returned to military service in 1987. He managed to command a battalion and at the age of 46 became brigadier general. He served in Baghdad and Mosul in Iraq and later on in Bosnia as part of NATO forces, and eventually became full general in 2007.

At that time, Petraeus was sent to Iraq to implement his counterinsurgency ideas. With support from additional troops, he managed to suppress the violence in Iraq and eventually took over the command of US Central Command and coordinated all US military operations. In 2010 he was appointed as commander of the US forces in Afghanistan and in 2011 as Director of the CIA. His career ended unexpectedly after his extramarital affair with his biographer surfaced in 2011.

When not in army gear, Petraeus had the appearance more of an academic than a warrior. His pleasant disposition and eagerness to explain allowed him to communicate his messages convincingly while displaying his deep understanding of the military practice. He would occasionally display a lack of empathy and he would never hide ambitions. His drive to win would get him to openly declare his objectives in an effort to add more pressure on himself and to commit to their achievement. In addition, he made every effort to ensure that his physical fitness matched his intellectual strength as he thoroughly believed in the balance of body and mind for effective leadership.

He was credited with the success of the counterinsurgent initiative in Iraq as he implemented a change of strategy with high casualties. He replaced the previous practice of US forces, which moved in armoured vehicles and barricaded themselves in fortified camps, with a mobile deployment of units in forward bases and patrols on foot. Of course, this exposed the troops to deadly attacks, but it proved to be the only effective strategy in flushing out the insurgents and stopping their advancement. Iraq at that time was considered a losing proposition and was a challenge that very few career generals would have accepted. His successful legacy allowed for a cultural and doctrinal change in one of the most rigid institutions, the army.

3.3.10 Angela Merkel

Angela Merkel was born in Hamburg in what it was at the time West Germany. Her father was a Lutheran pastor and teacher with Polish ancestry, and her mother was a teacher of English and Latin with roots in the Social Democratic Party of Germany. Following her father's pursuit of theological studies, the family moved to a rural area north of Berlin, where Angela grew up. At school she excelled in maths and became fluent in Russian. She entered university and studied physics, eventually receiving a doctorate in quantum chemistry. She became a published researcher and joined politics after the fall of the Berlin Wall and the reunification of Germany.

Merkel's move into full-time politics resulted in her election to the Bundestag in the first federal election since reunification and she has continued to be re-elected ever since. Following her first election, she was appointed as Minister for Women and Youth and later on she became Minister for the Environment and Nuclear Safety. After the defeat of the government in the 1998 election, she became Secretary-General of her male-dominated Christian Democratic Union party. Her election to the leadership of the party increased the party's popularity and after leading the opposition coalition, she managed to be elected Chancellor of Germany in 2005. She was the first female Chancellor and has held that position ever since.

Despite her socialist roots, Merkel was a supporter of market reforms that would allow the German economy to be more competitive, like removing barriers to laying off employees and increasing the number of weekly working hours. This allowed German business to reduce costs during economic downturns, sustaining their competitiveness until conditions improved. While she is considered less charismatic than other leaders and as possessing little style, she has managed to become the longest-serving elected female head of government. Despite this, she is not considered a good speaker, takes time to make up her mind (considering all possible risks) and seem to occasionally have a pliable ideology. A case in point is her U-turn from stubbornly supporting nuclear energy to completely abandoning it in favour of alternative sources after the Fukushima nuclear reactor disaster in Japan.

Probably as part of her character, upbringing and education, Merkel remained pragmatic and methodical at all times and true to her dogma of progressing, even by only a few centimetres at a time. She managed to successfully lead Germany through the economic crisis and is often regarded as the most powerful woman in the world. Her efforts to build a multiculturally diverse Germany have materialized with the refugee crisis that Europe faced as conflict in Syria, Iraq, Afghanistan and Africa continued. Her decision to open up Germany's borders and accept immigrants was radical and reflected her worries that refugee misery could lead to huge problems for Europe if it was not addressed properly.

3.4 Characteristics of leaders of the twenty-first century

While for the historical leaders we saw in the previous chapter we had an idea of their achievements throughout their lives, most modern leaders we have discussed here are quite active nowadays, so there is still room for the rise or fall of their 'empires'. However, what they have achieved up to now is quite impressive, so their place in this chapter's pantheon is deserved. Yet, identifying common characteristics that led to their success might not be as easy as with the historical leaders featured in the previous chapter simply because a lot of detail relating to them and their behind-the-scenes actions are unknown, and will require the passage of time to reveal details that might now be too sensitive to see the light of day.

Nevertheless, there are some characteristics about their early lives and their rise to leadership that can be easily identified. For one thing, they really didn't inherit anything, at least in the sense of a position of status. Their competence in their field of expertise in undeniable, whether it is technology, politics, entertainment or something else, and they have all worked hard to get where they are. Communicating their vision and attracting followers to their cause is another common trait, in addition to their ability to thrive on change and redrawing boundaries. In terms of integrity, the verdict might not be so clear with regard to some of them, but their competence in

Table 3.1 Leadership characteristics of twenty-first-century leaders

Leader	Field	Education	Leadership style
Alex Ferguson	Sports	Informal	Autocratic
Elon Musk	Technology	Formal	Autocratic
Vladimir Putin	Politics	Both	Autocratic
Pope Francis	Religion	Both	Inclusive
Carlos Ghosn	Business	Formal	Both
James Cameron	Entertainment	Informal	Autocratic
Indra Nooyi	Business	Formal	Inclusive
Mark Zuckerberg	Technology	Formal	Autocratic
David Petraeus	Military	Formal	Autocratic
Angela Merkel	Politics	Formal	Inclusive

leading their teams to success has been proved by their achievements. While some may appear autocratic in nature, they are all quite comfortable delegating tasks to capable individuals and engaging others in problem solving.

Readers should once again be careful in the impressions they form here as the sample size in this chapter is extremely small and is only meant to serve as a testament to the diversity of fields in which leadership can be observed. In addition, the sample is biased in the sense that only successful leaders are included. We should not forget that these leaders are still navigating in uncharted territory, so the final verdict on them might change. However, it is undeniable that they are advancing in their 'field' to new heights.

4   Theoretical perspectives

Having seen expressions of leadership in the previous chapters, we will deal here with the theoretical representations that were developed to explain its many facets. One might question why it is important to have theories with respect to leadership and what benefits would come from their development. Considering theories is a traditional approach to discussing practical implications in addition to advancing knowledge and our understanding of our world. The primary advantage that theories offer is that they allow for the development of models that as abstractions of reality allow for a much easier understanding and provide a frame of reference and experimentation. Models allow us to communicate efficiently complex phenomena and to see how variations of their parameters and variables can lead to alternative interpretations that will eventually suggest practical improvements.

While it is great to have theories that realistically represent phenomena, we should always be aware of their potential disadvantages. In the social sciences in particular, which is where the study of leadership mostly belongs, we always need to be aware of the abstractions theories provide, as they are not complete representations of the phenomena they model. The explanation and motives for leadership could be simple enough, like necessity or to provide an evolutionary advantage that increases the chances of survival for the leader, or even something like a call to arms. Allowing for some flexibility in what theories consider as motivations for leadership and how we adapt to what we are facing is probably the best we can make of these theories. As we will see in this chapter, this is the route that most theories of leadership follow.

4.1 Constituents of leadership

Factors that surround leadership can in general be classified according to three influential elements and the ways in which they interact and influence each other: the leader, the followers and the environment (see Figure 4.1). The latter includes the organizational/societal setting in which the leadership takes place, the projects and tasks the leader and the followers are involved in, and any stakeholders that influence the situation in any way. All three of these elements are dynamic in nature and are expected to change during the application of leadership. Existing theories of leadership usually focus on some of these elements and account to an extent for influences on the others.

Before we get into the core elements of leadership, it is worth mentioning the extended environment in which it takes place. This includes the internal features of the organization in which a group operates and the wider environment (stakeholders that influence the organization). The former might be seen as the micro-environment where the leader, the group and the goals are set, while the latter includes the macro-environment of the society, market or world that influences the organization. The interaction of these two perspectives (micro and macro) is greatly ignored in modern leadership theories, as we will see later on. However, the fact that they are there and provide the background to the expression of leadership make their consideration necessary. The main elements that identify an organization in its extended environment (stakeholders and the world at large) are its structure and culture. Since the focus of this chapter is on the popular theories and practices that have been developed to explain leadership and given that organizational structure and culture were not specifically addressed by these theories, we will refrain from discussing them until the next chapter, when we will attempt to put everything together into a cohesive framework.

The view of the three influential elements (leader, followers and environment) clearly places the leaders in a prominent place in the traditional treatment of the phenomenon of leadership and, according to popular belief, they form the core of the phenomenon. As individuals, leaders are expected to possess certain qualities and characteristics that distinguish them from the rest of the individuals in the group. These include personality characteristics like maturity, influence, strong will, extraversion, etc. and physical characteristics like appearance (being tall and strong),

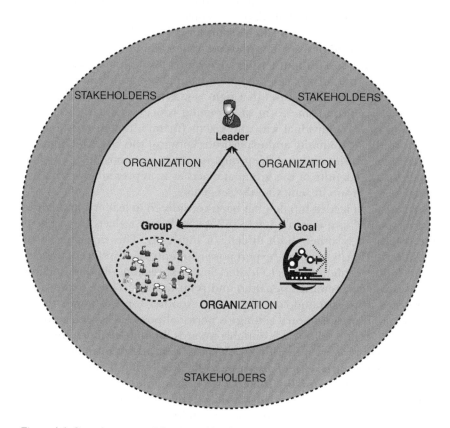

Figure 4.1 Constituents and factors of leadership

intelligence, fluency, etc. Obviously some individuals possess such characteristics more than others and one would expect them to be more suitable for leadership positions.

Another of the elements involved in leadership is the goal. This is expressed in the form of a common purpose that the leader and the followers adopt. The word 'common' here is key as it provides the ethical tone that leadership is an acceptable arrangement that benefits everyone. It also stresses the need for leaders to work collaboratively and within acceptable norms with the followers in order to achieve their goals.

Alternative perspectives where leadership is viewed as a process focus on the dynamic nature and interaction of the three elements. This emphasis on the process inherently implies that the three elements interact and affect each other during the application of leadership. Otherwise leadership exists in a social setting and a leader affects and is affected by followers and stakeholders. This approach emphasizes that leadership is not a linear, one-way phenomenon, but rather is an evolving interaction of its elements. One form that the interaction between leader and followers takes is influence. This refers to the ability of leaders to affect the behaviour of their followers and vice versa. When leadership is defined in this manner, it becomes available to everyone and appears as something that many can achieve, rather than being restricted to the formally designated leader in a group.

A basic question when studying leadership from the perspective of a process is how the leader is identified. Do they get assigned or do they emerge? When leadership is a function of a position within an organization, we consider this assigned leadership. This is typically what we experience in the organizational world where someone is raised to a management, head or executive position. When an individual is perceived as the central point in a group without having an assigned position, we consider this emergent leadership. In the former case, someone from above grants an individual the right to lead, while in the latter case, that right is granted by the leader's peers. While the former is based on some form of screening process, the latter is based on the involvement of the individual with the group (mainly though communication), the extent of their familiarity and expertise relating to the task, the interests of the group and their consideration of the group members' opinions. In a sense, an emergent leader fits the identity of the group and acts as its representative with the authority to engage the group in achieving the set goals.

A final characteristic of leadership that has been considered in leadership theories is the concept of 'power' as a contributor to influence. Power reflects the capacity to control the behaviour of others both directly or indirectly. This capacity can be appointed (position authority), gained (expert power) or entrusted (referent power), such as when the followers identify/elect a leader. Some expressions of power include the provision of privileges, rewards, penalties and punishments. These expressions are often considered as reward and coercive power. Another form of power that is identified in group and organizational settings is personal power. This refers to the capacity of leaders to incline followers favourably towards them. Role modelling best behaviour and practices is one way in which leaders can acquire this form of power.

A type of power that attracts a lot of attention in the leadership literature is coercive power. Coercion refers to forcing someone to do something against their will and includes both punishment and reward practices. While many theorists who study leadership refused to consider coercive practices as an ideal form of leadership, it is undeniably true that many leaders (both well-known and unknown) rely on this form of power to control subordinates. A case in point is Adolf Hitler, as mentioned in Chapter 2. Such leaders are self-interested and use coercion to achieve their personal goals instead of focusing on the goals of the group or organization they represent.

4.2 Leadership and management

In the context of organizational studies, leadership is best characterized in terms of its relationship to management. Before delving into the theories that have been developed to explain and guide leadership, we need to cover the distinction between leadership and management, if there really is one. Scholars often express the relationship as leadership versus management, but both managers and leaders can benefit from seeing the two as intertwined and inseparable. Leadership involves processes of management and vice versa. Studies of management do not have such a long history as attempts to theorize leadership. Academics became concerned with management in the early twentieth century at a time when organizations were becoming more complex in terms of their purpose, outputs and modes of production.

Early work by Frederic Winslow Taylor at the beginning of the twentieth century was one of the first approaches to scientific management that went on to influence models of mass manufacturing. During the same period, similar work by Max Weber on bureaucracies conceptualized the workings of large and complex organizations. A third strand to this work on management emerged later on in Taylor's principles of management, often referred to as Classical Management. He studied management holistically in the sense that he looked at the work of the whole organization rather than breaking down work into specific tasks. He identified five functions of management: planning, organizing, commanding, coordinating and controlling.

These classical functions of management were largely uncontested until, in 1973, Henry Mintzberg carried out an in-depth study into the nature of management, in which he and his team observed managers at work and asked them to keep work diaries. The analysis of these diaries revealed that the idea of the manager as a rational, ordered planner was misleading, as most managers 'worked at an unrelenting pace ... their activities are characterized by brevity, variety and discontinuity and they are strongly oriented to action and dislike reflective activities'. In contrast to Taylor's study, Mintzberg found that managers often carried out their work in conditions of extreme ambiguity and that much of their time was spent developing relationships within the organization. This study clarified the instances in which management and leadership intersect – when a team lacks clarity and needs direction, and when communication is crucial to success. Although at times they might both communicate similar information, the primary responsibility for leaders is the effective communication of a vision, while managers need to communicate the objectives for the accomplishment of that vision.

One of the 'deeper' conceptual differences is that while managers see mistakes as situations that need to be avoided and eradicated in order to sustain and improve efficiency, leaders see mistakes as opportunities for learning and growth. Another more classical and popular difference found in the literature is the long-term perspective leaders have (they work for the future) versus the short-term perspective of managers (they focus on the present). While this is typically true, a crisis situation or emergencies might force a change of roles in leaders and managers (see Figure 4.2). One needs to be careful crossing the boundaries between the two roles, as leaders can be in ineffective management roles, such as when they attempt

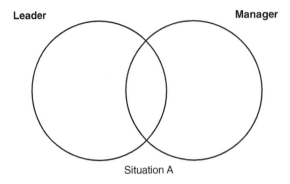

Situation A

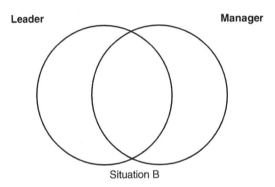

Situation B

Figure 4.2 Overlap of the roles of leader and manager

to motivate when instead they need to organize teams, and managers can be in ineffective leaders' roles, such as when they attempt to suppress change when instead they need to embrace it.

Of course, focusing on differences distracts from the similarities and overlaps that could be essential for the success of organizations. Prominent among these is that both leaders and managers work for the same organization and their purpose is to ensure that organizational goals are achieved. To ensure this success, they can motivate, inspire, discipline, plan, supervise, mentor, etc. It could be said that the two roles are not different and are probably two sides of the same coin. It could be that both roles are different expressions of leadership and that, according to the task at hand, the role of leader or manager is assumed. Hopefully, the rest of this book will provide a lot of material that will help to answer this question.

4.3 Early approaches to describing leadership

The scientific methods and practices as we know them today have not been with us for very long. In that respect, early attempts to describe leadership are mainly in the form of principles and guidelines for prospective leaders to follow. Often, these guidelines address specific situations like political engagements, fighting wars and building sustainable organizations. Some representative texts highlighting aspects of leadership as perceived by their authors will be presented here as a prelude to the more modern attempts to explain leadership and guide its practice. As we hope to see, the contrast between the old and the new is not so great. For these early approaches, only a descriptive presentation will be attempted without any critique of their advantages and disadvantages in describing the ideal leader. Given that the scientific approach was not fully developed during the times that the early theories were formed, the criticism will be reserved for those theories that appeared later on, which have no excuse for their shortcomings in that respect.

4.3.1 The Sage Kings

Early discussions on leadership come from Chinese mythology in the form of representations of culture heroes who set up civilization and were collectively called the Sage Kings. Their roots go back as far as records indicate (twenty-third century BC and beyond) and all the way up to the third century BC, as reflected in the *Analects* of Confucius and other Chinese scholars. Among the Kings, we can find probably the first account of a female leader (Nu Wa). While chief among their roles was delivering and enabling innovations like writing, music, agriculture and medicine, their political and leadership abilities extended to modern leader characteristics like meritocracy, team cohesiveness and harmony among the various components of society and virtue, to name but a few.

A case in point in terms of meritocracy was Emperor Yao, who as a conscious ruler saw his son as an unworthy successor and arranged for a competent and virtuous common man (Shun) to succeed him. He spent years training and coaching Shun, who eventually followed in his footsteps and established a meritocratic state where promotion was based on fairness, integrity and respectfulness when interacting with the public. Shun, like his predecessor, appointed his best official Yu as his successor towards the end of his life, conscious of the fact that his son wouldn't make for a good leader.

We see expressions of the Sage King in the writings of Confucius, where the leaders, in addition to their political function, also serve as educators for their people. This refers more to the form of teaching that leaders project as role models in their societies. In this way the teaching that is based on the learning of principles is enhanced by the real-life models the leaders portray by their behaviour and actions. Modern similarities exist in the terms of the maxim of acting towards others in the way you want others to act towards you. A noted difference compared to modern beliefs is that the educational Confucian policy is not about intelligence and skills, but about virtue. Any training and the skills one develops are all for the purpose of cultivating character and not just for the achievement of physical or intellectual strength. A noted example is the case of one of his disciples, Zi You, who as a magistrate emphasized the importance of music education for his people.

This eventually led to a system of practices and formal etiquette aiming to instil discipline and guide someone towards moral behaviour. To achieve this end, the leaders, according to Confucius, needed to work towards developing their own morality. Virtue, in the words of Confucius, is like the wind for the noble leaders and like the grass for the common person. When the wind sweeps over, the grass will gently bend. According to the Confucian philosophy, the greatness of leaders is directly associated with their concern for the good of the people.

4.3.2 The Philosopher King

At approximately the same time as Confucius is said to have written the *Analects*, in another part of the globe, in ancient Athens, Plato was developing his ideas on what a leader (ηγεμών) should be (fourth to third centuries BC). Plato's core idea of leadership was presented in *The Republic* and is expressed through the ideal ruler, a Philosopher King. According to Plato, in order for wisdom and political greatness to exist, either philosophers should be leaders or the leaders should embody the power and spirit of philosophers. Anyone who is not in either of these categories should stand aside if a sustainable community is ever to see the day of light.

The Philosopher King in Plato's view is distinguished by his prudence and virtue, in addition to his love for learning and understanding the eternal essence of his world. Among the traits he displays are his willingness to admit wrongdoing in any form and his passion for the truth. To these Plato would add decency, magnificence, bravery, moderation, grace and friendship. Above all, though, in order for an ideal state to exist, a sense of justice is the cornerstone principle of a virtuous leader. It is worth mentioning here that, according to Plato, educating potential leaders includes among other things military training, theoretical and practical knowledge, ethical principles and living a virtuous lifestyle. It is the responsibility of the state to select the appropriate individual as leader based on their education, intellect and character. We see here the democratic principle at work, in that leaders are elected and are not appointed in any other way.

These leadership traits reflect the philosopher in an ideal society who, as a balanced and virtuous individual, advances through education his physical and intellectual strength that nature gave him. This allows him to become a moral leader and to return to the society what the city did for him. In this way, the leaders surpass the commoners (non-philosophers) and naturally emerge as heads of the society. An interesting point to note here is that leadership is legitimized not only by expert knowledge but also by impartiality and fairness.

Plato also provides some insights for the followers, who are expected to go about their business and behave according to their natural strengths and abilities. This practice is reflected in the definition of justice as possessing and acting according to what one owns. The leader's trait of fairness contributes by acting as an integrator for the different members of society; in this way, understanding and cooperation among them enables the harmonious and sustainable development of the state.

It is evident that the two great thinkers Confucius and Plato shared many of the dogmas of a good leader, although they diverged in terms of the way they approached the subject. Confucius was more focused on how someone *becomes* good, while Plato seemed to be concerned more with what *is* good. Conceptually it is also worth mentioning that the focus of Greek thinking on truth suggests a more dialectic debate and engagement of opinions for the truth to emerge, while the Chinese thinking sees truth as more subjective and limited to the thinker's capability, so one should focus on being in touch with the whole that transcends human materialism. Apart from the differences between the two schools of thinking, it is evident that both believed that leadership needs to be based on morality and the innate nature of the individual. These characteristics form the main requirement for leadership in the pre-Christianity era.

4.3.3 The Rule of St. Benedict

In the fifth century AD, Benedict of Nursia developed a monastic guide (*Regula Benedicti*) aimed at organizing the life of the main religious organizations of his time: the monasteries. The book became quite popular as one of the first attempts to establish order while balancing the individuality of the zealot with the formality of an institution. The persistence of the book as a textbook for monastic life all the way up to modern times is a testament to its success in terms of establishing and leading monastic communities. In that respect, it is one of the first successful social models.

At the core of the Rule is the leader, whose primary virtue is humility. His vision, above all personal rewards and ambitions, is the vitality and health of his organization. Competence and ambition are complementary traits in support of his primary vision. The leader should also display grace, but should be quite firm and unbiased when it comes to disciplining and even expelling followers if this would preserve the health of the organization. The Rule also suggests more specific principles, such as leading by example, using actions instead of words and observing followers to resolve any arguments as soon as possible, as well as recruiting committed and dedicated individuals who would value stability and enrich the fraternity spirit of the communities.

As would be expected, ethics play a central role in leading the monastic communities. However, it was understood that the enforcement of ethical behaviour was not an effective way to enforce its practice and so it was up to the leader to support a culture where ethical decision making would be considered the norm. In addition to the expected focus on the Christian archetypes of ethics, the Rule covers organizational behaviour and structure with clarity. A flat hierarchy was the preferred operational structure to avoid centralization and bureaucracy. When the number of people was too high for an efficient flat structure to operate, it was suggested that offshoot groups should form independent and economically autonomous organizations with strong ties to the original communities.

An important aspect for the communities was their sustainability. It would be the leader's responsibility to ensure succession plans were in place to ensure a smooth transition to another competent leader. Even to this day, modern organizations struggle in this respect. According to the Rule, the process of selecting leaders should be democratic and based on merit alone, and not on seniority, despite its importance in relation to continuity and the maintenance of knowledge. Another element that would ensure sustainability was risk taking and challenging the status quo as a way to innovate. In that respect, it was considered appropriate for the front line (the lower levels in the community) to challenge and innovate within the existing paradigm, leaving it to the higher levels in the community to challenge the paradigm. Even innovations that would lead to paradigm shifts would be allowed as long as the stimulus came from the outside environment.

4.4.4 The Prince

In the midst of the turbulent politics of the early stages of the Renaissance in the sixteenth century), *The Prince* was written by Niccolo Machiavelli in an attempt to lay down the principles and practices that political leaders of his time should follow. The text aimed to be a guide for new rulers and is known for its controversial position that rulers must be willing to act immorally at times to maintain their position of power.

To that end, deceit and the extermination of political opponents were not unusual practices. Despite this radical stance, the text can be seen as a realistic reflection of the brutal reality of Machiavelli's time and of past centuries.

Regarding the qualities of the leader himself, while virtue is admirable for its own sake, acting on it alone could be detrimental to the state. In that respect, vicious actions can be justified if they benefit the state. Ensuring the benefit of the many at all costs is, according to this view, the best way to maintain power. When it comes to choosing between two extremes (like being cruel or merciful), Machiavelli always suggests the most despised option as the appropriate one. Self-interest is of primary importance for a prince and is a requirement for his survival as a leader.

The leader in Machiavelli's opinion is an efficient problem solver who acts before problems fully manifest themselves. This might result in an authoritarian ruler who crushes opposition in its infancy before it can develop into a sizeable threat. Seeking more is a natural state for a leader, but only when their current state is not at risk. Understanding the way in which the state functions and how wars are conducted is necessary in order to be a successful leader. To assist him in his rule, the prince appoints administrators who are dependent on him so as to reduce the risk of them forming alliances against him. For conquests that remained accustomed to their own laws, Machiavelli suggests destroying them to eliminate potential revolts unless the leader is willing to live there or let them retain their laws with a government that is friendly to him. While this was a reflection to the Medici rulers of the time, today we might see similarities of such practices in the mergers and acquisitions of modern corporations.

The first tasks of a new prince are the stabilization and enforcement of his power by shaping the political structure to his needs. Corruption can be used as a means to achieve the social benefits of stability and security. Unlike past accounts, which presumed that the role of leaders was to strive for an idealistic society, *The Prince* presents a realistic account of what can be achieved based on the subjective notion of what is right and wrong in the pursuit of universal stability. In a sense, the text seems to complement Machiavelli's *Discourses on Livy*, which in a series of lessons discusses the creation and structure of a new republic. Machiavelli is like a political scientist of his time who develops best practices for political regimes, leaving it up to the individual to make the choice of what they will pursue.

4.4 Modern approaches

In modern times, we see a more systematic effort to analyse the phenomenon of leadership and then formulate it in a theoretical framework. The select theories that will be presented here refer to the successful (at times) and most popular attempts at explaining and providing guidelines for leadership. The aim of presenting these leadership theories with their key characteristics is to allow for a comparative appreciation of their core principles and focus, as well as their strength and weaknesses in describing the phenomenon and practice of leadership.

4.4.1 Trait theory

At the beginning of the twentieth century, the turbulent political times and the Industrial Revolution brought about the need in leadership studies to define and explain leadership. One of the first systematic attempts, which was inspired by past perceptions of leaders as great men, focused on the traits that great leaders displayed. By identifying the innate characteristics of great politicians, military leaders and influential social and religious figures, one could seek to identify them in individuals who could be potential leaders. At the time and according to the theory, people were born with certain traits that predisposed them towards natural leadership actions. Based on this hypothesis, organizations needed to establish screening and evaluation processes to ensure that the individuals who possessed leadership traits were selected and advanced. The situation/environment and the followers are considered of secondary importance, and good leaders are expected to perform well no matter what they face.

The challenge of such a position was the identification of a universally acceptable set of traits that are distinctly associated with leadership. Some of the traits associated with charismatic leaders that help them attain self-actualization and social power include intelligence, persistence, insight, alertness, self-monitoring and self-motivation. As the thinking of the theory progressed and in an attempt to explain the rarity of great leaders, an association was made with the environment where leadership was to appear. Relevance to the situation where the leader functions became in this way an important factor in the expression of leadership. In this respect, successful leaders in one situation were not necessary successful in a different situation. In addition, the effect of followers also became apparent and traits that supported a more engaging working relationship with their group members became the focus of studies.

Developments of the traits approach began to be more specific and included drive, persistence, risk taking, self-confidence, accountability, tolerance of ambiguity and frustration, and the ability to influence others and formalize social structures. Later on, traits perceived by followers as important included masculinity, adjustability, power, intelligence, conservatism and extraversion. The dominance of male role models in those times greatly influenced the perception of leadership and continued to do so subsequently.

The trait approach was revived in the twenty-first century under the label of charismatic leadership, with Barack Obama as one of its modern representatives. The traits of charismatic leaders, according to the modern perspective, include self-monitoring, engaging, motivation in the pursuit of social power and self-motivation. Social intelligence became another popular trait identified in research studies, along with the verbal and perceptual abilities of the leader.

While the traits approach seems intuitively appealing, provides benchmarks for evaluation and is supported by a century's worth of research, it has been criticized for its reliance on a diverse set of traits that subjectively have been adopted by different researchers. In addition, this approach focuses exclusively on the leader and completely ignores the followers or the context in a direct way. It makes no suggestion as to the type of leader who would be appropriate for a particular situation, instead insinuating that a great leader would do well in any situation.

In organizations, the traits approach suggests having people in managerial positions who fit designated leadership profiles. This makes professional development and training efforts in organizations difficult to identify and implement as the particulars of the organization and the environment always seem to crop up as influential factors. According to this view, someone is born a leader and there is very little that society and organizations can do other than recognizing these individuals through screening and promoting them to leadership positions.

4.4.2 The skills approach

While the traits approach is based on the inherent characteristics (mainly personality traits) of leaders, it became apparent that certain skills and abilities that people develop over time greatly contribute to leadership effectiveness. The skills approach originally considered technical, human and conceptual skills that leaders can master, contrary to traits that show what leaders are. Skills in this respect represent abilities to accomplish goals and objectives using knowledge and expertise.

While the need for technical skills might be easily understood as it provides leaders with competencies relating to their domain of activity, relating to the domain of their group's activities, human skills were meant to address the ability to collaborate with others across the organizational hierarchy. The modern expression of such skills (people skills as they are frequently called nowadays) includes being aware of their own perspective as well as that of others, being adaptable and sensitive to the needs and motivations of others, and being capable of engaging and inspiring others to accomplish a common goal. The third category of skills includes conceptual skills like analytic capabilities, reasoning and the ability to process abstractions (ideas and concepts). More specifically, such skills, when complemented by an understanding of economic and political situations, help to effectively articulate a vision and devise a strategy to achieve goals and objectives.

Based on the premise that learning from experience can help in the acquisition of leadership, major organizations like the US Army and the Department of Defense built on the skills approach and created development programmes to suit their needs. In addition to the individual attributes and competencies, such programmes took into consideration the performance of individuals in problem solving, their career experiences and the influences of their environments. Career experiences are regarded in the skills approach as contributing to competencies and, to an extent, to attributes (at least with respect to their expression), while the influences of the environment affect every aspect of leadership.

A critical set of skills identified in the skills approach is social judgment skills, which include the capacity to understand individuals and groups. These were further delineated into social perceptiveness (understanding how others will respond to a proposal), perspective taking (understanding the attitude of others towards an issue), social performance (communication and persuasion) and behavioural flexibility (adapting one's behaviour). Another important factor is knowledge in the form of the organization of data and information into an effective mental structure, which is also something that can be acquired and is part of the skills approach. When knowledge is expanded to efficiently cover more complex structures and the realities they represent, it ascends to the level of expertise. Knowledge is seen here as complementing the inherent and acquired cognitive abilities of the individual.

Coupling the aforementioned skillsets with motivation as an attribute, we end up with individuals who are capable and willing to tackle organizational issues for the benefit of the organization. Overall the skills approach emphasizes the leader's capabilities and suggests that leaders perform and grow by gaining skills and an understanding of their operational environment and context. This thinking allows organizations to place the emphasis in leadership training on categories of skills and abilities that can be learned and developed, like technical, social and organizational.

Compared to trait theory, we need to be aware that while traits are indications of what leaders are, skills show what leaders can accomplish.

The skills approach allows for a consideration of leadership as a process that can be structured and controlled while still intuitively attractive and potentially available to everyone. However, the abundance of skills that might be considered necessary for leaders to possess makes the approach problematic at times. In addition, its resemblance to trait theory cannot be overlooked, as many of the individual attributes closely resemble traits, while the development of the remaining attributes cannot be effectively used to predict a leader's success.

4.4.3 The style approach

Focusing on leaders' actions and reactions became the basis of the style approach to interpreting leadership. In this way, the interaction of leaders with their followers and their surroundings becomes critical. This activity can be subdivided into behaviours relating to the task and facilitating the accomplishment of a goal and those that concern relationships like ensuring commitment and engagement amongst followers. By adopting the appropriate behaviours, leaders ensure that followers are committed and participate willingly in the accomplishment of the set goals.

Examples of task behaviours include establishing a command and control hierarchy with clear role assignments, planning and scheduling, and organizing task and work

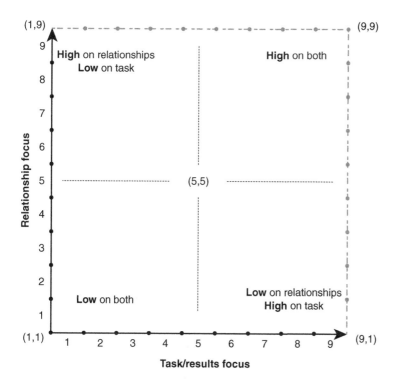

Figure 4.3 Leadership emphasis

activities. Relationship behaviours include activities for building team cohesiveness, collaboration, trust and team identity. In essence, leaders need to create a structure that allows the build-up of a culture of constructive engagement and participation for the achievement of a commonly accepted goal. While a leader can apply both types of behaviour to achieve the set goals, an emphasis on either task or relationship will depend on the circumstances and the environment in which a team is operating.

Based on the findings supporting the style approach, a behavioural grid was developed in the 1960s (and revised afterwards) to explain how organizational leaders practise their styles. This was nothing more than a pictorial representation of the two types of behaviour identified previously (Figure 4.3) graded from low (1) to high (9). According to the grid, a (1,9) style (high emphasis on relationships and low emphasis on task) is a case such as a club, where building strong relationships among the members is a priority for a leader, while a (9,1) style (low emphasis on relationship and high emphasis on task) could be managing a task force with strict deadlines.

Effective leadership is the culmination of personal style and the individual's behaviour. The focus of this approach is exclusively on leaders' behaviour and reactions. A more flexible form of leadership is considered here based on how a leader perceives a situation and the decisions they make. In that respect, leadership behaviours can focus on organizing followers in terms of the accomplishment of a task or in the building of an environment of trust and cooperation that in itself will address what needs to be done.

The broadened scope of this approach allowed leaders hip to be viewed as a balance between task and behaviour relations. However, this relationship still hasn't produced a universal leadership style that can be successfully applied to any situation. In addition, while the style approach provides a heuristic framework for studying and understanding leadership, there are situations where the theory's suggestions for high task and relationship focus cannot address the complexity of the situations that leaders face, for which a more adaptable leadership style should have been considered. In that respect, the behaviour and style approach overlaps with the situational approach that we will examine next.

4.4.4 The situational approach

The impact of the situation on the expression of leadership became the focus of the situational approach. According to this approach, leaders need to take into consideration the capabilities of their team and the environmental factors that will affect the situation. The theoretical foundations of the approach are the directive and supportive dimensions (Figure 4.4) that define the leader's intervention in their teams. In order to be effective, a leader needs to adapt their style to meet the commitment and competence of their teams with the demands of the situation they face. In terms of leadership style, we consider here directive and supportive behavioural patterns to reflect the followers' motivation and skills as they change over time.

Directive or task-oriented behaviours include planning, establishing goals and procedures, assigning roles and responsibilities, and providing guidance and anything in the form of a one-way communication from the leader to the followers. Supportive or relationship-oriented behaviours instil a feeling of comfort in the team members during the execution of a task and include two-way communication, where the followers can provide feedback and share information, and the leader praises and invites

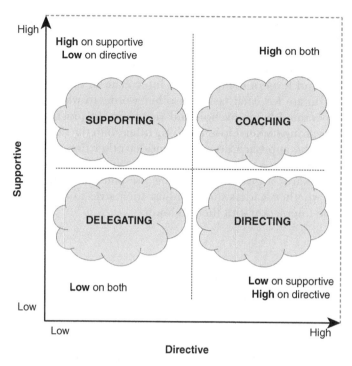

Figure 4.4 Supportive and directive leadership dimensions

participation in problem solving from the followers. The combinations of the emphasis placed on the two behaviour dimensions result in the four leadership style categories in Figure 4.4.

The directive style is dominated by a focus on goal achievement with minimum attention to supportive behaviours, while the opposite is true of the supportive style. In the directive style, leaders spend a lot of time providing instructions and supervision, while in the supportive style, leaders transfer control to their subordinates and provide social support and recognition. When a leader is heavily involved in directing and supporting, we have the coaching style. The focus of this style is both on providing support and also on controlling the decision-making process by having the leader provide guidance on how things are going to be done. On the diametrical opposite quadrant of Figure 4.4, we have the more democratic delegating style, where the subordinates act as a group and collectively decide on and take responsibility for how to proceed to accomplish a task.

In addition to the behavioural dimensions of the leader's intervention, the situational approach also addresses the development needs of subordinates in terms of the competencies and commitment required to accomplish a task. At a high development level, we find team members who are developed professionally and are confident and motivated in engaging in the team's task. On the other end of the spectrum, we have employees who lack the appropriate skills for the task, but have the motivation and will to acquire it. These developmental aspects made the situational approach very popular in the marketplace. The approach was appealing in terms of being practical, easy to understand, diverse and prescriptive enough to be used to train leaders. It stresses the importance of understanding subordinates and treating each one differently based on their capabilities and the task at hand.

Some of the challenges that the situational approach faces include the assumptions regarding the categorization of subordinates in terms of their development needs. It is not clear how commitment and level of competencies interrelate in defining the development level of a subordinate for each task – in other words, to what extent the lack of skill can be compensated by motivation and vice versa. In practice, the approach is unable to consider group leadership as anything other than the dominant subordinate level. In addition, the approach does not consider other demographic variables like education and experience that might impact a leader's style and the disposition of a subordinate towards a given task. Among the potential issues not addressed by the approach is whether leaders should adjust their style to the group average or focus on one-to-one interaction with their followers.

4.4.5 Fiedler's contingency theory

Contingency theory sees leadership as a match between a leader and a situation. The introduction of context becomes a defining characteristic of the leadership style that needs to be adopted. Similar to other theories, the leader's style is defined by the dimensions of the task and relationship with the additions or the leader's position of power that is introduced here (Figure 4.5). The relationship dimension reflects the leader's ability to establish a positive and supportive working environment, while the task dimension reflects the level of formalization of the task. Tasks that are highly structured are more accepting of the leader's control, while tasks that are vague and unclear might lead to role confusion, which diminishes the leader's control.

The third dimension of the model concerns the amount of control leaders have in terms of exercising their power. More specifically, the position power expresses the freedom leaders are allowed by organizations in terms of making reward or punishment decisions for subordinates. A CEO, for example, could easily be perceived as the ultimate power when it comes to making such decisions, while a lower-level project

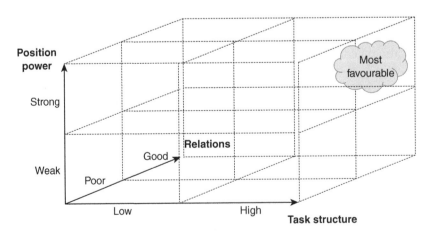

Figure 4.5 Contingency theory dimensions

manager might be in the weakest possible position to do so. Taking into consideration all three dimensions, we can predict the outcome of situations. Obviously when relations between the leader and followers are good, the task is clearly defined and the leader is in a strong power position, we would expect a favourable outcome, while the opposite will be true in the reverse situation.

In order to make the contingency theory more practical in its application, the Least Preferred Coworker (LPC) scale was developed to categorize leaders as relationship- or task-focused. The scale is meant to indicate the appropriateness of a leadership style for a particular situation. Leaders with high LPC scores are considered as relationship-motivated and are expected to be effective in situations with moderate uncertainty where they exert some degree of control while those with low LPC scores are expected to be more effective in situations with a low or high degree of uncertainty.

The rationale behind these conclusions is based on the assumption that in a mismatch between leader and situation, the leader could be overwhelmed by stress and anxiety, which could result in unpredictable behaviour and poor decision making. Ideally an organization should consider LPC scores with the three dimensions of Figure 4.5 as predictors of a leader's success in a particular situation. An obvious conclusion of the theory is that not all leaders are suited to all situations.

While contingency theory has received a great deal of support from empirical research, it fails to explain why a leadership style matches a specific situation better than others. For example, it is not clear why task-motivated leadership seems to be more effective than relationship-focused leadership in extreme settings. This limited understanding also becomes problematic when considering training and professional development in organizations, as the uncertainty of situations suggests that leaders will be more prone to influence and change the situation in order to fit their style. Despite this limitation, the predictive nature of the theory and the ability of organizations to change leaders according to the situation at hand make it extremely popular.

4.4.6 The path-goal theory

The way in which leaders motivate followers to enhance their performance became the focus of the path-goal theory. This is based on the premise that followers will be motivated if they believe they can manage the task and will benefit from its accomplishment. According to the theory, the leader's primary responsibility is to motivate their followers in accomplishing the task. They achieve this by adapting their style and behaviour to provide guidelines, information and any type of support that will ensure follower commitment and dedication in overcoming obstacles and reaching goals.

According to the path-goal theory, leaders are more like coaches who train and guide their teams to accomplish their goals, while also working towards removing any obstacles on the road to success. To ensure motivation is successful, leaders adopt styles like supportive, participative, directive and achievement-oriented behaviours to match the characteristics of their subordinates and their task.

A supportive leadership style is completely focused on the needs of the followers. The leader is open to subordinate requests, shows respect and consideration for what the followers are going though, and makes sure their needs are considered. Followers with strong needs for affiliation prefer this style as a source of satisfaction for them. When the leader considers subordinate feedback and invites them into the decision-making process, we have a participative leadership style. This is considered ideal for subordinates with an internal locus of control (when they feel in control of their fate) as their participation in the decision-making process enforces their feeling of being in control.

When the leader wants to be in control and is more instructive on how things are going to be done, we have the directive leadership style. In order to be effective, this leadership style requires that leaders are clear about their expectations for their teams and the rules and regulations that will guide behaviour. This style is suggested as being suitable for uncertain situations or when subordinates are strong minded and authoritarian. Also, it is appropriate for subordinates with an external locus of control, as it parallels their belief of being controlled by external forces. Finally, the achievement-oriented leadership style focuses on trusting and challenging followers to continually improve themselves and reach the high standards that the leader sets in the accomplishment of their goals. This style is considered ideal for ambiguous tasks where the subordinates believe that their efforts will have great results.

While the path-goal theory is practical and provides a clear explanation for the role of motivation and the impact that the leader's behaviour has on subordinate performance and satisfaction, it has been criticized for its complexity and partial support from empirical research. In addition, while it provides some 'recipes' for leaders' behaviour, it doesn't go far enough to explain why the 'recipes' work and how leadership styles like directive and supportive styles help in motivating subordinates during ambiguous and tedious tasks, respectively.

4.4.7 Transactional leadership

Many of the theories discussed here consider leadership as some form of transaction between the leader and the followers. In its pure form, transactional leadership is a rewards-based approach that to a great extent is closer to management than leadership. The practice mainly refers to setting expectations and goals for task completion that are associated with rewards and recognition. It is a form of dependency building that ensures that the success of a task is directly related to the success of the individuals who are involved in its completion. During the process of monitoring and controlling subordinates, rational means (economic and other) along with disciplinary threats and punishments are employed to ensure performance and accomplishments of goals.

The focus of this theory is explicitly on the exchange between the leader and the follower. The leader is indifferent to the needs and development of subordinates unless they are part of the exchange. Leadership works like a contractual agreement where the leader exchanges value (monetary or other) for expertise and work from the followers in accomplishing a task. The power and effectiveness of this theory comes from the fact that the interests of both parties are considered. It also reflects the realities of many work situations, where individuals are involved either as freelancers or are diverted to a task only for the duration of that task.

The leader's role according to transactional theory is to ensure that proper individuals agree to participate in the completion of the task and what their rewards will be. In cases where the subordinates do not perform to the agreed expectations, the leader is expected to take corrective action either by providing negative reinforcement and feedback or even by releasing subordinates from the agreement. This is a management-by-exception practice and the leader can act either proactively when performance deteriorates (active form) or when results deviate from what is expected (passive form). At the extreme end of transactional theory we find what is usually called *laissez-faire* leadership. This is the case where, after the initial assigning of roles, responsibilities, rewards and penalties, the leader disappears from the scene. As the translation of the French term suggests, it is a 'let do' attitude where the leader 'lets' followers 'do' as they please. In order to be effective, such a practice needs to rely on strong, competent and independent followers who can take over and follow up with what is needed to accomplish the goal at hand.

While the great advantage of the transactional approach is its clarity and simplicity, its motivational philosophy is quite simplistic, as the leader can view job performance as an exchange of effort and excellence, with rewards limiting in this way the need for praise and recognition. The rigidity of the approach and the transfer of responsibility for the success of a task to the subordinates further restrict the applicability of the approach when high levels of participation and commitment are required for a project.

4.4.8 Transformational leadership

One of the most popular theories of modern times is transformational (also called developmental) leadership. The theory was developed to an extent to contrast with previous theories that viewed the leader–follower relationship as a form of transaction between leaders and followers. The emphasis of this theory is on follower transformation through motivation and development (similar in many respects to the path-goal theory). Leaders are expected to be exceptional in terms of their influence over their followers to the level of pushing them to excel. Influence in this case should not be confused with power, because the needs of followers are inseparable from those of leaders and the two grow together towards the accomplishment of their commonly accepted goal. The theory is often considered a form of *charismatic leadership* and covers a wide spectrum of influences, ranging from the individual to the organization and even to the society as a whole.

According to the transformational theory, leaders focus on raising the level of morality of their followers. To distinguish between the abusive and unethical forms of follower transformation (Adolf Hitler is a case in point) that self-absorbed and power-hungry leaders pursue, the term pseudo-transformational or personalized leadership was developed. Such leaders are interested in themselves and show little concern for their followers. At the opposite end of the spectrum, we have authentic and socialized transformational leaders who place the collective good above everything else.

Another term that is sometimes used in relation to transformational leadership is charismatic leadership. This is meant to mainly reflect exceptional leaders (like Alexander the Great or Gandhi, for example) who are gifted and strong personalities, and inspire followers to excel even by their mere presence. These types of leaders appear competent and confident, have excellent communication skills, serve as strong role models and elevate the followers' sense of achievement toward specific goals. In its ideal form, this type of leadership gets followers to put aside their own needs and self-interests in favour of the movement/task.

In practice, the transformational leadership style is suggested for situations where a radical change in direction is required (especially when things go wrong) and collective effort and enthusiasm is necessary to provide that direction. The focus of leaders is then on motivating and helping followers to develop their full potential. One of the ways in which leaders can ensure the trust and respect of their followers is by role modelling high ethical and moral values. By displaying strong ideals and values, leaders can provide the sense of vision and mission necessary to engage their followers in the achievement of their goals.

Another approach that transformational leaders follow, especially in those cases involving highly qualified teams, is using intellectual stimulation and individualized consideration. The former includes suggesting that followers challenge their assumptions and values, and even those of their leader and the organization, with the aim of inducing creativity and innovation that will overcome obstacles and achieve the desired outcome. The latter involves the development of a supportive environment where followers feel comfortable sharing their concerns and needs. In these situations, leaders act more as coaches and mentors who help followers to grow through their personal challenges to reach their highest potential.

Support from case studies of prominent leaders and academic research enhanced the intuitive appeal of transformational leadership as a description of the interaction between leaders and followers. It provides an expanded view of leadership that supplements and augments other leadership models. Despite its popularity, transformational leadership has been criticized for lacking conceptual clarity and being too broad. The theory fails to be specific enough in its application to stand on its own and provide measurable outcomes. In addition, it treats the 'transformational' capabilities of individuals as a form of a personality trait rather than as a behaviour that can be developed through training and practice. The potential connotation of the term 'transformative' as a leader's inherent ability that either exists or cannot be developed also worked towards an elitist view and a bias towards heroism for the theory.

4.4.9 Servant leadership

With an exclusive focus on followers, servant leadership is a counterintuitive approach to leading followers. The impression of many of today's leaders contradicts the concept of them being willing to be servants. This theory focuses on the behaviour of leaders in addressing the concerns of their subordinates and supporting them by empathizing with and nurturing them.

Followers and their needs become the primary goal of leaders and, in addition to empathy, leaders' characteristics include the ability to listen, heal, persuade, provide a clear sense of direction and take responsibility for the role that is entrusted to them. This role includes as a primary duty the development of the team identity as a community of individuals who are bonded together by shared interests and pursuits, and something that they perceive as greater than themselves. Only by helping subordinates develop their full potential can leaders achieve their goals.

Servant leadership has strong ethical preconceptions and leaders are seen as working towards the common/organizational good. At the conscious level, it is assumed that leaders' inclinations and intentions to serve drive them to seek leadership positions that allow such individuals to accomplish their mission to help others to meet their needs and grow to their full potential. A basic assumption here is that the good of the organization or the group that the leader 'serves' takes precedence over the leader's self-interest and any other issue for that matter. Leaders in this respect are dedicated to the success of their followers in accomplishing the commonly accepted mission.

Given the nature of the endeavour and that 'serving' comes more naturally to some than to others, servant leadership has been viewed by many as a trait than an individual either possesses or doesn't. There are, though, a great number of researchers and practitioners who view it as a form of behaviour and in this way it is something that can be learned through training and awareness. To that end, clear and honest communication can greatly help a leader establish consensus and the alignment of group interests with task and organizational interests. This communication is viewed in servant leadership as an interactive process and the leader first learns to listen and consider the perspectives and viewpoints of their followers. This listening takes the form of empathy for what the followers believe and feel and, in this way, leaders validate the existence and importance of their followers. Eventually, leaders use persuasion to communicate their views persistently and convince followers to actively engage in the accomplishment of their goals.

In engaging with their followers, servant leaders show interest in them and assist them even in their personal issues, helping them to develop and mature as individuals. To be able to show such understanding, leaders need to be well aware of all aspects of their environment (social, political or physical), display foresight and stewardship (remaining accountable for their actions), provide a sense of belonging to the community of the group, and show commitment and dedication to the development of their subordinates.

However, a criticism of servant leadership is that the promotion of altruism as its central theme is considered counterintuitive to the traditional preconception of power. While the notion of sharing control and influence suggested by the theory as an alternative way of achieving control might seem revealing, it is nevertheless paradoxical and it suggests reliance on a multitude of traits and behaviours. In addition, while the theory itself suggests that it is context-appropriate and might not be suitable when subordinates are not susceptible to guidance and empowerment, it is unclear why some of its conceptualizations can be regarded as cognitive abilities or behaviours.

4.4.10 Leadership theories continued

In addition to the theories we have presented here, there are many more attempts to explain leadership and guide its practice. One such theory is *authentic leadership*, where the convictions and originality of the leader in the application of leadership are of primary importance in the perception of leadership as genuine and 'real'. Important elements of the theory are the intrapersonal, interpersonal and developmental perspectives that are built and nurtured by leaders and followers (in the case of the interpersonal). The theory sprang from the social need for trustworthy leaders and, as such, it remains current, while providing guidelines for people who want to be labelled as authentic and as possessing a strong moral dimension. The distinction from other theories that authentic leadership seems to seek often led to the consideration of aspects like positive psychological capacities that have been challenged in research, as well as the lack of strong support from positive organizational outcomes, which remain as challenges that the theory needs to overcome.

A similar theory in nature but with a focus on creating value and interest in followers is *stewardship leadership*. The premise of the theory is that beyond profits and wealth, people seek something more from their participation. This includes the drive to excel, intellectual stimulation and achievement in the face of hardships, among others. By effectively communicating shared values and principles, leaders can advance their groups beyond the mere accomplishment of their goals towards a sustainable satisfaction and sense of accomplishment that positively impacts both their professional and personal lives. This approach is mission-focused and the leader in essence acts as a steward who helps subordinates grow in all aspects of their lives. A clear and mutually accepted vision and values along with shared decision making and commonly accepted ethical practices lead to follower commitment and enthusiasm. To reciprocate, followers take ownership of their responsibilities and accept account-ability for the results of their actions. In essence, leaders and followers commit to a mental contract by agreeing to task competencies, performance expectations and act-ing in the organization's or the community's best interests to ensure the achievement of their set goals with short- and long-term benefits.

While most of the theories discussed here focus on the leader or the followers, the *leader-member exchange* (LMX) theory (also called the vertical dyad linkage theory) views leadership as a process of interaction between leaders and followers. The theory highlighted the individualities of followers and the need for leaders to vary their lead-ership style according to the individual instead of applying a style that targets the average of the group. In this way, leaders form an individualized (dyadic) relationship with each of their followers. These relationships can either be in the form of a con-tract that formally defines the role of both the leader and the follower (out-group) or could be based on a negotiation of expanded responsibilities (in-group). Followers become part of the in-group or out-group according to how good their cooperation with the leader is and their intention to offer more (in-group) in exchange for some-thing the leader can offer. The in-group in essence affords privileges like information sharing in exchange for benefits beyond their contractual rewards. In some ways, this is considered a form of empowerment that moderates the interaction between leaders and followers in an effort to increase job performance and satisfaction.

The importance of teams in organizations in improving productivity, quality, inno-vation and effectiveness, among others, led to the development of the *team leadership* model. Teams are more organized than groups in that they are driven by a common goal. This creates an interdependency between their members, who need to coor-dinate their activities in order to accomplish their goal. This institutes in the team capabilities and cultural characteristics. While here we consider the classic model where the leader is appointed, we need to remember that there are other forms of leadership in teams, like *shared* or *distributed leadership.*

Team leaders start by conducting a formal evaluation of the internal (team members and the organizational processes and culture) and external (task and stake-holder-specific) operational environments, then move on to build a mental model of how the roles in the team will be distributed and then proceed to communicate the plan of action. During the execution of the plan, the leader monitors and controls team performance to respond to issues and adjust the plan of action.

The interaction of leaders and teams can be either immediate, as in the case of small teams, or through a proxy, especially in large organizations, where it is physi-cally impossible for leaders to engage with followers on a one-to-one basis. This reality led to the development of the *indirect leadership* model. According to this model, lead-ers use influence to communicate their intentions and implement the plans they have formulated. This influence is exerted in their immediate circle, who has direct contact with followers. They serve as the 'link' (individually or as a group) and their role is to act as the leader's proxy and to pass the leader's communication (formally or informally) on to their subordinates or peers. This process of message propagation is complemented by the demonstration of favourable or unfavourable behaviour by leaders and their proxies. This type of role modelling aims to visually project the intentions of the leader. The extent of the information that is intentionally communicated or miscommunicated is left to the leaders. A precondition for the success of such a process is the existence of trust between followers and leaders.

Another group of theories that made a significant contribution to the understanding of leadership followed a *psychodynamic approach*, where the emphasis is on the personality and the thoughts and feelings that drive the actions of individuals. The approach takes the position that certain personality types are better suited for leadership positions or situations than others. In order for leaders to be effective, they need to be aware of their personality characteristics and those of their followers. Given that personality is formed during the early stages of development in individuals, where it is greatly affected by the family environment, the approach posits that changes are thus impossible, so the best that can be done is to be aware of its effect on the perceptions and decisions of individuals. In addition, it is necessary to pay attention to the feelings and drives that are hidden within the subconscious and have been influenced by past experience. The state of maturity of an individual will be reflected in the way in which they lead or interact with others.

A final theory that will be briefly mentioned here is *followership theory*. This theory investigates the nature and impact of followers on the leadership process. This can be viewed from a positional (role) point of view or as a process point of view. The former sees individuals as adopting the role of the follower and through their influence affecting leaders' behaviour, attitudes and outcomes. In essence, the followers cause leadership to exist. The latter sees leadership through a constructivist lens where leadership is co-created as a result of the interplay of the following and leading actions. In this respect, leaders are granted the right to lead by the followers. Although the differences might sound semantic, what the theory tries to do is eliminate the negative connotation of the word 'follower'. It attempts to bring power and control to the followers who, through obedience, subordination, resistance, influence and proactive behaviour, define and influence the leader's behaviour.

Combinations of approaches (*blended*) have also been considered in the application of leadership. These have aimed at taking advantage of the strengths of a particular approach in eliminating the weaknesses of another. One such popular combination suggests the application of transformational and transactional leadership for alternating between empowerment and control (Figure 4.6). Using praise and recognition behaviours also reflects a blend of both styles. These behaviours can be categorized as a personal interaction (transformational) because it involves individual attention and as an impersonal interaction (transactional) because it can be based solely on employee performance. One recommended practice is to use transactional behaviour as a foundation and display transformational behaviour for motivation and support.

The benefit of blending the two approaches is that leaders can easier adapt to different situations and can be more flexible in the execution of their command as it allows personal interactions and exercise of authority as necessary. The blend can also prove effective at communicating information and vision at the organizational level, and can convey high expectations while appealing to the core values and creative

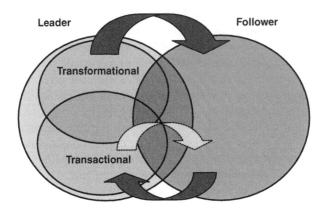

Figure 4.6 Combining transactional and transformational styles

nature of employees. One of the challenges with the blended approach, if the leader is not experienced enough, is that one style might be applied to situations that are in fact suited to the other. Also, it might be conceived as an attempt to deceive and leaders might look unstable when they switch abruptly between styles.

Other combinations, like combining transformational, authentic and indirect leadership, have also been proposed, but it is beyond the scope of this book to exhaustively cover them all. In addition, many blends appear under a different name, while in reality they are amalgamations of existing theories. An example of such a case is the *full range leadership model*, where transactional leadership behaviours like contingent rewards and management-by-exception are combined with transformational characteristics like idealized influence, inspirational stimulation and the individualized non-leadership consideration of *laissez-faire* leadership.

4.5 Comparing and combining theoretical perspectives

The theories presented in this chapter are not meant to exhaustively present the plethora of leadership theories that academics and researchers have developed to explain leadership, but to display the diversity of what has been developed to address the complexity of leadership as a phenomenon and practice in organizational settings. Obviously there has been a tremendous amount of research in this field, but, as we will also see in the next chapter, there are still many challenges that must be faced in order to further advance our understanding of the phenomenon.

Distinguishing the alternative representations that each theory supports can be difficult as the overlaps amongst them are extensive, while the diversity of situations that need to be addressed is affected by multiple dimensions like the power position of the leader, the team size and structure, the maturity of the followers, the nature of the task, the dependencies of the leader with the stakeholders involved in the task, etc. Table 4.1 attempts to highlight some of the characteristics of the theories presented previously.

Considering the initial breakdown of the constituents and factors of leadership presented in Figure 4.1 and the focus and points of view of the various theories

Table 4.1 Comparative leadership theory characteristics

Theory/approach	Theory's emphasis	Leader's primary focus	Leadership tool
Trait theory	Leader's personality	Leader	Inherent traits
Skills approach	Leader's capabilities	Leader	Acquired skills
Style approach	Leader's behaviour	Situation	Behaviour adaptation
Situational approach	Situation	Situation	Style choice
Fiedler's contingency theory	Situation	Followers	Style, power position
Path-goal theory	Task	Followers, task	Motivation, clear obstacles
Transactional leadership	Leader–follower transaction	Transaction	Agreement
Transformational/ charismatic leadership	Leader	Followers	Influence
Servant leadership	Leader's behaviour	Followers	Behaviour adaptation
Authentic leadership	Leader	Leader	Convictions, originality
Stewardship leadership	Achievement	Followers	Communication
Leader–member exchange	Leader–follower interaction		
Team leadership	Followers	Followers	Monitor and control
Psychodynamic approach	Leader's personality	Leader, followers	Self-awareness
Followership theory	Followers	Followers	Follower

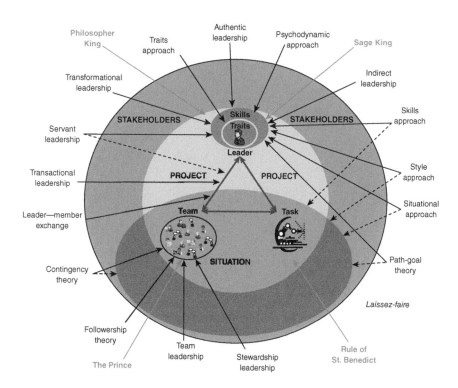

Figure 4.7 Comparative depiction of leadership theories

discussed in the previous sections, Figure 4.7 attempts to put everything together to comparatively depict their similarities and differences. The focus of each theory (solid arrows) is complemented with the point of view where action is taken (dashed arrows). As was expected, given the presentation in the previous sections, the main focus of most of the theories is the leader as the centre of the phenomenon. Leaders are viewed as possessing characteristics that when applied to the situation result in the accomplishment of a goal. Leaders develop their characteristics (traits and skills) and adapt their behaviour to influence their followers towards the direction they want to follow.

5   A leadership framework

In this chapter we will develop a theoretical framework that explains the appearance, evolution and practice of leadership. Before going further, though, we need to consider the motivation behind the development of a leadership theory and whether one is even possible. Regarding our motivation, we need to remember that theories are good as conceptual abstractions of practices and, as such, help to convey their message in a concise and convenient way. Being aware of them will hopefully make us more flexible in their adoption depending on the scenario we are facing. What we do with them is of course up to each of us. We have seen in the previous chapters that as a distinct and identifiable characteristic of human behaviour in social contexts, leadership is observed and, as such, it exists as a discrete phenomenon with an underlying cause and effect relationship, meaning a representation in the form of a theory.

The research process we will follow here will be both analytic and systemic. The analytic approach will seek to break down the components of leadership into atomic theoretical constructs/elements that when combined together form higher-order complexes that represent observed behaviour. Their modifications and assembly should be able to explain the diversity of leadership characteristics and behaviour we observe and to predict its expression. Analytic approaches are ideal in themselves when the various elements of which a phenomenon is composed are simple enough in their interaction to allow for their synthesis in order to reconstruct the phenomenon and accurately enough represent reality. This is not the case with leadership, as we saw in the previous chapter. To cover for the deficiencies of the analytic approach, the development process of our theoretical framework will be supplemented by a systemic approach that considers the complexity of the phenomenon and the various factors that affect its expression.

As we saw in the previous chapter, the theoretical attempts to explain leadership have made significant progress in terms of identifying the elements that make up the phenomenon and the way in which they interact, but to a great extent failed to provide a comprehensive understanding of its appearance and evolution. While the majority of the older attempts focused on leadership from a static perspective (something that is) of either the leader or the follower, there are modern approaches that view leadership as a process (something that happens). The latter is something we will adopt in this chapter as we strongly believe that any form of interaction that evolves over time and includes conscious and subconscious thoughts (feelings, emotions, etc.) that influence individuals is far from static. Someone might be a leader and a follower at the same time according to their position in an organization. In essence, what we will basically assume in this chapter is that there are no leaders and followers, just positions/roles that individuals adopt and degrees of influence they exert through their behaviour.

In considering the development of a framework that will allow for a useful enough representation of the various elements involved in leadership – and one that will provide a satisfactory explanation of their interactions – we will choose to start from the lowest conceptual level (the sub-factor level) that, like atoms and molecules, is beyond empirical observation. This simply means that we will not choose to extend or use as our basis any of the leadership theories developed up to now. Everything we have discussed in previous chapters will hopefully alert us and will serve as pointers and hints to supplement inspiration and rational thinking in the development of a working framework for approaching leadership. Through this process, we will eventually end up with a sufficiently abstract model that captures the core and details of leadership as well as its application in as many diverse scenarios as possible.

One last point to make before we delve into the exploration is that we are discussing here a framework and not a 'standard'. Developing a 'leadership standard' would be a great idea if it wasn't for one problem: the fact that it is a 'standard'. By default, this means it is unchangeable. The challenge with leadership nowadays is that everything changes. To give one example, there were no virtual or distributed teams in the past, while now this is common practice. While a standard may be good when it comes to evaluating and training individuals, it is developed and represents the realities of the past and to an extent the realities of the present, but never the realities of the future. A framework, on the other hand, works like scaffolding upon which leaders can build the details that will reflect their preferences and the realities of their environment.

5.1 Case study

Let us first consider the phenomenon of leadership in all its glory, as it is depicted in the mosaic of Figure 5.1. This represents probably one of the most expressive domains of leadership: the battlefield. Two organizations/armies compete/clash for market share/territory. The mosaic depicts one of the battles of Alexander the Great against Darius. The particular moment depicts the turning point of the battle where Darius orders his troops to retreat after the onslaught of the Macedonian army. This becomes key in the interpretation of the battle dynamics as the Persian spears are still facing the enemy, unaware as yet of the retreat order and fate of the battle.

The mosaic is considered a masterpiece of presentation and of the dynamic interplay of the situation. On the right side, the Persian army seems to dominate the painting (probably in an attempt by the artist to realistically represent the sizes of the two armies). The two armies (we will creatively extrapolate the Macedonian army for the missing pieces in the mosaic) appear in formation in the background, so there is a definite structure where the leaders occupy a prominent position. Apart from the structure, it is evident that the two 'organizations' differ in their appearance in terms of clothing, armour and equipment (with Darius in the chariot). We can deduce that the cavalries clash on a somewhat plain field and we also see casualties for the Persian site lying on the ground winded and about to be run over by the Macedonian cavalry.

Most of all, the focus points of the mosaic seem to be around the two leaders. We have Darius in his chariot, distinguishing him from anyone else in his army,

Figure 5.1 Alexander Mosaic from the House of the Faun, Pompeii

resembling by analogy modern leaders sitting in the back of their sports cars (a sign of their high power status) with their drivers following their orders. Darius looks surprised, worried and fearful almost at the same time. He was obviously unprepared and had not even remotely considered the possibility of losing. There is no apparent plan B on the horizon.

Alexander, on the other hand, is in full control of his vehicle, the Ferrari of his time one could say (a special horse he himself tamed). His posture displays determination and confidence, and his eyes are locked on Darius, the head and heart of the opposing army. He is at the forefront of his troops, leaving no one who sees the mosaic in any doubt that he is in control of the battlefield and is going in for the kill. One could say that he already sees Darius defeated and moves with the confidence of someone who has written the future for himself.

From the above observations, we can see that leadership is expressed in structurally organized groups (organizations in our modern terminology) of individuals with certain common characteristics (culture) and an acknowledged hierarchy of authority, with control in the hands of certain individuals we call leaders. The groups compete to dominate each other and establish control over their environment (both natural and social in this case). In modern terms, we would probably have an infographic instead of a mosaic and we would say that we have two organizations with relatively similar structures, but distinctly different cultures and leadership.

Moving from the description/analysis of the phenomenon given above to building a model/theory that will explain its evolution/outcome, we can see that the elements that we need to consider in any representation we attempt to formulate include groups of individuals (followers) with some in a prominent position (leaders) organized into a formation (structure) and displaying a certain behaviour (culture) in an environment (market/competition in time). Of course, there might be other elements that we need to consider, but at least for now, the basic ingredients for developing an explanation have been identified.

5.2 Individuals

As we saw above, in order for leadership to appear, there need to be followers (and a leader of course). This means that individuals as human beings need to be involved and we need a way to represent them in terms of their properties and characteristics. Otherwise, we need some variables that can express the particular 'being' (essence or substance if you like) that drives individuals who are involved in the phenomenon under investigation. In the same way as when we study gravity we adopt mass as the property that represents entities in gravitational fields, we need a concept that incorporates the characteristics of individuals that contribute to their interactions with the entities that comprise the phenomenon. Traditional ways of representing individuals are based on the constructs of *human* and *social capital.*

Human capital is usually defined as the potential human beings accrue through their life in terms of qualities and competencies that can support their future aspirations and endeavours. In simple terms, it is an abstract representation of human beings as transactional agents in economic environments. Although the term has been adopted for economic purposes, one can easily see extensions to its use that would include emotional and spiritual dimensions, especially when these dimensions are known to act as drivers and motivators for the attitudes of an individual towards life and their purpose of being.

Traditional human capital approaches also consider contributions to an individual's potential from education and past experience. Notably, education has been an important source of knowledge that boosts self-confidence and improves critical thinking and problem-solving abilities. It sharpens the analytical abilities of individuals and advances their skills in terms of anticipating obstacles and devising appropriate strategies to overcome them. Adding experience to the mix of human capital, we can see that it can provide the coping mechanism for individuals to deal with adversity and succeed in overcoming obstacles. Human capital can be accrued through experience and the acquisition of skills that could further enhance an individual's ability to survive and grow in their environment.

The accumulation of human capital can be seen as a conscious and calculated process, although it is now believed that cognition should be included. In that respect, bounded rationality is probably the better-suited candidate as a proxy for cognition. This allows us to account for the cognitive limits of individuals in information processing and, in this respect, it makes the inclusion of cognition in human capital a necessity. One can see this as an endowed human capital inherited from their parents and strengthened by the society in which they live. In this way, cognition and its expression through rational decision making can also be viewed as a form of human capital. Rationality is a form of information funnel through which individuals filter their attention and prune the conformation space of possibilities to efficiently discover solutions. Although cognition follows the psychological paradigm, it can help explain how information (as recorded following sensory stimulation) is processed and stored for later retrieval and use. It also serves as the dominant influence over our performance in decision making, and shapes experience and attitudes towards learning and information processing, resulting in the way we think and act. Differences in cognitive processing help us make sense of the world around us and are at the root of the behaviour we display.

Since cognition directly influences decision making, it is no wonder that it can be shaped by experience. Adjusting judgement is necessary for individuals and those who are successful make it a 'habit' to base their decisions on past experience, creating a dynamic circle of learning. These successful individuals are bound to have repositories of information that allow them to use heuristics to simplify strategies and make effective decisions in the absence of complete information. In this way, they can outperform novices who lack internal benchmarking capabilities and have to rely on exhaustive and analytical searches to find an optimum strategy in order to deal with challenges. This effort, by its very nature, costs more, requires time and puts novices at a disadvantage compared to successful individuals in competitive situations. This disadvantage could become an advantage for novices in new situations where the more experienced individuals might show an over-reliance on heuristics that no longer work in the new domain. The tendency to confirm prior beliefs and overconfidence can constrain individuals from making correct judgements and can act as a barrier to new and potential useful perspectives.

Considering individuals in isolation is far from realistic, at least in theory development. Since followers and leaders function within social groups, the effect of the influences of others on each one of us needs to be expressed in the form of a variable. For this purpose, *social capital* has been introduced by researchers to represent the accumulated value we derive from participating and interacting with other individuals, groups and organizations (governments, businesses, clubs, etc.). This form of capital can be used in a variety of ways for the benefit of individuals, including the use of others in achieving an objective, saving time and effort and reaching out to greater goals. A leader like Alexander the Great, for example, made excellent use of his social capital (position and status) to engage his troops and convince them to follow him in his conquests.

The notions of human and social capital, although they allow for some of the observed characteristics that drive behaviour to be expressed, do so in a way that divides them in an overlapping and not complementary way. That is primarily because the boundaries between the two seem blurred due to differences in their interpretations by various researchers. Instead of using these traditional notions, we will here introduce a division of the followers' and leader's attributes and characteristics into two mutually exclusive categories—*internal* and *external* capital. This division, as we will see, facilitates the conversion of one to another and will later prove to be useful in explaining leadership. The two categories are mutually exclusive, so we will focus here on describing what internal capital is and assume that everything else will be considered external capital.

Similar to human capital, in internal capital, we include all the innate or acquired capabilities of the individual that are part of them during their lifetime and that serve as guides in their decision-making process. These include, among others, any genetic traits they inherited from their parents, skills that they acquired through education and training, and the knowledge they gained/accumulated during their life (including in a professional capacity). We include here the individual's intellectual and cognitive capabilities, their emotional and personality attributes, along with any other competencies and skills they might have. As a variable, internal capital represents an individual's state and, as such, it characterizes their place in time, meaning that there is a value that internal capital has at every instant in time for every individual. Figure 5.2 displays potential contributors to the internal capital. More on what specifically could be included will be discussed later on.

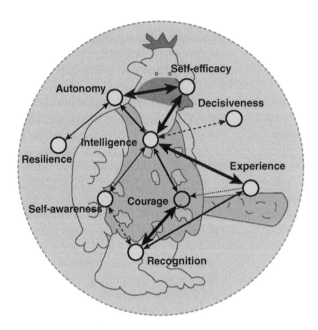

Figure 5.2 Internal capital as a network of traits

A reference to self-awareness as a contributor to internal capital needs to be considered here. This is important in addressing the difference between perception and reality from the point of view of an individual. Normally there is a difference between what we perceive our traits and capabilities to be and what they really are. We might think, for example, that we are exceptionally smart when in reality we are average in this respect. In the leadership case, we might believe we are persistent and insightful enough to succeed when in reality these qualities are not strong enough in us to make things happen. A usual misconception many people have relates to their communication skills. The plethora of disputes stand as testimony to that. By introducing self-awareness as part of internal capital, we can move away from the complication of introducing separate variables for real and perceived trait values. Self-awareness always acts as an internal filter modifier to self-efficacy and other traits required for leadership, such as devotion, savviness and networking and communication skills, to name but a few.

Including entities in internal capital does not mean that these entities are completely independent of each other. Given the range of personality and physical traits that appear in the literature, we can naturally assume there will be dependencies. For example, an individual can be logical and mature, but it is unlikely that they will be considered mature if they are illogical. In that sense, there is a direct connection between the two, and this is what Figure 5.2 tries to display for some hypothetical parameters of internal capital. The thickness of the connecting lines indicates the strength of the dependence between traits – the thicker the line, the stronger the relationship. If we wanted to make the diagram more representative of reality, we could even adopt dashed lines for tentative relationships and coloured lines to emphasize patterns of connectivity specific to particular activities such as leadership (Figure 5.3).

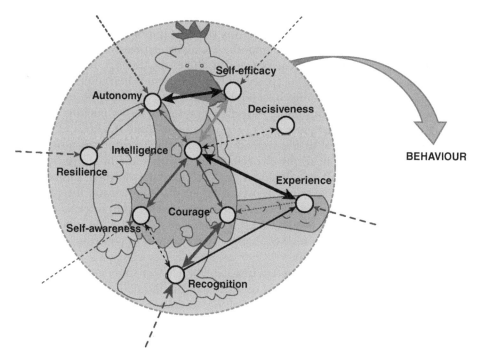

Figure 5.3 From stimuli to behaviour

Armed with their set of interconnected traits and capabilities, individuals process the signals they receive from their environment and make decisions. As they move on in life, certain patterns emerge and their ideal response establishes patterns (the thick lines in Figure 5.3) of preferred behaviour (expertise) for specific stimuli.

Ideally, and if all the attributes could be measured and expressed in quantitative terms, we would be able to adopt a mathematical formalism that would express internal capital in the form of a formula. In terms of the parameters we use today, this formula would be a combination of what we describe as intelligence quotient, emotional quotient, knowledge, beliefs and aspirations, social networks, and physical state and resources (including monetary) under the control of the individual. Given all that, we also need to mention here that humans – being vessels of human capital – will have limitations on the amounts of each parameter they can afford. Seen as a vessel with various compartments of fixed size, there are limits to the 'quantities' of each trait (for example, intelligence) as well as limits to the total of these quantities that individuals can carry. This is a very important consideration as it places limits on what we can do in accordance with the physical and mental limits of our species.

In order to make the distinction between human capital and internal capital more clearly, we will summarize their most common characteristics:

- Human capital is primarily meant to address traits and qualities accrued through life experience, such as coping, cognitive management and leadership skills. Although these traits also imply that there is a foundation of genetic and emotional personality traits upon which the acquired traits are built, their existence and impact is not directly addressed and considered in building theories of leadership. Internal capital, on the other hand, considers accrued and genetic predispositions as vital and equal in terms of their importance to leadership. Attributes such as intelligence, imagination, creativity, expressiveness, the ability to conceptualize and abstract, senses (sensing the environment), temperament, physical appearance, birth rights (place/citizenship) and inheritance have been marginalized (in terms of being considerably addressed) primarily because there is very little one can do about them, especially in terms of policy making.

- Internal capital (or at least parts of it) is considered a 'fluid' quality and can be disposed of at the control of the individual, while human capital is more conceived as unchangeable in terms of exchanging it with something else. In our notion of internal capital, an individual can exchange part of their capital with other individuals or entities, such as organizations, the market and the physical world. The potential to provide labour, which is also included in internal capital, is one case of exchange for food, money or other valuables. Sharing ingenuity in the form of ideas with others in exchange for their support or contribution is also an exchange in internal capital.
- Human capital is usually conceived as invariant, at least for short periods of time, while internal capital is dynamic and differs from one moment to the next, even if that is by the simple act of living/breathing, as energy (physical and mental) needs to be exchanged to sustain life.
- Internal capital includes many aspects of social capital as it includes the effect of the individual's network and social circles. The influence one can exert on others in the form of control over them is leverage at the disposal of individuals in making things move in the way they desire. It belongs to them to use as they please.

An important aspect of internal capital that is vital for our interpretation of leadership is the weighing of the various traits that it includes in terms of their importance in the existence and behaviour of individuals. Naturally, safety is more important than pleasure (rationally thinking anyway) and so we would expect that activities to ensure an individual's safety take priority over any higher-order needs such as becoming a leader. This brings into focus the notion of the hierarchy of needs that we usually see in theories of developmental psychology. A classic representative of this case is the hierarchy of needs that Maslow developed in 1943. In his scheme, which we will also adopt and extend here, a description of human motivation is outlined in terms of fulfilment of needs in order of their importance for an individual's survival and growth. Starting from the basic and fundamental needs, we move on along the hierarchy of needs to the emotional, and to the more conceptual and abstract, the various levels include the following:

- *Physiological needs*: necessary for the functioning of the human body, such as food, water and air for metabolism, clothing and shelter for protection from the elements and sex for reproduction and sustainability of the species.
- *Safety needs*: to protect against infrequent natural and human events such as natural disasters, social disruptions such as economic crises and various forms of violence and abuse.
- *Social*: involving interpersonal needs such as feelings of belonging, acceptance, intimacy, friendship and love.

- *Cognitive:* including the desire to be accepted and valued by others in social, professional and personal settings – in simple terms, the need to make a positive impact on other people's lives. The value of this need can be measured by the self-esteem and self-respect one has for oneself.
- *Self-actualization:* the need to realize one's full potential and accomplish everything that one can.

To the aforementioned list we will add one more that expresses the need for someone to be something beyond what they are:

- *Legacy:* the need to be remembered as someone important and significant to the lives of future generations. Remaining in the memory of others in time is an important drive that is not directly addressed by the other needs listed above.

Although as a trigger and motivator of actions, legacy could be considered as part of self-actualization and the cognitive needs, we believe it deserves a separate mention as the motivations behind it are different philosophically, since it addresses metaphysical needs. Being accepted by others as a cognitive need could potentially include legacy, but the level of reward and feedback an individual gets from the fulfilment of a cognitive need is directly perceived by them, while the notion of legacy, at least from the individual's point of view, is purely a mental dimension that can differ in expression from a cognitive need. In addition, reaching one's full potential is personal and private in essence and has a mark or a point in time beyond which there is nothing more anyone needs or should want to do.

Leaving a legacy is a need that projects the impression that the individual in some sense will continue to exist in the minds of others. For example, while a cognitive need might trigger someone to donate to charity, a legacy need might drive them to create a fund that will provide ongoing help and support to a cause past and beyond their lifetime. Seeking breakthroughs is another example of a legacy need, as it addresses the need to go beyond the recognition of the living and extend into the future of an individual. Wanting to be remembered in the same way as, say, Einstein, Beethoven or Michelangelo are remembered is something that the need for legacy tries to distinctly encapsulate.

Of course, each individual is different from another, has different life experiences and perceptions of themselves, and consequently the breadth of each individual's needs will vary. In our discussion here, we will consider the needs as the parts of the

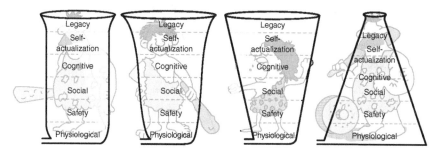

Figure 5.4 Hierarchy of needs for different individuals

internal capital that drive the flow of thought through the network of the traits and attributes of an individual, while being themselves attributes. Figure 5.4 shows the hierarchy of needs for different individuals as represented by different shapes of containers. The leftmost container is closer to the representation of a hierarchy that most people are familiar with and shows how Maslow imagined it.

Differences in the social and natural environment in which an individual is raised and functions along with the various influences upon them allow different amounts of needs to be satisfied. The more able an individual is and the more opportunities the environment provides, the more needs they can fulfil (the liquid level in the vessels of Figure 5.5) and the higher they are in the hierarchy. Satisfying needs is not exactly the same as filling a bucket, as we have a constant demand for them and we have to satisfy them from environmental sources. In an analogy with the container of needs, it is more appropriate to imagine the vessel as a container with a hole at the bottom. We need to constantly keep fulfilling our needs if we are to stay alive and rise in the hierarchy. As long as the inflow matches the outflow, we can remain in a steady state. If, say, the economy is not doing well (a suppressive environment) and we lose our job, the inflow will be less than the outflow and our physiological and safety needs will be at risk. When our activities eventually become 'profitable', the surplus of inflow will raise the level of the liquid in the container and higher-order needs will be satisfied. The opposite will be true if we were, say, on a small desert island. The rewards (traces of food probably) will barely cover the physiological needs despite the behaviour we would display, risking potential emptying of the vessel and death.

Something that is beyond the scope of this book and is more in the realm of philosophy is the idea that this hierarchy of needs is not set in stone and, for some reason, human beings have an amazing capacity to shift them up and down according to their situation. Take, for example, the extreme case of a Buddhist monk. His social needs are apparently zero, while his self-actualization needs have been transcended to another level. Similarly, while his physiological needs still remain, the need for safety is not of primal importance to him. He could very well be an exceptional leader if he wanted to, but he is content and happy in his own choices.

By combining the needs (Figure 5.3) with the traits and attributes mentioned above (Figure 5.5) as internal capital, we get a more complete picture for representing individuals as they interact in their natural and social environments (Figure 5.6). The external pressures (the dotted arrows) and the rewards individuals receive from

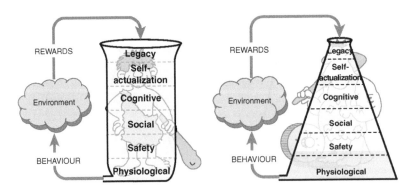

Figure 5.5 Hierarchy of needs for different individuals

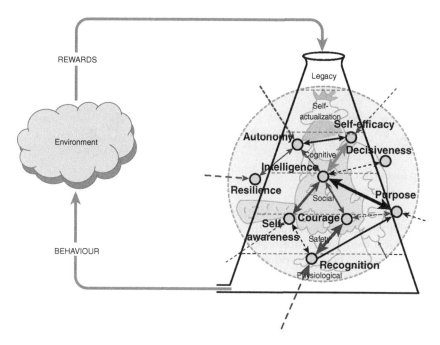

Figure 5.6 The individual as a theoretical construct

the environment trigger their decision-making process, which materializes as behaviour. The network nodes in the representation should be seen as floating around the various need levels, as the same attribute – such as autonomy – can be used to satisfy different types of needs.

5.3 From groups to organizations

Individuals coming together to form a social entity for one reason or another are said to have formed a group. The reason for the creation of such social forms can be found in the pressures exerted by the environment (physical or human) and can include security and protection from threats and social drives such as recognition, prestige and status, to name but a few. When individuals share or decide to share a common characteristic, they come together and identify each other as part of their group (Figure 5.7). Organizations like clubs, online communities and even industries are examples of such groups. Groups capitalize on the synergies of their members to effectively create a mechanism for exercising power and controlling their environment (external pressures and opportunities) to ensure the survival and growth of their members.

Like any gathering of objects/humans, there must be certain ingredients or behaviour that individuals display that brings them together to form a group. Critical among these is the development of trust and acceptance of others. Concessions might be made (behavioural and otherwise) to allow someone to become a member of the group and influence others in that group. As the potential members come together, communication and decision-making mechanisms are agreed upon and set in motion. As time passes, these will eventually create commonly acceptable behavioural norms,

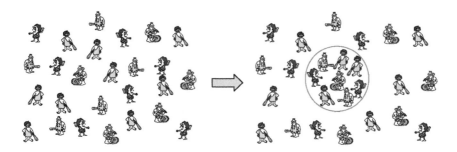

Figure 5.7 Group formation

and consideration and concern for each other's interests will develop. As members get comfortable in the group, working efficiencies of scale will materialize that will promote cooperation over competition between the members of the group, eventually increasing the group's overall productivity.

Eventually a hierarchy or governance structure will need to be established to allow for a better coordination of member activities and to prevent deviations from the norm. A hierarchy is nothing more than the identification and establishment of roles that group members are asked to play. As roles we consider here associations between individuals with specifically identifiable responsibilities. Coordinators, guards, healers, etc. are examples of such roles. Another categorization could include checkers, knowers, doers, solvers and caretakers. This organization will allow for agreement of the more efficient and effective allocation of responsibilities according to skill and expertise, and in response to the external pressure the group is experiencing.

A more specialized form of a group is the team (Figure 5.8). These are usually limited term formations with a specific focus or goal. Although the terms 'group' and 'team' are used interchangeably in the literature and in practice, there are some distinctions that at least from a theoretical point of view are worth mentioning. Team members tend to complement each other in terms of skills and hold themselves accountable for the achievements of the team. Like groups, teams can be seen as knowledge-integrating mechanisms that undergo the same lifecycles as a group, with the only addition being the adjournment of the team after it has achieved or failed to achieve its goal. Characteristics that are attributed to successful teams include commitment, cohesiveness and supportiveness.

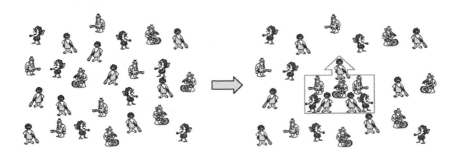

Figure 5.8 Team formation

From a theoretical point of view, one approach regarding group and team evolution has suggested the stages of forming, storming, norming and performing. Later, adjourning was also added at the end to make the theory specific to teams. Individuals are selected to be part of the team based on their specializations and experience, among other things. In this forming stage, the team members agree on goals, the roles each one team member will perform and their responsibilities. The interactions among members at this stage are formal and positive, while emotions can be mixed, ranging from excitement to anxiety and even resentment at times. In the next stage (storming), the team interactions are stronger and continuous as they are expressing their opinions and concerns about the team tasks in an attempt to test the limits of their influence and control and to establish themselves in their roles and positions in the team. Gradually, this dynamic situation will settle into negotiated norms and practices, and acceptance of each other's space and authority. This balanced stage is the norming phase and it is in this phase that the personality and character of the team takes shape. Having established its identity, the team transitions into the performing stage, where the actual work on the tasks takes place. Everybody knows what to do and how to communicate with the rest of the team effectively. The team structure and culture (as we will see later on) are clear and established, and the team now operates like a well-oiled machine. Eventually the team will reach the adjourning state, where the goal has been reached or abandoned in the event of failure. This is the closing phase where the team dissolves and each member returns to their occupation before the team or aims to join other teams.

Teams come in different forms and can include transient teams, which have a short lifespan (often in the role of a task force), distributed teams that are loosely coupled individuals and groups that are spread across physical locations and the modern type of virtual teams. The latter case is quite important and is growing in popularity as it can achieve high levels of interdependence and cooperation among its members regardless of their location. The ability to recruit expertise from around the world comes at a price, as there are many challenges that virtual teams need to overcome before they can become efficient in the achievement of their goals, especially from the point of view of the team leader. The lack of a physical location where the team can come and build connections is prone to causing issues relating to trust, commitment and accountability. Building a sense of real teamwork needs to overcome the barriers of separation, national and professional cultures, language, time zones and technology limitations (like broadband speed), among other things. Organizations and team leaders in virtual teams have devised many ways to surmount the challenges by blending the communication mode with some face-to-face interaction.

The flexibility of assembling and dissolving teams makes them ideal for the execution of projects. Project teams in general differ from other organizational teams in that they are multidisciplinary, they frequently have transient members who come and go according to the needs of the project at each stage of its lifecycle, and they might include outside experts, consultants and members from more than one organization. In addition, their temporary nature is more clear and their members are often spread across different geographical locations. The practice of establishing project teams has gained tremendous momentum and a whole science of managing projects has been established to formalize and disseminate best practices. Developing a team to complete projects is of major importance and organizations nowadays even have dedicated units like project management offices (PMOs) to efficiently develop and support teams. These offices also ensure that the project deliverables are timely and of the appropriate quality.

The role of the leader of the project team is pivotal for the success of the team. The challenges that leaders (project managers) face are more intense than those facing leaders of other teams, as they often operate under extreme time pressures and with limited resources at their disposal. These conditions leave very little room for the long-term effects of good leadership to appear. Apart from proper planning and staffing for their project, leaders achieve their objectives by establishing trust, facilitating support and clearly communicating the roles, responsibilities and expectations for each member of the team. Typical daily project manager activities include negotiating with project stakeholders and influencing their teams to accomplish project milestones. Some of the skills required for such a function include communication and negotiation skills, the ability to motivate and engage team members, knowledge of the project situation and its operating environment, and tolerance for pressure and ambiguity.

Teams and groups occasionally evolve into more complicated structures that persist over time. This is the organizational level (Figure 5.9) and it is one of the most basic social structures that has existed for as long as historical records have been recorded. Organizations come in the form of business entities, religions, political parties and countries, among others. They include assemblies of groups, teams and individuals adopting a common mission and organized under some type of structure that allows them to work. The organization forms a vision of where they need to go and adopts a commonly accepted value system to inspire its members to work in that direction. We will see more of the interplay of the various organizational statements when we discuss culture later on. For now, it is worth mentioning that a more formal

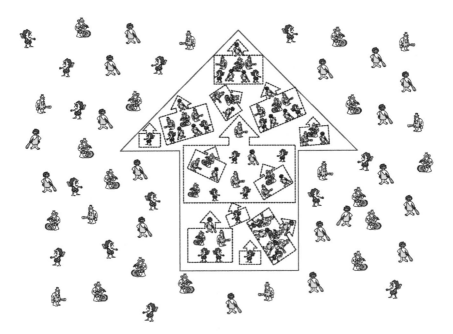

Figure 5.9 Organization

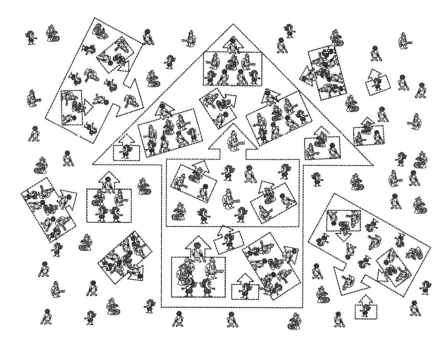

Figure 5.10 Society or market view

term for organizations is bureaucracy, which simply means they are based on rational-legal principles and are defined by rules and hierarchical relationships.

For the time being, we should also consider the view of society as a whole, where multiple organizations, individuals and teams coexist (Figure 5.10). Their motives and goals as they form groups, teams and organizations would naturally collide and contradict each other as they move in the direction that each one deems appropriate for them. Naturally, some will overcome the obstacles (other organizations and the environment) facing them and will move on, while others perish, are absorbed or change direction. In the business world, this interaction takes the form of competition in a market environment, where entrepreneurs form businesses and compete with other entrepreneurs and established businesses for market share.

5.4 Organizational structure

What was missing from our description of group, team and organization formation were the specific reasons behind their creation. To address this, we need to consider the environment in which individuals operate. This includes the physical and social environments (Figure 5.11) where these individuals exist. The physical world includes the organic and inorganic resources that planet Earth makes available to us, whether in the form of minerals and energy or in the form of living organisms, while the social environment includes the labour, products and services that we make available for ourselves and others to use. To take advantage of the available resources, we build organizations that specialize in mining, manufacturing, energy production, agriculture, transportation, entertainment and many others.

Figure 5.11 Physical and social environment

While there are popular analogies of organizations as machines or organisms, here we will view organizations as structures that are built for the benefit of their members on top of the physical and social resource layer of their environment (Figure 5.12). As such, these formations assume physical forms (buildings, equipment, etc.) and adopt a belief system based on agreed-upon principles, rules and guidelines in the form of policies and operational procedures. These are designed to guide their members and influence the way in which decisions are made and executed. This is not a static arrangement, but an evolving one following the organization's interactions with its internal and external environment. The limited resources lead to the establishment of multiple organizations that compete by exerting influence on their environment (Figure 5.12).

Through role distribution and the breakdown of organizational activity into functions that address specific needs, the organization acquires a structure. As shown in Figure 5.13, this is the form of a hierarchy that governs the relationships of its members. At the bottom of the hierarchy we have the low-level employees who deliver the products and services to the market/environment, while they import resources (raw and support materials and services as well as monetary and other rewards) into the organization. Some of these resources will be consumed in the form of rewards and

Figure 5.12 Competitive view of organizations

benefits by the members of the organization, while the rest will be processed using labour and expertise to develop other products and/or services that will be released on to the market. This cycle of imports and exports will sustain the organization as long as the exchange is efficient enough for the environment to provide resources and accept the products or services that the organization produces. In essence, the market/environment is like a separate entity with which the organization is in constant negotiation.

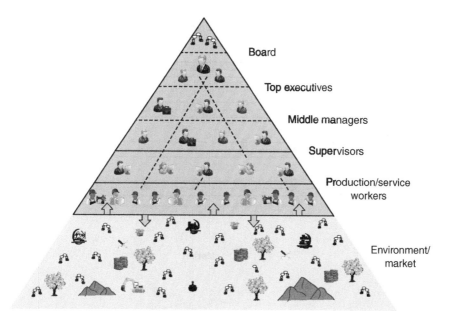

Figure 5.13 Organizational structure

As we move towards the top of the hierarchy in Figure 5.13, we find the supervisors and decision makers (middle management) who deal with the day-to-day and short-term issues facing the organization, while at the very top we have the executive team, which is responsible for the long-term planning and the strategy that the organization will follow to ensure its future survival. At the very top we have the Board. This is not a standard organizational component as some organizations (especially for-profit ones) may choose not to have one. The role of the Board (often called a board of directors or a board of trustees) is usually to oversee and advise top executives to make sure they function for the benefit of the organization and promote the organization in the communities and the public and private sectors.

Hierarchies and operating procedures create invisible structures (noted by the dotted lines in Figure 5.13) that often correspond to physical structures like office buildings, factories and office spaces. In addition, they correspond to socially constructed ways of controlling behaviour by connecting and organizing their members into working groups with reporting and authority relationships. The physical and social structure of organizations results in identifiable patterns of regularity that identify the overall structure of the organization. What distinguishes one organization from another in terms of structure includes the way in which they coordinate their activities and exercise authority (centralized or decentralized), their breakdown into levels of authority and functional units, and the formalization of their policies, rules and procedures.

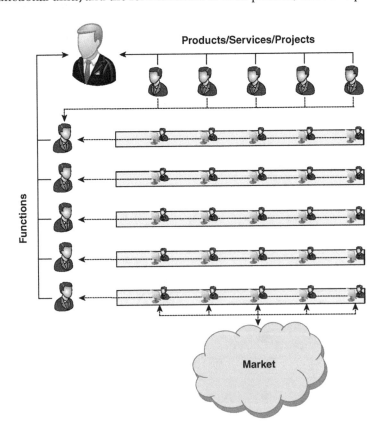

Figure 5.14 Functional organizational structure

Traditionally, organizational structures are built to correspond to organizational functions like manufacturing, production and accounting. When these functional areas have their own distinct governance bodies/executives, we say that the organizational structure is functional or horizontal (Figure 5.14). These structures focus on specialization and they consider the specialist in each functional area in charge of all activities and personnel of the organization under that area. In this way, the structure becomes dominant in terms of how the organization operates. Due to its focus on functions, the advantages of this type of structure include simplified management control, better division of labour, economies of scale and efficiency in function execution. Some of its drawbacks include a lack of coordination, control and accountability of multifunctional activities. When functional units operate as silos, friction between them can degrade operational performance and cost the organization in terms of the maintenance of specialists and product/service efficiency. An evolution of the functional organizational structure is the multidivisional structure. This is ideal for big organizations that operate globally and can organize their divisions according to a specific product and/or region.

To alleviate the deficiencies of functional structures and to address the need for flexible structures in response to the changing and highly competitive market field, many organizations have adopted matrix structures (Figure 5.15). These structures organize employees into dual reporting relationships according to both function and

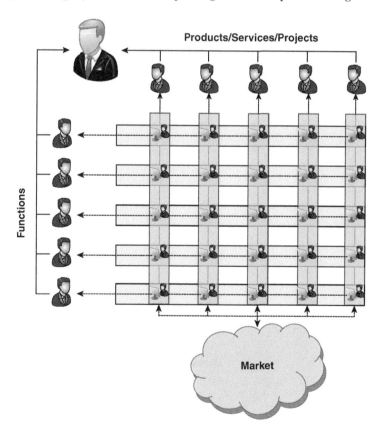

Figure 5.15 Matrix organizational structure

product/service or project. The structure allows for good coordination across functions/ divisions and aims to respond to market needs fast by expanding and leveraging on employees' competencies. By allowing specialists within an organization to be used in a number of project teams, the organization makes effective use of its resources and, in particular, enables the best deployment of those skills that are in short supply. While this is an effective use of people by the organization, the transient nature of these employees' work can be demotivating. This can get worse if there is an imbalance or friction between the sides of the matrix, so in order for the approach to be effective, clear coordination and management is required.

Another structure we will consider here is projectized (Figure 5.16) and this is appropriate for project-based and research organizations, where central control is relinquished in favour of specialization. This type is extremely efficient in terms of responding to market needs, but it requires clear communication lines between management and team members. As teams are created and dissolved frequently, a major concern with this structure is its alignment with the organizational mission and vision. Team loyalty builds within the project, but following the completion of the project, team members return to the organizational pool or are let go. To handle such drastic changes and the accompanying job insecurity, individuals need to be quite entrepreneurial and self-sufficient skill-wise in themselves. The challenge with projectized

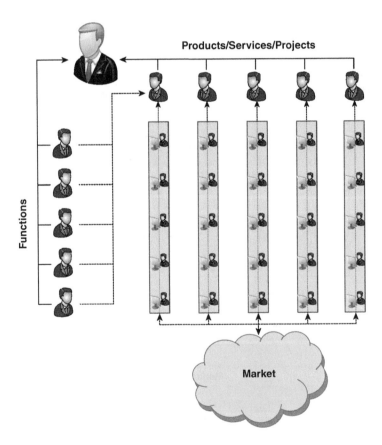

Figure 5.16 Projectized organizational structure

organizations is the redundancies in certain forms of expertise (like budget controllers, engineers and supporting personnel) that is required for every project that could have been avoided with a more functional grouping of experts.

In addition to the classical organizational structures we have discussed here and in response to globalization, an emerging form of organization has gained popularity: networked and virtual organizations. These types of organization are coordinated by a core and maintain a flexible structure that allows them to process information quickly and rapidly respond to changes in their environment. To achieve these benefits, they need to overcome the challenge of coordinating a location independent, diverse and multicultural employee base that is often spread across time zones, geographical locations and social groups. Establishing trust and lines of authority also becomes vital for team identity, coherence and alignment with the organizational mission and vision. Despite these challenges, such organizational structures seem promising for a future with no economic and market boundaries across the globe.

When viewing organizational structures, we need to bear in mind that they are not static and very often they evolve from one form into another under pressure in order to become sustainable. This pressure might occasionally push organizations to become flexible, expand or contract, and even change ownership. These changes among others, could lead to power struggles and could influence the organization size and its strategy, changing the way it operates and affecting the distribution of labour and management. If everything goes well, the organization will settle into a new structure that allows for ideal performance given the environmental realities of its market.

5.5 Organizational culture

The importance of organizational culture has attracted a lot of attention from researchers and different theories have been developed for its study. A structural and interpretive view of culture was among the first attempts to frame it theoretically. The structural view focuses on how roles are structured in an organization and has created a categorization of cultures into power cultures (usually observed in small organizations), where communication is informal and in compliance with the attitudes and norms of the central power source; role cultures (usually observed in larger bureaucratic organizations), where coordination is provided by the elite and employees are given clear roles, as reflected in their job description; task cultures (usually observed in matrix-type organizations), where power lies at the intersection of roles; and person cultures (usually observed in professional organizations), where the individual is the key element.

The interpretive view adopts a strategic outlook and focuses on the various design features (like culture and structure) and human qualities that enable managers to make sense of the world in a restricted/specialized way. The problem with this model is that it considers culture and strategy as independent variables. Another theoretical attempt considered culture from the perspective of a web where 'hard' structural and system characteristics of organizations are interwoven with 'soft' symbolic features. In order to make changes, both hard and soft elements need to be considered.

Shaping culture can be done in both direct and indirect ways. Setting up formal statements (Figure 5.17) that can be communicated across the organization is probably the first step towards consciously identifying and dictating the desired culture. Core among them is the organizational mission statement, which describes the reason for

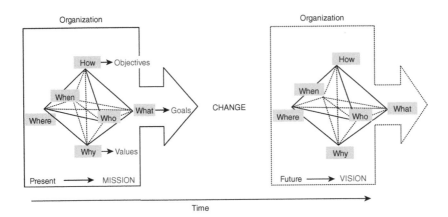

Figure 5.17 Organizational statements

the organization's existence. Its purpose is to define the operational objectives of the organization and to depict the qualities and values that the organization represents. In this way, the organization aids members in following goal-directed behaviours and performance standards that will ensure its survival and growth. While the organizational mission aims at the present, the organization's desired future state is expressed through the vision statement. This ensures that its members are aware of a forward move towards a sustainable future for them as well as that of the organization.

To achieve their mission and vision, organizations set up goals and identify core values that they will follow. Values represent everything that is considered valuable to the organization and are expressed as goals or strategic objectives, views and philosophies that are shared across the entire organization. They act as inspiration for employees, customers and other stakeholders of the organization, and manifest themselves as assumptions that members of the organization make regarding the way they do and should behave. In addition to imprinting the 'personality' of the organization upon these people, values also assist in decision making as they can be used in recruitment, marketing and quality control, among other areas.

In addition to the formal ways used by organizations to define their culture, there are informal ways that persist over time and are characteristic of social groups. These include norms, rituals and stories, to name but a few. Norms represent the way in which things are done in the organization and include rules, procedures and standards, while rituals represent the activities that provide a sense of belonging and inclusion, like when the members of the organization take part in celebrations, organizational retreats and other activities that encourage teamwork. Finally, stories express points of view as narratives of past events. Their effect is often subliminal and greatly overlooked, but they can be powerful forces that shape and strengthen the work culture of an organization while emphasizing its values. They anchor the organization's past to its present and they strengthen its culture as they reveal the history and development of its culture. They add back content, helping people reflect and learn as they can place themselves as the 'heroes' of a situation. This is an alternative way of telling people what to do by cultivating and creating expectations towards the organization without instructing them in terms of what to do.

The distinction between organizational structure and culture that is observed in traditional research raised the question of which one influences the other and how the cause and effect relationship started (Figure 5.18). Organizations have their origins in groups and it can be argued that social interactions and subsequently some form of pre-culture or cultural elements existed that initiated and created organizational structure. Alternatively, it can be argued that organizational culture is different from the cultures of individual members and groups, and that it cannot exist before an organization acquires some form of structure, so in that sense organizational structure precedes organizational culture. Despite the different positions, no one disagrees that structure and culture influence each other in many ways. One way in which this interplay can be expressed is by saying that culture legitimizes structure, while structure institutionalizes culture. For instance, it can be argued that establishing a strong hierarchy will create an autocratic culture that will provide legitimacy for the structure, while a flexible structure will allow for more transparent communication, leading to a more inclusive structure that again provides legitimacy for the structure.

From our perspective here we will consider culture as a way of restricting and supporting behaviour according to established norms. In that sense, it suggests restrictions and ways of movement within social groups and, as such, it interrelates and influences organizational structure. As people begin to interact in predictable ways, they become acquainted with the personalities of their peers, subordinates and leaders, and the routines each one is following. This settling into predictable norms and behaviours

Figure 5.18 Which came first?

Figure 5.19 Organizational culture

forms the organization's culture. In essence, it is another *form of structure* as it affects movement and expression. Employees learn, for example, to avoid their supervisors when they are in a bad mood or to engage them when their office door is open. While this form of structure might not be as clear or visible as the structure we described in the previous section, it can nevertheless be as critical and important, and at times can either make or break the organization.

From our perspective and in addition to considering culture as a form of structure, we will also include in it the formal and informal communication between the organizational members. Behavioural norms, values and the rest of the elements mentioned above are also included in this form of communication simply because they are all in reality exchanges of messages in one form or another (text, speech, body language, etc.). Figure 5.19 attempts to capture the fluidity of organizational culture as arrows that communicate written and unwritten rules across the various organizational levels. Down arrows represent orders, suggestions, feedback, stories, values, etc. that supervisors try to communicate to subordinates, while up arrows communicate information, responses, reports, feelings, etc. that subordinates project to their superiors.

Another important contributor to organizational culture that is often overlooked in organizational research is the *peer culture* (the horizontal arrows in Figure 5.19). These usually act as suppressors or enhancers of the other forms of culture discussed above, but they do have their unique contribution to make and so we will deal with them as separate cultural elements. A distinction need to be made between peer groups and peer culture. By default, individuals will belong to some form of peer group due to their specialization, role, experience, etc. Peer culture, though, is something that is collectively created by various social circumstances and settings, for example, participation in group and team activities.

A final contributor to organizational culture that again is greatly overlooked in research is the culture injections that organizations receive from their environment. For practical reasons, we will refer to this here as *ambient* culture. Organizations do not operate in isolation and, as such, they interact with external stakeholders like customers, suppliers, other organizations, the government, etc. that directly influence organizational culture through choices, preferences, policies and regulations. In addition, each member of the organization is part of social groups like their families, friends, clubs, associations, etc., which influence their beliefs and attitudes. These are carried into the organizational environment and actively influence the work culture. In Figure 5.13 ambient culture is represented by the arrows at the interface between the organization and the market/society.

In consideration of the view of culture as structure, the arrows in Figure 5.19 need to be seen as part of the structure and not as some passive elements that can be crossed or overcome with no resistance. In fact, in many cases, overcoming and changing organizational culture is far more difficult than changing the organizational structure (in its traditional sense). Overall, anything that carries some form of inertia and can resist change acts as a form of structure and, in that sense, culture can be treated as some form of structure. From the leader's point of view, as we will see, all forms of structure can serve both as opportunities and challenges that need to be considered when successfully exercising leadership.

5.6 The leader

We are now coming to the core of the leadership phenomenon: the leader. Although the same aspects we discussed in relation to individuals also apply here, we are going to focus here more on the role that leaders play. For this purpose, we will need to identify any special characteristics that are required for leadership that are new or more pronounced than is the case for individuals (see Section 5.2). We are more interested here in influence and its variants like power and control. The latter have occasionally been seen as separate forms of influence, but we will consider them here as extremes of influence. When individuals control the behaviour of others, we can say that they have total influence over them, while when their impact is non-existent, we can say that they exert no influence. In this way, every level of control on another's behaviour becomes a level of influence.

In our view, *influence* as the capacity to affect behaviour is in many ways like gravity. Two objects/agents attract/influence each other and affect each other's movement/behaviour. Agents can be individuals or entities (also called agents from now on) like organizations, groups, societies and even the world as a whole with its universal trends and practices. In addition, an agent can be a property like a catalyst that accelerates/influences reactions without actually being affected by the reactants. For example, that gene that results in an individual being tall and robust could easily influence them to become a basketball player or could make them more aggressive than others.

As human beings, leaders are shaped and grow personally and professionally under the influence of a variety of genetic and environmental factors. Such factors are responsible for the transformation of the signals and stimuli they receive in response to their interaction with their surroundings into perception and knowledge of how the world around them operates. For the purposes of our analysis, we will consider a systems perspective of four generalized layers, each one affecting the way influence travels to and from an individual.

Starting with the inherited genetic traits that are passed to each of us in the genes we inherit from our ancestors and moving on to the family and social environments, we are influenced by various groups (the concentric cycles in Figure 5.20) as we grow and become exposed to more and more of the world. As microcosms inside nations, regions and the world at large, these groups influence individuals at different times and stages in their development, and leave marks that in some people trigger and nurture the expression of selective attributes that could eventually support the expression of leadership. More specifically, the layers shown comprise: (1) inherited personality and intelligence (imprinting through our genes); (2) the family environments where we grew up and matured and that conditioned us to certain beliefs and values; (3) the society in which we live that imposes cultural traits onto us and (4) the world at large, with its global trends and influences. Some of the influences that penetrate and guide our perspective and purpose in the world are education and personal experiences. These influence personal style and build intellectual abilities and coping skills throughout our lifetime.

As individuals are affected by the influences of the environment, they react by trying to exert influence to control their environment. Influence radiates from ourselves into the social environment around us, diminishing in strength the further we go from ourselves in terms of social connections in space and time. Figure 5.21 identifies four distinct regions of influence that individuals exert. The innermost circle, that we call here *circle of constitution*, represents the influence an individual has in terms of controlling and even changing their own behaviour. In a way, this is the most critical form of influence, as without this, individuals will be unable to extend their reach to other individuals. Immediately after this we have the *circle of conduction*, which includes the people with whom we have direct contact (face-to-face and though

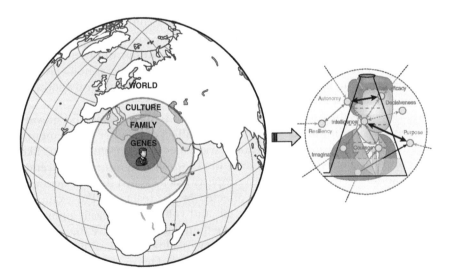

Figure 5.20 Regions of influence on individuals

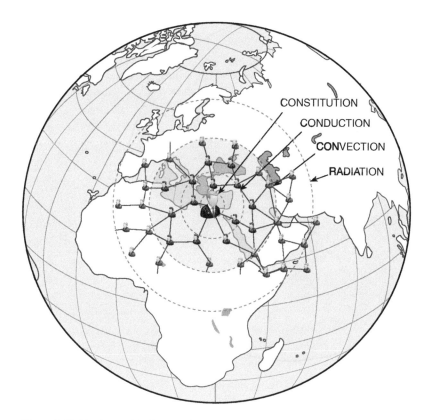

CONSTITUTION
CONDUCTION
CONVECTION
RADIATION

Figure 5.21 Regions of influence from individuals

immediate communication) on a daily or regular basis. These could be family members, subordinates and superiors, business partners and any other business stakeholders that we communicate with directly. This circle is followed by all other individuals that our direct contacts can influence. We call this the *circle of convection* and, in an analogy with how heat dissipates, includes a more fluid social group. Eventually, we have the *circle of radiation*, which includes all those individuals that, in essence, we influence by reputation. This is the circle where the stories about us exist, rather like the organizational stories we discussed in the previous section.

The incoming and outgoing influences shown in Figures 5.20 and 5.21 are interrelated as their reach and extend to affect each other, as Figure 5.22 demonstrates. The shading scheme is also preserved in relation to the proximity of the influence to the individual's core. The exception to this rule is with respect to the circles of constitution and genes, as the latter is impossible to change, while the former can to an extent be controlled by the individual.

It should be evident for a reader familiar with the way heat dissipates in physical systems that the three outer circles of influence are an analogy to the way in which heat is transferred. We have the exchange of heat between objects that are in contact (conduction), like when we touch a hot object; we have heat that is transferred by the movement of hot molecules, like in the case of hot air (convection) and finally we

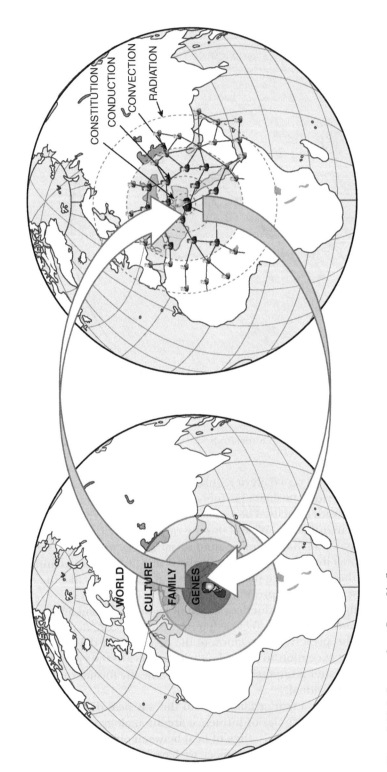

Figure 5.22 Inflow and outflow of influence

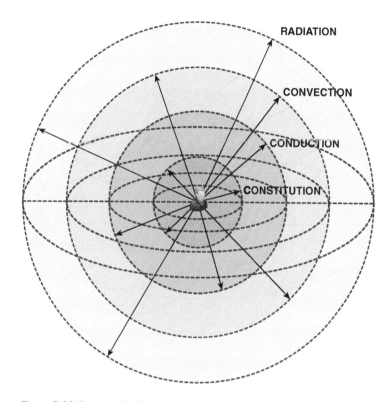

Figure 5.23 Spaces of influence from individuals

have heat that is transmitted, like in the case of the radiation we receive from the sun. A more representative image to reflect the analogy would be to consider the influence type in three dimensions, as shown in Figure 5.23.

One important aspect of the four types of influence that we need to keep in mind is while their reach is limited, they do act on what is inside their space. Radiation, for example, which can be seen as corresponding to reputation, also traverses the conduction and convection spaces. A person's reputation in an organization influences those in contact with them and, by proxy, spreads across the organization. It even influences one's perception of themselves (constitution) as they become self-aware of its reach.

Another important characteristic of the circles of influence is that the expansion and compression of each circle can to a great extent be independent of one another. An individual, for example, a floor manager in an organization, can have similar-sized circles of conduction and convection if their subordinates do not have any subordinates of their own.

Two important distinctions regarding the circles/spaces of influence that we need to make here is that they are not static in terms of size or position and that they are permeable in terms of the individuals that they encircle. An individual might be in our circle of convection, one instance and later on (for example, if they get promoted or become our business partner) move to our circle of conduction. Another important characteristic of the circles of influence is that the expansion and compression of each circle can to a great extent be independent of each other.

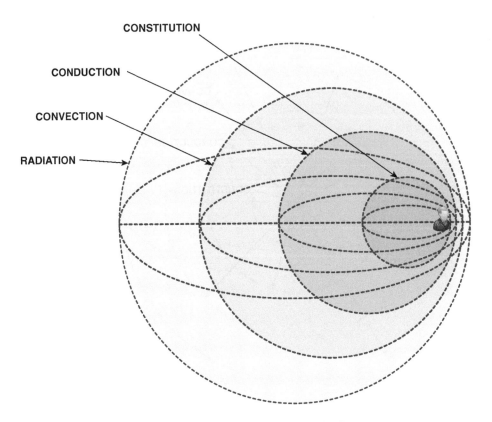

Figure 5.24 Directional application of influence from individuals

In addition, as we move to accomplish our goals, we might need to exert influence in a certain direction (Figure 5.24). This will require the movement of our influence spaces, which is not analogous to the direction of movement, as people do not instantly get influenced. In that respect, the control we exert in our various circles diminishes as their distance from us increases and this will lead to a form of inertia (or time lag) in the way in which our influence grows and moves.

To complete the picture, we need to consider other leaders/individuals who might be interested in influencing us (Figure 5.25). What we end up having in this way is a 'collision' of influences. It could be a head-on collision, as depicted in Figure 5.25, it could be at an angle or we could even have one supporting the other, such as when two partners are working together for a common goal. Obviously the influence spheres, while permeable, are elastic to an extent and although they might overlap, indicating that other third parties might be known and influenced by both the colliding individuals, the innermost sphere would be harder to compress. For example, penetrating one's sphere of constitution might very well be a case of physical abuse, so we shouldn't expect it to be the norm when individuals interact, at least from the organizational point of view that we are interested in here.

In the case of organizations where the various individuals exert their influence, the representation of culture shown in Figure 5.19 will now look more like Figure 5.26. Presuming that the influence of the leader is strongest, the tendency of all other

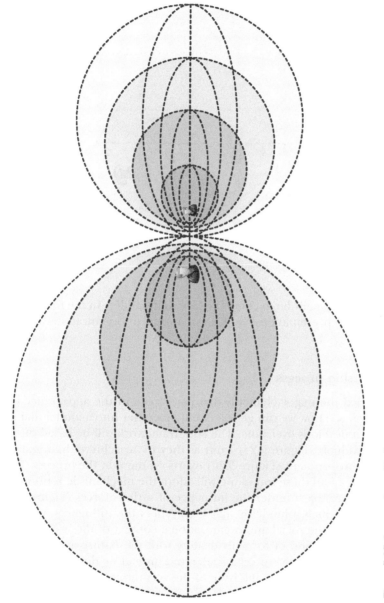

Figure 5.25 Interaction of influences

Figure 5.26 Influences in organizations

influences would normally be to climb the hierarchy ladder. In the following section, we will see how a representation like this can appear in organizations and in groups in general.

5.7 The leadership process

Having identified the major elements that participate in the appearance of leadership, we will now see how we can get everything together into a model that describes the process as it develops over time. The core framework will be based on the influences that individuals (Figure 5.24) exert as they try to achieve their goals and the influences the environment (Figure 5.20) exerts on them in the process. To address the directionality of all these forces, we will adopt the mechanistic representation of an individual as an object under the influence of various forces (Figure 5.27). The great advantage of such a model is that it considers the influences as forces of all other individuals in the social and organizational context of the leader. In this way, we avoid the complication of formally dealing with the nature and strength of the influence that each entity exerts on a leader and instead we deal with its representation as a force arrow. However, the issue of the accuracy of such representation will be discussed later on.

The various forces included here are indicative and by no means cover everything that can be involved. The lengths of the arrows are meant to indicate strength, while their orientation indicates the direction of the force within the organizational context. In our example in Figure 5.27, F8 could indicate the individual's application of influence to move upwards (organizationally), F4 and F2 could be influences from

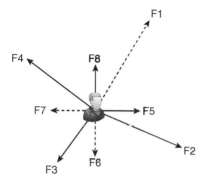

Figure 5.27 Influences as forces on individuals

subordinates that might want to move the individual upwards or keep/pull them downwards correspondingly, F3 could be influences from superiors to keep them from moving upwards, and F5 could represent influences from peers.

Another group of influences/forces has been included here as dashed arrows to indicate the internal nature of some forces. F7 could, for example, be an attraction/ loyalty an individual might feel towards a peer group, F6 could be fears and insecurities that prevent someone from daring to move upwards, while F1 could indicate the individual's need to be recognized and appreciated. You will notice that F1 and F8 are different, although the goal might seem the same. This was done on purpose to indicate that, often, we are not really aware of the extent and direction of our inner drives and of the influence they exercise. Knowing ourselves is not easy, as philosophy will testify.

With the representation of influences as forces that act on an individual/leader, the next step will be to consider how individuals move as a result of their application. One way to calculate the resulting force is to see each force analysed in an axis system. For simplicity's sake, here we consider horizontal and vertical components (Figure 5.28). When we add (those in the same direction) and subtract (those in opposite directions) the components along the individual axes, we will end up with a horizontal and vertical component that we can synthesize to get the resultant force on the individual. The direction of this force will represent the direction of movement for the individual, while the strength of the force (arrow size) will suggest the magnitude of movement.

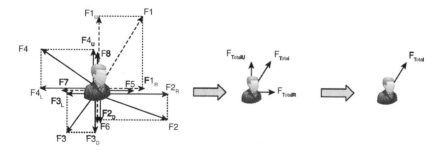

Figure 5.28 Influences as forces on individuals

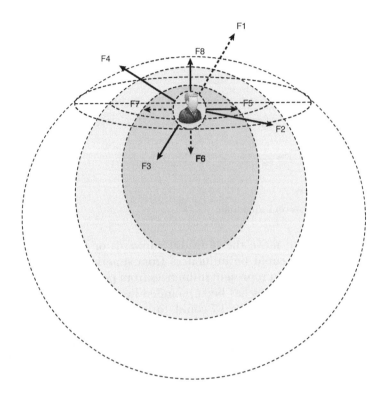

Figure 5.29 Influences on individuals in real settings

Superimposing Figures 5.24 and 5.27, we obtain the representation we will use from now on for individuals in organizational positions (Figure 5.29). In the follow-up discussion we need to keep in mind that the purpose of this book is to primarily explain leadership. It is anticipated that an outcome of this explanation will be an understanding of what makes an individual a leader in a situation when others fail. To a great extent, this will depend on the types of forces that leaders generate on them and those contributed by the environment.

Having developed a representative enough picture of the potential leader, we need to consider the organizational structure where they are at a given time (Figure 5.30). We can see here the advantage of using the force modes in simplifying the image of the alternative we saw in Figure 5.26. Under the influence of the total force on the individual, they move upwards through the organizational structure into middle management (Figure 5.31) and executive (Figure 5.32) positions, and finally the leadership position (Figure 5.33). As they move upwards, external capital becomes internal capital for the individual. The excess capital is represented by an expansion of their circles of influence, which can subsequently be used to contribute to the upward direction of movement.

A good analogy would be to consider capital as air that when moved from the external environment to the internal environment of the influence circle blows them,

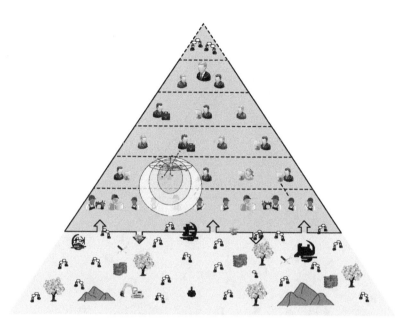

Figure 5.30 Initial position of the leader in the organization

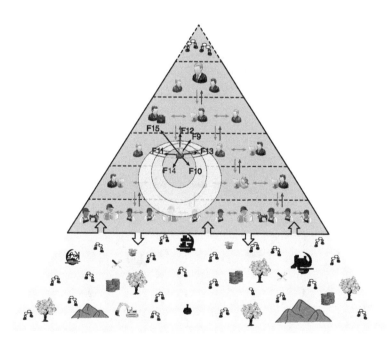

Figure 5.31 Moving up into middle-management positions

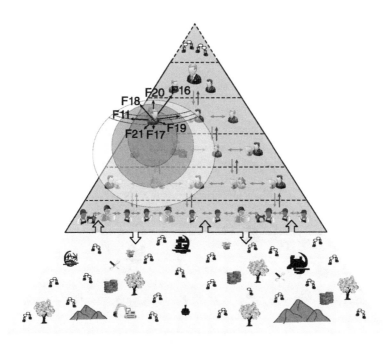

Figure 5.32 Moving up into executive positions

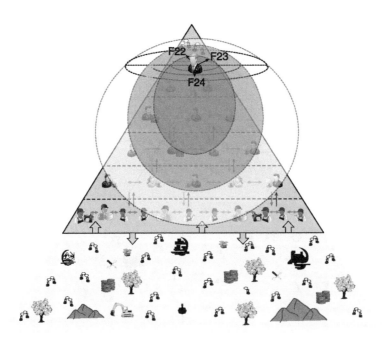

Figure 5.33 Moving up into the leadership position

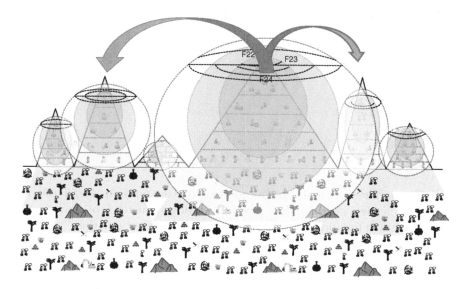

Figure 5.34 Spreading the leadership role

expanding their reach. In essence, this extra air comes from the influence circles of other individuals (represented as forces) as they lose in their competition with the leader. This is the result of the interactions shown in Figure 5.25. Combinations of influences could occasionally support upward movement, while in other cases they could result in sideways or even downward movements.

Reaching the top leadership position is not an end to the process, but rather a dynamic point of temporary equilibrium. If a leader's potential or internal capital, as we adopted here, is more than what the organization needs, leaders could venture/ expand their circles of influence to other organizations (Figure 5.34) and could either lead them as separate units or merge them into one organization. In the business world, situations like this can occur in mergers and acquisitions and in the formation of conglomerates. The influence leaders exert does not have to be in isolation, but it could be shared – like in partnerships – to enable greater reach. Influence in this sense can be contagious, allowing one to move around in the world of social entities (individuals, groups, organizations, etc.).

A final point about the dynamic nature of the leadership position is that it takes effort to maintain. Other individuals or entities might continually challenge the leader by exercising their influence to move them downwards. A constant exchange of capital will need to be maintained, sufficient to suppress threats and maintain the internal and external forces acting upon the leader. In the next chapter we will see how leaders can maintain their position in the face of the forces that the internal and external environments exert on them.

6 Application of leadership

Having described a framework that explains how to rise to the position of leader, here we will discuss how leaders maintain their position. Staying at the top is of course relative to the time spent at the top and the way in which leaders conclude their 'career'. Some of the leaders we discussed in the earlier chapters are testimony to the fact that staying at the top is much harder than rising to the top. This reality suggests that the two situations require the practice of somewhat different leadership qualities or at least the selective application of leadership behaviour. As a result, the best approach would be to see leadership as dynamic and evolving in a way that allows individuals to successfully 'influence' their teams within the operational environment they face. As the environment changes, so does the practice.

The way in which leaders act or need to act has been extensively studied, and there are literally thousands of books and research publications out there on the subject for anyone to read. This chapter does not aim to replace or enforce that wealth of knowledge, but rather to point out some of the elements that contribute to the application of leadership, especially through the prism of the framework we developed in the previous chapter. To recap, two of the elements discussed in the previous chapter that define the playground of leadership in organizations are the organizational structure and culture. The former provides an organization with a hierarchy or roles and authority, while the latter provides the social norms that guide the behaviour of individuals. Organizational culture is also seen here as a form of structure as it 'restricts' and guides behaviour (in a fuzzy and unspoken kind of way) just as organizational structure does. In addition to these two elements, organizations have established processes for their members to follow in order to convert raw material and energy (human and other) into products and services.

An additional aim of this chapter is to show that leadership is not as easy as might be imagined. Hopefully, a reality check about the skills, knowledge, experience and commitment required to succeed in leadership will show, to anyone aspiring to be a leader, how difficult and circumstantial the role can (sometimes) be.

6.1 Leading organizations

In acting out their role (exercising their authority as widely known), leaders manipulate the elements that define organizations (Figure 6.1). By changing (*upgrading* might be a less threatening term) the organizational structure, culture and processes, leaders can steer the organization away from current and future threats towards a

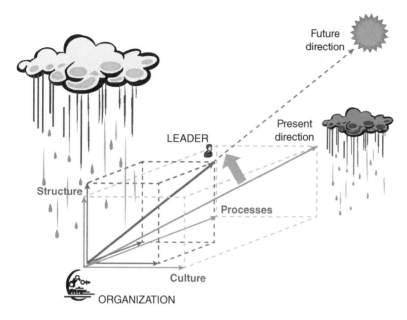

Figure 6.1 Organizational upgrade

direction that ensures its survival and sustainable growth. In order for this to be successful, they need to be able to 'see' the future and successfully perform that 'upgrade'.

Considering the ability to perform the upgrade first, we need to keep in mind that a leader's primary function is to lead others. In that sense, they affect physical and social change through others. We do have leaders who are also involved in the front line (like Alexander the Great or a modern executive making sales or writing a piece of computer code to build Google), but this is usually done to get a sense of the battle rather than critically influence its outcome. Alexander the Great killed a few of his enemy's soldiers in battle, but it is unlikely that this influenced the outcome of his battles in a direct way. However, it did inspire his troops to trust and follow him, as they saw him risking his life like everyone else. They were willing to trust him because he never asked anyone to take risks he wouldn't take or to do something that he wouldn't do himself.

Modern organizations operate in an environment affected by a multitude of stakeholders, as shown in Figure 6.2. The representation is an alternative to that given in the previous chapter, as it emphasizes the entities involved in affecting leaders' goals at an instance in time. At the edges of the sphere of influence, we have those that are external to the organization stakeholders, like clients, suppliers, partners and competitors. All these create conditions that can be either opportunities or threats for the organization and, by extension, for the leader. They provide the sources of the signals that the environment sends to the organization and are the subjects of the impact that the organization makes in the world.

From the external stakeholders, we move on to the internal stakeholders, which include every entity within the organizational boundaries. Traditionally, organizations

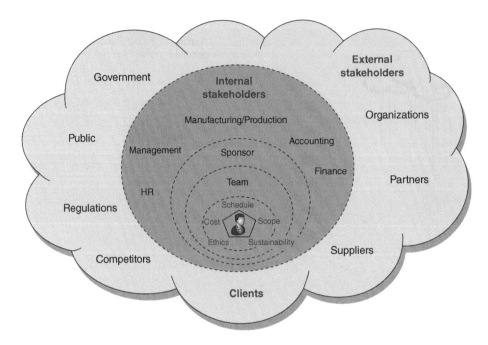

Figure 6.2 Organizational stakeholders from the leader's perspective

are broken down into five main functions: accounting, finance, manufacturing and production, human resources and management. Depending on the organizational structure, authority and control might typically be horizontal, vertical or matrix, as we saw in the previous chapter. As we get closer to the leader, we have the individuals they directly interact with, like their subordinates/team and supervisors (sponsors in project management terminology).

In addition to the entities discussed up to this point, there are other conceptual entities that remain the subject of the leader's focus and relate to the goal they try to achieve or the project they supervise. These appear in the form of constraints (the labels at the corners of the pentagon in Figure 6.2) and include the traditional constraints relating to scope, cost and schedule that form what is usually called the 'iron' triangle. In addition, we might consider others like sustainability and ethics. Whether they form triangles, pentagons or any other polygon is up to how the leaders organize their priorities and focus their attention.

We now need to consider the time domain, as it uniquely defines the situation leaders face in the present and the future. For the remainder of the discussion here, we will adopt the stance that the practice of leadership is dependent on their situation. If this were not the case, then anyone who had risen to power would have stayed there as long as they wanted. What we will need to do before moving further is to define 'practice' and 'application', as we will use these terms to explain what we hope will be considered a sustainable leadership behaviour. Practice is any intended and regularly applied action that could be driven by an idea, belief or method that is not an explicit expression of a theory.

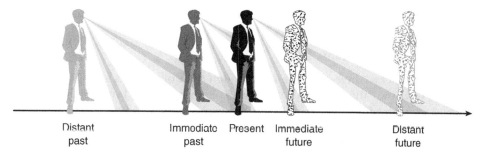

Distant past   Immediate past   Present   Immediate future   Distant future

Figure 6.3 The time continuum of an individual

Application here is nothing more than the action to put something into operation. The benefit of actions always has a time perspective, as some actions target present situations, while others aim at affecting the future. Given that humans are learning organisms that live in a universe where time moves forward (from past to future), our concept of who we are extends beyond the present we experience (Figure 6.3). We tend to learn from our past and apply this knowledge to anticipate and predict the future. Our focus shifts like a light beam illuminating an instance/spot of time as we imagine it to be – clearer at the centre of our attention and getting fuzzier as we move away from the centre.

Considering every instance of time is impractical because our capabilities are limited and because life does not change that much from one moment to another (at least as we usually experience it in our lives). Based on the signals we receive from our environment and our influences from our immediate and distant past, we react to our present and plan for our immediate and distant future. In that sense, we will consider here the time domain broken down into the 'distant past', 'immediate past', 'present', 'immediate future' and 'distant future'. This is a rough subdivision and is influenced by an individual's perception of time based on their life experiences, personalities and situation, among other factors. The labels are also adopted to emphasize the nature of the focus and avoid subconscious overlaps in terms of their meaning.

The general breakdown of time periods that we will consider here will include the aforementioned time continuum categories as they also reflect the organizational point of view when it comes to time planning. To get a sense of what timeframes we mean in our discussion, 'near' (past or future) might refer to days or months, while 'distant' might refer to months or years in the future. 'Present' will be reserved for the minutes, hours and even days that comprise the 'now'. We take the philosophical stance here that the 'now' doesn't really exist, as the moment you define something as 'now', it has already become 'then'.

Given the adopted time breakdown, it might be argued that the 'immediate' domain is for managers and is different from the leadership domain, but as we have also seen before, this classification is merely an issue of proximity to the time horizon and action type rather than a clear distinction of the two roles. Leaders do not live in isolation doing their leading. Whenever they interact with their immediate subordinates, they are in essence managing, since they directly affect behaviour. Some classification in terms of leaders in the various time domains might be frontline employees reacting to customers for the present domain, floor or frontline managers coordinating and organizing for the near future domain, and top executives planning for the distant future.

6.2 The action playing field

Organizations react to their environment through their operations and deal with the fear of the unknown that the future poses by planning tactics for their immediate future and strategies for the distant future. Strategy is considered here to be any plan of action aimed at achieving a goal in the future. Considering the adage that 'no plan survives first contact with the enemy', an intermediate form of action is required to deal with the immediate future. This is where tactics come into play. Tactics, as the name implies, are there to ensure some order and regularity in dealing with a situation based on pre-existing and well-tested 'manoeuvres'/practices to ensure optimal behaviour in the face of the enemy/challenge. In essence, they can be viewed as strategies that target the immediate future.

Generic strategies in the business world focus on differentiation and cost. These are mutually exclusive in terms of resource usage and are meant to emphasize the interaction between minimizing costs, differentiating products and focusing/targeting specific market segments. Tactics are often seen as means of achieving strategies, but since they are suggestions for action, they are in essence plans for operating in the immediate future. A marketing plan or a project organization and execution could be considered tactics.

The space of action types available to leaders along with the time domain can be illustrated by the chessboard representation given in Figure 6.4. The board is meant to highlight the ideal targets (the shaded squares) of each action, as our understanding comes from our distant past and we learn from our immediate past. Based on what we have learned and understood, we react to our present, plan our tactics to address what we expect in our immediate future and strategize in terms of what our distant future could be.

While we are in the present, we can spend our time reacting to requests and emergencies from our environment, acquire information and learn new skills, and review our past to understand our present and imagine the future.

We need to consider here that while humans have evolved to communicate rich information between each other and adopt innovations better than any other species, we have not yet evolved beyond our basic need for security and safety (physiological needs, as mentioned in the previous chapter). We are still trying to adapt what we know to unknown situations that we fear. The future, in that sense, with its uncertainty, looks threatening and it is treated as a physical threat.

Another form of action in which we engage concerns planning our tactics for our immediate future and our strategies for our distant future. Of course, there are cases like when we are anxious or depressed, for example, where our body might be in the present, while our spirit might be in the future or the past. While sometimes it might be beneficial to do this, for example, in the face of an upcoming crisis, spending too much time out of the present could result in us missing the events we actually experience. The fear of uncertainty caused by an ambiguous future could result in 'safe' decisions that constrain creativity and preserve the status quo. 'Visiting'/recalling the past might provide insights about the situations we have experienced, while 'visiting'/imagining the future allows us to safely test-run our plans.

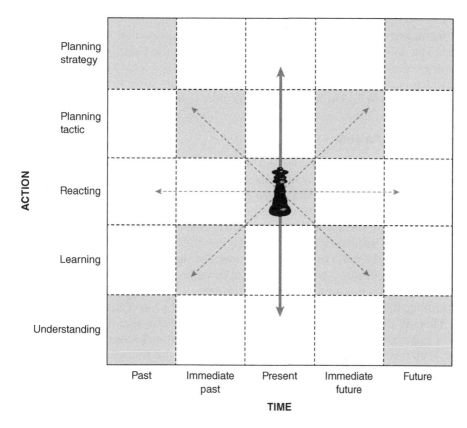

Figure 6.4 Space of action types

Synchronizing and timing our actions so as to reflect the realities of present, the lessons of the past and the prospects of the future might not be as easy as it seems. If, for example, instead of reacting to a situation in our present, we remain passive, living in either our past or our future that is not there, then we end up becoming prisoners of our present, unable to control what is happening around us. Similarly, if instead of planning our strategies when the present allows for that, we end up micromanaging/ reacting to our present, we will be unable to prepare the organization for what might be coming up in the future.

In forming tactical and strategic plans, organizations often rely on tools like SWOT and PESTLE analysis to correspondingly deal with their micro- and macro-economic environments. A SWOT analysis is regularly used to organize information in the context of a situation from an internal perspective according to organizational strengths and weaknesses (internal view) and an external perspective considering the opportunities and the threats available in the operational environment. With a view of the external environment and the organization's capabilities, leaders can plan the immediate and near future tactics/strategies they will need to implement in order to ensure the success of their organization.

When it comes to the macro-environment (operations on a global scale), a more inclusive approach is required. A PEST analysis in such cases will provide information about the political, economic, sociocultural and technological situation in which the organization operates. Political stability, taxation, inflation, unemployment, education and technology influences are among a variety of aspects that such an analysis will reveal. This information is valuable for planning for the future and the distant future strategy of an organization. Additional components like legal and environment (PESTLE) factors can also be considered in such efforts in order to provide a more thorough and focused evaluation of an organization's environment.

6.3 The life-cycle of a goal

In discussing the application of leadership while combining the time and situational dimensions, we will follow a project management life-cycle perspective at least in terms of the life-cycle of a goal that a leader sets and pursues. This approach more or less covers the range of phases that leaders go through in achieving their goals. While leaders might delegate the accomplishment of the goal-related work and activities to their proxies, we will assume here that they are the ones in charge of accomplishing the goal. Hopefully, this will convey to the reader the magnitude of what is involved in relation to accomplishing a goal (of a tactical or strategic nature) in terms of traits, knowledge and capabilities on the part of the leader.

In describing the life-cycle of a goal, we will follow a project management perspective. This will enable us to explore all the possible phases that leaders could go through in terms of accomplishing their goal. The traditional waterfall style model (Figure 6.5) that is used in project management will be the framework that we will use to analyse the evolution of a goal and the requirements it places on leaders. The reader can expand on what we will discuss here by consulting the Project Management Body of Knowledge (PMBOK) by the Project Management Institute (PMI).

Regarding leaders in the business world, at the beginning there is the leader and their operational environment (organization, group, team, etc.), and signals flow between the leaders and the environment. Leaders process the signals and identify a case (opportunity, threat, etc.) that needs to be addressed. This is where a goal (a project in project management terminology) will begin to form. A feasibility study will normally be conducted, either in the leader's mind or through research. This is where the validity and probability of success of the goal will be determined. In this case, the leader will evaluate the need for the goal, will clarify its description, will ensure it aligns with the organizational or departmental vision and will estimate its impact. In addition, the requirements for its accomplishment (regulations, compliance, etc.) might be considered and alternative solutions evaluated to ensure its appropriateness in addressing the case at hand.

If the outcome of this process shows promise and deems the goal to be feasible, the formal process of pursuing the goal starts (*initiating* in Figure 6.5). During the *initiation* phase, leaders communicate with key stakeholders that will be affected by the goal or involved in its pursuit, identify the specifics of the goal, such as expectations and the types of resources that will need to be involved (human, equipment, facilities, etc.) and consider the formalities that will need to be addressed, like policies and procedures. A lot of communications will take place during this phase and this usually materializes in the form of an announcement of a kickoff meeting with the immediate stakeholders.

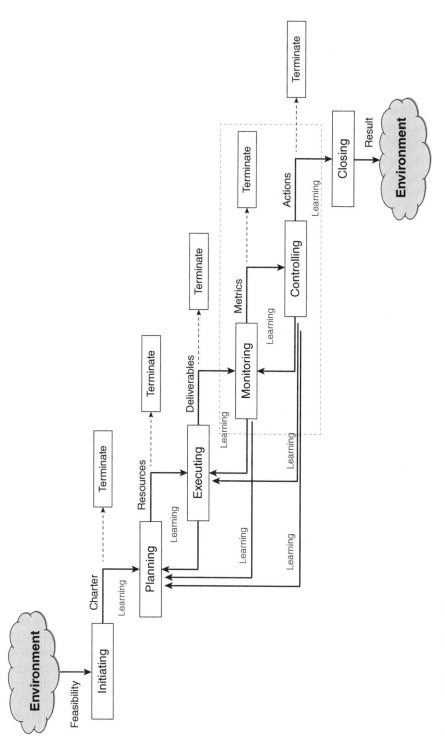

Figure 6.5 Waterfall model of goal management phases

The outcome of the initiation phase is usually a form of a charter (mental, oral or print) in which the various aspects of the goal are identified. This includes a detailed description of the goal, justification or purpose for pursuing the goal, expectations, measurable objectives, requirements, resources needed (human, monetary, etc.), risks and anything else that is needed to make the goal a reality for those involved and the organization. Key players will also have been identified and classified during this phase based on their involvement and influence. Some of them might have a legitimate interest in the accomplishment of the goal and some might be considered supportive, necessary, dominant, dangerous or whatever other adjective appropriately classifies individuals or entities. For the completion of the initiation phase, leaders need to display certain knowledge and skills like the ability to organize the various elements of the charter, to identify the stakeholders that are affected and those that will be involved, and to identify potential risks and limitations. In addition, leaders need to highlight and support that the benefits that will be achieved will outweigh the costs involved. Overall they should be able to sell the goal to those that need to support the initiative and participate in its completion.

6.3.1 Planning

Having set in motion the process of pursuing the goal, leaders now need to be engaged in planning how they will achieve it. As an example, here we will consider the outline of the actions that need to be coordinated for the accomplishment of the goal. Such outlines need to clearly define the baseline of the scope, steps and resources that will have to be involved for each action, subsidiary plans for the specific elements that will be involved in the execution of the plan, such as requirements, communication and quality, and the strategies and tactics that will be adopted.

Expanding a little more on the development of a plan, some of the 'ingredients' that need to be considered to ensure that it is going to succeed include managing its scope and schedule, ensuring that resources (including people, money, facilities, etc.) are adequate, considering potential risks, making sure quality is as expected, and ensuring that it is effectively communicated among the stakeholders. These could be in the form of subsidiary plans that will address the specifics of each factor in addition to the general planning philosophy, how status and progress will be measured, and the organization of command and control, among other things. A brief account of some of the critical ingredients of a good plan follows.

Directional control: Like any human endeavour, goals could be modified either intentionally (new information might create better understanding) or unintentionally (obstacles or opportunities might emerge in the process). The plan itself needs to have checks and controls to account for drifts and diversions (scope creep in project management terminology) from its initial direction/objectives. Focusing on the scope of the goal will ensure that only the work that is required is included in the plan. This might sound easy, but scope creep is one of the most frequent reasons for goal failure. 'Know thyself' should be seen here as 'know thy scope' if it is to accurately express the importance on staying on track. Among the various factors that could affect the direction we want to follow are the structure, culture and operating procedures of the organization, as well as the environmental/marketplace conditions at the various points in time as we move along in accomplishing the goal.

Scope management (or directional control as we have termed it here) requires detailed and accurate documentation of the requirements that surround the goal to ensure that they all address the need (business or otherwise) that gave birth to the goal. Requirements cover a wide range of elements and could include business requirements like the rules and guiding principles of an organization, stakeholder requirements like the impact of the goal to internal and external entities, solution requirements like compliance, training and support, functionality, quality and reporting, and goal requirements like performance, safety, levels of service and completion criteria. In addition, we might also have assumptions, constraints, dependencies and transition requirements.

To overcome the challenges that directional control poses, leaders need to be able to exercise expert judgement and facilitate an effective communication in engaging the various stakeholders. They should also be able to bridge the gap between objectives and deliverables by using tools (for example, traceability matrices), to perform a value and systems analysis, and often to apply design and engineering techniques. They could finally benefit by considering alternatives and breaking down the goal into units and/or atomic elements that could be pursued separately and synthesized at the end.

Scheduling: Once we have the clear requirements and a breakdown of the work that needs to be performed in accomplishing the goal, we can then move on to defining and scheduling activities and tasks. Initially, at this stage, we need to describe the necessary activities, their sequencing and relationships with each other, as well as the resources each one requires. We also need to identify constraints, assumptions and potential time restrictions imposed by internal and/or external stakeholders. An important point at this stage is the identification of milestones that will act as markers of completion for tasks and other units of work.

The process of estimating the duration of each activity in terms of work periods is complemented by estimations about the resources required for the identified activities and includes estimations for human resources, equipment, material (types and qualities) and other supplies. To produce such a scheduling of activities, leaders can use expert judgement (theirs, their groups and of other experts), historical information about similar activities or more sophisticated algorithms depending on the type of the goal. Eventually, a schedule will be developed, either manually or with the use of software. Critical activities and milestones will be identified.

Scheduling actions requires a lot more than estimating their duration and organizing one after the other. When the plan unfolds, things tend to happen (remember the adage 'no plan survives first contact with the enemy'). Crises unfold, interventions from unexpected sources arise, politics gets involved, the team underperforms, the quality of the product or service might be below standards and overall Murphy's law (anything that can go wrong will go wrong) might shadow every step of the way. Being able to plan for sensing and dealing with the unexpected is the make-or-break factor in the accomplishment of most goals. Leaders need to ensure that the quality of what is pursued is ensured, while at the same time the realization of potential risks has been properly considered in their plans.

Along with estimating the duration and sequencing of activities, we also need to make sure that what is delivered at each stage is of adequate quality. Planning quality checks involves the identification of quality requirements and standards that need to be met for each deliverable and developing the documentation that will prove the compliance with and achievement of the expected quality. Eventually the leader will have to establish metrics and checklists that will reflect the quality of deliverables, as well as the processes that will have to be implemented in the event that improvements or updates need to be made. To address such concerns, leaders need skills and knowledge in quality control management, familiarity with quality control tools and techniques like benchmarking, process flowcharts, control and Pareto charts, assembly checklists, force-field diagrams and cause-and-effect diagrams (like fishbone diagrams), to name but a few. In addition, knowledge of group decision support systems like nominal group techniques and brainstorming would be of great benefit to leaders.

Quality checks and scheduling in the planning phase are predictions and controls in anticipation of the future. However, the unpredictability of the future requires that leaders consider the risk involved in the various action they plan. Risk accounting involves the identification of potential risks, analysis of their influence and impact on goal activities, and eventually developing responses to mitigate, respond and recover from emergencies. Identifying risks requires the determination of the characteristics of actions that may affect the goal activities. A risk register is an ideal output for this process and should include, along with the identified risks, the responses that will alleviate their impact. The tools and techniques that leaders might apply at this stage include collecting relevant information and historical data, reviewing and researching, performing checklist and assumption analysis, and SWOT analysis, to name but a few.

The challenge with analysing risk is that not all of them can be quantified numerically. If they could, then one could apply some form of probability and trend analysis or develop a prioritization that would make it possible to organize the risks according to their impact and to develop strategies to deal with them. When dealing with risks of a qualitative nature, some form of quantification, even in the form of an ordinal variable (like very low, low, medium, high or very high impact or probability) will be needed in order to assess and prioritize risks. Assigning proper values is the real challenge in such situations.

While risk in itself carries the negative connotations of something bad, we should not forget that there is also positive risk (opportunities in another respect), which needs to be considered to avoid undermining additional potential gains. Strategies for addressing positive risk, apart from accepting it and passively waiting for it to happen in order to act, include exploiting opportunities when they arise or working to ensure that the opportunity happens. In addition, we can increase the probabilities of key drivers in creating positive impact and share ownership of risk with another party to increase the probability of the occurrence of the positive risk.

Skills and knowledge required in performing risk analysis include, among others, the ability to gather data (like interviewing and researching), familiarity with modelling techniques (like sensitivity analysis, expected monetary value analysis and simulation), responsibility assignment matrices (RAM), and applying expert judgement. It also helps leaders to make sure that highly creative and talented team members are involved in the process (especially for realizing positive risk possibilities) and a form of feedback loop exists to capture information that will suggest changes to the schedule baseline.

Management of resources: This includes human and non-human resources like money (usually treated separately), equipment and facilities. Money/cost is of critical importance as it is one of the most visible aspects of a goal, so a good plan should include a realistic budget with allowances for the unexpected. In the planning phase, leaders need to establish the procedures and policies for assigning, managing, expending and controlling costs. As a result of this process, a cost management plan will be established that will assign a budget for the various activities associated with the goal with allowances for variances and monitoring processes, as well as a reporting structure and format.

Calculating cost is relevant to the procurement process and also includes the identification and evaluation of potential suppliers, dealing with contracts, timing purchases for when they will be needed (considering potential lead times) according to the activity schedule, ensuring insurances are acquired and auditing is scheduled. Some of the skills and knowledge that are required for procurement and cost estimation of activities, in addition to expert judgement, include estimation techniques (like analogous, parametric, bottom-up and three-point estimates), reserve and vendor bid analysis, financial techniques like return on investment (ROI), payback periods, discounted cash flow, internal rate of return, net present value and earned value management (EVM). Familiarity with the relevant software and group decision-making techniques will also enhance a leader's arsenal in this respect.

One of the main categories of expenses in all budgets that requires special mention is salaries and compensations. This means that a consideration of all the people who will be involved in accomplishing the goal is needed. Identifying the required human resources for each activity and documenting their roles and responsibilities is of critical importance. This process will usually result in an organizational chart and staffing management plan that identifies what skills each individual needs to have to perform their job, their level of authority and their reporting relationships. Staffing will need to account for staff acquisition and release, training, compensation and rewards, as well as compliance and safety requirements. For such activities, the skills and knowledge required include, among other things, an understanding of organizational theory, the ability to develop charts and position descriptions, networking and, of course, expert judgement.

Stakeholder communication: Managing the communication process of team members and all other stakeholders is a vital component in the successful accomplishment of any goal, and a proper plan needs to account for this requirement. Communication should to be based on stakeholders' information needs and requirements, and available organizational assets like historical data and policies and procedures. It should make sure that potential barriers are identified and managed effectively as early as possible.

In order to develop a proper communication plan, leaders need to be aware of the communication technology capabilities and to understand the communication process, like how information is encoded, transmitted, decoded and acknowledged between emitter and receiver. This will ensure that a proper feedback and response mechanism is in place and that all parties are clear and up to speed with everything that is going on. Leaders also need to be efficient in terms of conducting constructive meetings and engaging stakeholders according to their needs, interests, level of involvement and importance in the activities and accomplishment of the goal.

6.3.2 Executing

Following the planning phase, leaders need to move on to the execution phase. In this phase, the team will need to be assembled, responsibilities and tasks assigned, and material and equipment procured. Everyone will be set to follow the plan of action and communicate status and progress updates between the team members and any other stakeholders involved in the various stages of the goal activities. Communication is now mainly in the form of reporting progress, issues, changes, etc. to leaders and stakeholders. Performance reporting can be based on the analysis of goal forecasts and benchmarking with past performance when pursuing similar goals, In addition, the status of risks and issues as a function of the work completed and the approved changes needs to be part of the reporting information.

Leaders need to focus on directing and managing the work for the various goal activities, to meet the needs of the involved stakeholders (their team primarily) and to foster their active engagement throughout the life-cycle of the goal. A balance between interpersonal and management skills is required at this stage. Interpersonal skills include, among other things, the build-up of trust, conflict resolution, active listening, engaging all stakeholders and overcoming resistance to change. Familiarity with communication technology is also a great asset during this stage. Management skills include the ability to facilitate consensus towards goal objectives, exercising influence, negotiating agreements and modifying organizational behaviour to accept the activity outcomes. Because influence and negotiation are critically important, we will dedicate more discussion to them later on.

For now, it is worth emphasizing that acquiring the right team will make or break the efforts to achieve the goal. Ensuring that the right team members are engaged requires negotiation with other leaders (including functional and project managers), promoting positions, recruiting and the acquisition of expertise from inside the organization and from outside contributors (contractors, freelancers, etc.). Alternative options here include the consideration of the participation of virtual or distributed team members. Leaders need to exercise their judgement in appraising talent availability, experience, skills, ability, character and attitude, as well as appropriate compensation levels, incentives and rewards.

Acquiring the ideal team within the available budget and goal constraints might not be a realistic expectation, so effort might need to be dedicated to development activities so that the team grows to the level of coordination, coherence and collaboration required for accomplishing the goal. Integrating teams is quite a challenging endeavour and it requires a variety of skills from the leader. Along with the interpersonal skills mentioned above, leaders need to able to address team training and team-building requirements (like the forming, storming, norming and adjourning mentioned previously), set ground rules, provide appropriate recognitions and rewards, and be familiar with personnel assessment tools (attitudinal surveys, structure interviews and ability tests, among others).

Managing the team when the work starts involving activities like managing the composition of the team, tracking team member performance, providing feedback and resolving issues. Leaders need to be good at observing behaviour and evaluating performance, managing conflict, influencing, analysing available information, staying focused on the goal at hand, stimulating creativity, managing risk and establishing transparency and reliable decision-making processes. Displays of confidence and competency will help establish the leader's authority and credibility among the team members and will further assist in the development of trust in the leader's ability to manage the tasks required for the achievement of the goal.

6.3.3 Monitoring and controlling

As the goal activities and tasks are executed, leaders begin to operate more in a monitoring and controlling capacity. Among the elements that keep their attention is making sure that activities are aligned with the goal and no deviations are unaccounted for; that the schedule is on track; that the quality of the work is as expected; that costs are not overrun; that necessities are procured, are delivered on time and are of the anticipated quality; that the communication among the team and other stakeholders is clear and constructive; and that potential risks are under control. These activities might look numerous, but the reality is even worse. The execution phase is where the goal will take its physical form either as a product or service and will impact the recipients of the goal outcomes.

When monitoring activities, we usually compare present with past performance or with a standard that plays the role of benchmark. Considering processes as requiring some kind of input (work, material, etc.) to produce some kind of output (product, service, etc.), leaders can use leading or lagging metrics correspondingly to monitor performance (Figure 6.6). Leading metrics (like the level of team expertise and quality of raw materials) are usually seen as proactive, while lagging metrics (like the quality of a product or service) are seen as reactive. Variance analysis is a technique that could be applied here to determine the cause and degree of difference between baseline and actual performance. Deviations from what was originally planned will eventually lead to going back to the execution phase or even the planning phase, as the back arrows in Figure 6.5 demonstrate.

If the deviations are dramatic, they could even lead to the termination of activities and the pursuit of the goal. Factors that can lead to termination of the pursued goal include cost overruns, scope creep, unrealistic expectations, poor planning, lack of support from the top, overestimation of the leader's and the team's abilities to address the complexity of the goal activities, unexpected (and obviously unplanned) changes in the environment (political, economic, social, technological, legal, etc.) or shifts in organizational priorities. To these we can also add the loss of enthusiasm after the initial phase and requirements changes (from the client), among others. Less subtle factors can also be at play, like the loss of reputation shown in Figure 6.7. Reputation might be an important influencer in sticking with a goal that should have normally been terminated.

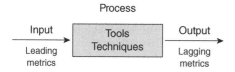

Figure 6.6 Performance measurement

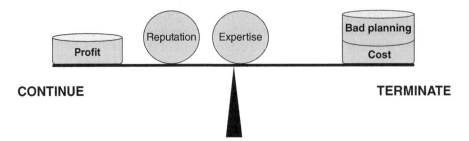

Figure 6.7 Performance measurement

Among the things that need to be monitored, the status of activities in terms of sticking to and updating the schedule is critical. This requires leaders to be able to conduct performance reviews, apply modelling and resource optimization techniques, identify and/or plan schedule leads and lags, and be comfortable with scheduling and software tools. These skills will allow leaders to forecast schedule variances and act on what needs to be changed (schedule, cost, scope, procurement, communication practices, etc.).

Controlling and monitoring goal activities requires an extensive skillset for leaders. Experience and familiarity with similar goals can greatly contribute to better control of the changes than need to be established. Keeping costs under control, for example, might require understanding and familiarity with techniques like earned value management (EVM), forecasting and reserve analysis, to mention but a few. Controlling procurements might require skills in inspections, audits, payment systems, contracts, claims and performance reporting, among others. Other control requirements like controlling quality and risk might require additional hard skills in quality tools (like affinity diagrams, prioritization matrices, activity network diagrams, etc.), statistical sampling, risk audits, variant and trend analysis, etc. In other cases, like monitoring and controlling communications and stakeholder relationships, soft skills like negotiating and organizing meetings might be more important.

Eventually, all goal activities will be completed and the goal will be considered to have been achieved (hopefully). The end here is not like 'death', but more like the beginning of a new phase that can be called either operations or maintenance. New goals might be conceived based on the results of the achieved goal, or the sustainability of the achievements might be necessary. If the latter is true, then outcomes/results of the goal (product, service, etc.) need to be maintained for as long as they are necessary. As time passes, modifications or changes might be required to keep the achievements up to date in order to ensure that the intended benefits continue to exist. This stage could still be overseen by the leader or assigned to another individual. Regardless of who is in charge, the life-cycle of a goal should result in additional benefits like learning (Figure 6.5), networking, professional growth, maturity, etc. For these to materialize, a reflection process needs to exist (usually in the communication plans) where the results will be disseminated for the benefit of the leader and the organization. Reflecting on the process is a great way to recognize the contribution that the achievement of the goal has made to the leader's experience and to those involved and affected by its accomplishment.

6.4 Leading teams

While in the previous chapter we saw the formation of teams as an evolutionary step towards building organizations, here we will discuss the formation, development and management of teams from the perspective of the leaders (as we briefly saw in Section 6.3.2 above). Choosing the right team members is so important that it can make or break leadership. Whether a team will succeed or fail under our leadership will reflect on our ability to act as leaders. In that respect, the acquisition and engagement of proper team members is of critical importance to leadership.

When it comes to teams, what we need to keep in mind is that *the total should be greater than the sum of its parts.* This means that the synergies between the team members and the complementarity of their skills and traits should magnify their contribution to achieving the goal or task assigned to the team. Excellence in this way will lead to superior results and outcomes, and work and camaraderie will transcend the lives of everyone involved. Coming down to earth now from the ideal we have set, we need to focus on the elements that affect team membership, performance and leadership effectiveness.

Team membership at the individual level usually involves a balance between expertise, competencies, costs and personality characteristics in the context of the situation/goal that the team pursues. At the group level, the number of skills and personalities needs to be balanced so one does not exist in excess of the other. There needs to be a common baseline understanding of the team's purpose and function, a complementarity of skills, and a smooth interface among team members and team subdivisions (cohesiveness). In organizational settings, team membership will usually include a variety of expertise levels as less experienced members need to learn and acquire skills to mature as professionals in their respective fields and as potential future leaders.

Ideal teams operate like complete organisms (or well-oiled machines) where there is a division of labour and integration of effort so that the organism can survive and grow. There needs to be an internal organizational structure and clearly assigned roles with no overlapping responsibilities (like muscles, bones, etc.), a shared communication network (a nervous system), a control process (like the lymph and endocrine systems) and a shared purpose that will form the collective identity of the team (a form of consciousness). Finally, a leader in the role of the mind then knows when to lead, when to follow and when to stay out of the way and let others do their job. The second (and third) characteristic is not something that traditional leaders are familiar with, but its importance is unquestionable.

A team in this sense operates in the subconscious space and the leader's role is to keep the team organization healthy. A well-built subconscious knows how to manage the organization of the team and react to the environment and only requires the leader's attention for guidance in critical situations. The analogy with the organism breaks as the collective is stronger when individuality is promoted. This allows professionalism to thrive and, as a result, the team experiences a collaborative and supportive spirit that empowers and engages individual members, while holding them accountable for their actions.

Integrating individuals who have gone through the same experiences and have been exposed to the same culture is relatively easy, but in today's globalized organizational environments it is not easy to accomplish. The cultural constitution of teams nowadays can be so diverse that the challenges this poses for leaders become critical. These include, among others, communication issues like language fluency and communication medium and mode preferences (direct versus indirect), norms and procedures (especially when it comes to decisions) and attitudes towards authority and hierarchy. Possible solutions to these challenges include the adaptation of common value and principle systems (in order to make them closer to the dominant culture), delegation of authority to leadership representatives or proxies for subcultural groups, cross-cultural education and training, and the reorganization of the team structure to eliminate interpersonal friction.

Leading by proxies or representatives, as mentioned above, is one way to deal with diverse and large teams, especially if they are also distributed across different geographical boundaries and functions. When team members are from a variety of cultures, there are different expectations in relation to authority, communication and expression norms, decision making styles and attitudes towards risk. If we add to cultural diversity the different organizational cultures to which the various team members have been exposed in the past, we can see that in diverse teams, there might be more than one way to lead. Each member will influence and be influenced by the other members' cultures, and each might have their own perception of leadership style and behaviour.

To address the wide variety of team members, leaders might be required to understand cultural and personality differences and to develop strong social connections with their teams in addition to providing practical, technical and strategy-related guidance. This becomes especially important in cases where leaders might not be able to choose their teams. Occasionally, team members may also leave, thus creating the need for leaders to intervene and reiterate objectives and norms to new recruits and the remaining team. The leader's role and responsibilities remain with their team and any deficiencies in the team will have to be addressed and compensated for by the leader.

6.4.1 Influence revisited: the good, the bad and the ugly

Influence as the means of controlling behaviour to achieve a goal is one of the fundamental activities of leadership. Controlling behaviour in essence means overcoming resistance. The influence continuum can be seen as ranging from forcing followers to do something by using authority and power to inspiring and motivating them to do it willingly and enthusiastically. In leadership we need to distinguish this from power, which usually represents the capacity to influence. In our discussion here we will focus more on the 'good' side of influence. More precisely, we will consider the means of influence in a threefold continuum (Figure 6.8): the 'oppressive'/suppressive (the bad), the 'necessary'/traditional (the ugly) and the 'sophisticate'/modern (the good).

While Figure 6.8 displays a selective list of tactics that leaders can employ to exert influence, the true continuum includes a great many more options spread between the three attractors. Near the 'good' side, we can have, among others, role modelling behaviour and collaborating, showing respect, building trust, using persuasion and appraising, making personal appeals, developing reputation, negotiating and bargaining, legitimating, charming, inspiring, displaying emotions, consulting and forming coalitions. Towards the 'ugly' side, we can have ingratiating, entertaining, upwards appeal (getting someone with more formal authority to influence), co-opting antagonists (sharing the potential spoils), incentives and rewards, to name but a few.

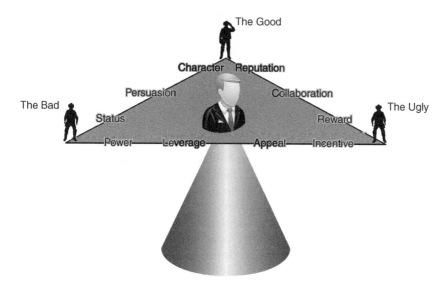

Figure 6.8 Faces of influence

Finally, the 'bad' side can include the use of power and status, and manipulative tactics like deception, coercion, manipulation of people and situations, bribing to achieve compliance, threatening and debasement, among others.

While discussing all the aforementioned forms of influence is beyond the scope of this book, a selection will be discussed here and in the following sections, simply because they help to explain how leadership grows and functions. Persuasion, for example, is an important tactic for influencing others, especially when combined with rationality. Presenting factual evidence with assertiveness in a logical and consistent way and without contempt or arrogance can be quite an effective and convincing way to ensure commitment. A moderating factor in the success of persuasion is the leader's credibility. In this respect, reputation will greatly assist in establishing the leader as a credible source. The reason why persuasion leans towards the 'bad' in Figure 6.8 is that in some cases, it might be seen as a manipulation and control mechanism.

Another significant influence tactic is role modelling behaviour (leading by example or acting as a positive role model). This is displayed by working long and hard while assisting subordinates to complete their tasks, and is an indirect way of exerting influence. This type of leadership is expressed as 'do as I say and as I do', displaying perfect alignment between words and actions, where one serves to explain and clarify the other. To be effective, this leadership practice needs to be based on mutual respect between the leader and the followers (no one wants to do as a crazy person does) and trust shown by the followers that the leader will follow through.

Although influence tactics have up to now been considered in isolation, we need to keep in mind that they can always be applied in relation to each other and in tandem. Combinations of tactics like persuasion, appeal and consultation might be effective in strengthening commitment to a task. The ordering of influence tactics is also important and, conditions permitting, their application should begin with the 'good' as much as possible, reserving the 'bad' for when everything else fails. The importance of the outcome is a potential indicator of the ordering that leaders could follow. Low-cost and low-risk tactics might be followed by higher-cost and higher-risk tactics if the desired outcome is not achieved.

Caution is needed when combining tactics, as some might have the opposite effect from what was planned. For example, using formal authority and forming coalitions combined with the exercise of pressure might lead to resentment and the sabotage of task activities. Other combinations of tactics might work in some situations and not in others – for example, applying incentives and bribes might work for subordinates, but might not be effective for superiors. In general, tactics that are effective in a downwards direction are not effective in the opposite direction. Overall, combinations of non-coercive tactics with rational justification might be more effective in ensuring compliance than threatening or manipulative tactics.

The tactics considered here should always be seen in the context of the situation and individual(s) they target, as well as the leader who applies them. Figure 6.8 tries to indicate this by showing the delicate balance between the three categories. In essence, what the image is trying to convey is that the characterization of tactics is not suggestive of their need for a particular situation. Oppressive ('ugly') tactics, for example, might not be ideal for normal operating conditions, but in the event of a crisis might be more effective than others ('good'). Power and exercise of authority might be more appropriate for effectively responding to a crisis than collaboration and bargaining. Also, the target's status in terms of motivation might suggest a different tactic than the one traditionally recommended. In general, when we distrust people, we tend to control their actions.

A final point here with respect to the effectiveness of an influence tactic is the relationship between the leader and the follower, and the skilfulness of the person who applies it. If the relationship is poor, followers might interpret appeals to their beliefs and motives as empty and might resist following the leader. Instead, a tactic like consultation might be more effective in such situations. Regarding skilfulness, even 'bad' tactics can be effective if the leader knows how to deliver them and how to follow up on them. The exercise of power, for example, in a crisis situation could be followed by expressions of gratitude and appreciation, with rational explanation of the motives behind the behaviour after the crisis has passed, in this way alleviating any negative impact on the followers.

The reason why most of the influence tactics mentioned here work is because they target emotions. Emotions are nothing more than expressions of our feelings towards what we perceive in our environment (including our body). They are the building blocks of feelings and are often considered instinctive feelings. There are eight generally accepted emotions (five according to the Pixar movie *Inside Out*) that can potentially be grouped into three categories. Anger, fear, disgust, sadness and shame are considered to be survival emotions and usually operate at the subconscious level, triggering fight or flight responses. Joy (often considered excitement) and trust (love according to Aristotle) are considered to be attachment emotions, while surprise as a regulator (a category by itself) plays the role of activator or suppressor between the survival and attachment categories.

Another categorization that allows for the inclusion of many more emotions is separating them into positive and negative. Humans experience positive emotions like pride, self-confidence, sympathy, generosity, love, attractiveness, joy, gratitude, relief, hope, surprise, interest and curiosity, to name but a few, and negative emotions like anger, fear, sorrow, panic, disgust aversion, frustration, shame, guilt, envy, cruelty and hate. Looking at how each of them is triggered and how leaders can use their emotions and intellect to trigger selected emotions in others is beyond the scope of this book. What is important, though, in the application of leadership is how and why they actually manifest themselves. This insight, along with knowledge of who we and others are, can help leaders to intelligently apply selected emotions to themselves and others in order to enable their influence to spread in the desired direction.

By 'knowing who we are', here we don't mean acting like our true self, but more like understanding who we are in terms of our capabilities. What defines us can be broken down into what we have been throughout our lifetime. This is expressed through our thoughts and emotions in the environment we operate. At the root of it all, we are organisms that are regulated by chemicals. We receive signals through our senses from the environment (including our bodies), which trigger the release of chemicals like hormones and neurotransmitters, which are picked up by organs (the heart, the brain, etc.), which result in actions in other organs (for example, muscles), which materialize as work/response to our environment. The difference between one human and another is in the way in which the various pieces are organized throughout their lives. For example, one person might be born with a more efficient neuron network to organize memories and process information, resulting in heightened intelligence, while another person might have glands that produce excess growth hormones, making them tall.

The chemical reactions in our brain will manifest themselves as emotions that will influence our behaviour. While emotions are normally firing signals separately, there are cases when they could be firing at the same time, like in the case of jealously, where love and anger could be firing at the same time. No good can come from such competition and this can result in confusion and even violent behaviour. The category of attachment emotions is vital for leadership as they promote the bond between leaders and followers. Trust in particular has been widely accepted as a cornerstone emotion as it suppresses the perception of threat, and it is the responsibility of leaders to inspire trust in their followers if they are to succeed in their role. Today's workforce is educated and highly skilled, and trust becomes vital in motivating and committing followers to the organizational goals established by leaders.

While the previous discussion might seem to some like a diversion from the topic of influence, the truth is that it is at the heart of it, as all decisions are influenced by emotions. Knowing what is going on internally and externally at the level of emotions is vital for effective leadership. While we take it for granted that there is very little we can do about the raw material (mind and body) we were born with, there is a lot we can do to sharpen and keep healthy what we have. We can educate and train our mind to become smarter, we can reflect on our experiences to become wiser, and we can acknowledge our physical limitations and make sure our body is healthy enough for our brain to function at optimal capacity. Balancing all these is not as easy as it might seem for most of us.

Working towards 'developing' our influence, traditionally we build influence (we will avoid the 'bad' side here) by demonstrating strength, promoting achievements to project credibility, creating dependencies, adding value (such as by contributing expertise) and owning information. The latter is quite important as it allows us to 'sell' answers. By providing useful information/answers, we become the hub of a network of others who value and depend on our information and are willing to exchange this for influence on their respective others. However, one tricky point with answers is that their value is fixed, in that when you provide them, there is no future need for them. To counter this issue, leaders need to continually replenish their pool of answers with new ones that might be of interest to others. By supplementing this with resources that others might also need, we have an effective influence arsenal with which to exercise leadership.

6.4.2 Tools of the trade

Leaders can influence their teams in a variety of ways, including by exercising authority, role modelling behaviour, collaborating and sharing the workload (leading from the trenches), building trust, using persuasion, teaching, mentoring, coaching, motivating, negotiating and managing conflict. With the exception of negotiating, which we will examine in the next section, we will briefly discuss here some of the aforementioned elements for the purpose of completeness of the text and not in an attempt to thoroughly and exhaustively cover all of them.

If many of the aforementioned elements sound like they should be part of management, it is because they are. Managing is not something left to someone else while the leader has a 'dream' about where an organization should go and then interprets its symbolism convincingly for others to execute. The heavy involvement of leaders is required, either in the form of guidance and supervision of their immediate team and the managers they supervise or even through direct, hands-on involvement in the task at hand. The latter is not meant to take the form of micromanaging everything, but rather to show involvement and interest in achieving the set goals.

This also is meant to indicate that being a leader is not an easy job. When done right, it is a highly stressful occupation most of the time. An extreme way of describing the ideal leader is to consider one who is responsible for everything that goes wrong and for nothing that goes right. This says a lot to subordinates as they can feel that their back is covered and their efforts are appreciated. Subordinates will always rise to the occasion for such a leader and will even go out of the way to be part of the community the leader builds.

Motivating: In relation to motivation, we need to break down as much as possible what it is and how it works. In short, motivation is the drive behind the actions and behaviour of individuals. This drive usually includes what individuals consider important according to their personal values and in the context of the organizational environment in which they operate. For example, importance could be placed on recognition, monetary gain, teamwork, intellectual challenge and stimulation, results achievement, affiliation, power, learning, experience, etc. All these drive behaviour as they are strongly attached to emotions (as we have seen in the previous section) and the safety that individuals feel when they act according to their value system. For example, regarding some of the social elements of the previous list, achievement focuses on the desire to be recognized as capable and effective, while affiliation addresses the need to feel associated with the status and allure of a particular environment. As with all practices, caution is required when considering different types of motivation as their advantages can always be associated with side-effects. Achievement motivation, for example, could in achievement-driven individuals lead to obsessive behaviour (they might not know when to stop), which could lead to oversights, errors and even collapse. Overplaying affiliation may not work in environments where personal interactions are not encouraged as it could lead to groupthink in decision making.

Alternative expressions/definitions of motivation include the will to perform, persistence of one's efforts in a certain direction, a reflection and instinctive response to environmental stimuli (behavioural approach), and rational and purposeful act based on goals and behaviour (cognitive approach). Regardless, the way one defines it, motivation is valuable because it leads to commitment. In studying motivation, theories have been developed to explain what it is and how it works. Some focused on content and tried to identify what moves people to commit in a certain direction, while others focused on the process and how personal characteristics interact and influence human behaviour. An interesting insight comes from expectancy theory, where motivation is considered as the product/interaction between expectation and valence/preference ($M = E*V$). Valence here refers to the worth or attractiveness of an outcome, while expectancy is seen as an individual's assessment of the probability that effort will lead to the correct performance for the task. A supporting concept here is that of instrumentality that represents an individual's assessment of the probability that performance will lead to certain outcomes. Finally, goal theory suggests that motivation comes from setting specific goals that, while challenging, are acceptable as long as the effort expended is supplemented with appropriate and frequent feedback. In this way, goals direct attention and focus to a course, mobilize and dedicate resources, and engage self-evaluation, self-monitoring and self-adjustment in the pursuit of the goal.

In practice, motivation is closely linked to incentives, rewards and a feedback loop to ensure its effectiveness. There are some significant differences between incentives and rewards, and one way of distinguishing between the two is that the former is given before while the latter is given after something is achieved. The real difference is that incentives are like promises (which may or may not materialize) in advance of something, while rewards are always real, either in the form of recognition or benefits. Another difference is that incentives are usually given to raise performance (when it is presumably below expectations), while awards are ideal for exceptional or targeted performance beyond some expected 'average'. The way in which we use them is usually dependent on what we are trying to achieve. If, for example, deadlines are tight, we might consider incentives to encourage everyone to work faster, while if innovation or quality is an issue, we might want to consider rewards for those who pay extra attention to delivering quality work.

Occasionally motivation is confused with inspiration. Although both drive individuals in a certain direction and can be used by leaders, they work and act differently. While motivation works on emotions (the heart) in support of actions, inspiration is cognitive (the brain) and aims to stimulate perceptions or feelings that will lead to actions. Inspiration can exist/happen regardless of how one feels and closely relates to insight. Being a mental process, it theoretically stays longer than the emotion-based forms of motivation and it becomes the possession of the individual as soon as it is ignited by the leaders. Motivation on the other hand is owned by the leaders all the time, so it needs constant investment on their behalf to sustain the levels required to keep a team motivated. In a sense, motivation can be seen as a 'push' mechanism that will need frequent replenishment, while inspiration is more of a 'pull' mechanism that acts like a spark that fuels the fire. If the appropriate 'wood' is there, it will develop into a full-blown fire.

The aforementioned differences can be seen in the way in which stories are used by leaders to engage their teams. Sometimes, stories trigger feelings that could fuel the motivation for individuals to act, while at other times inspiring them to act. Before we had the written word, we had stories. They were how tribal wisdom and history got passed down. A well-told story not only communicated; it taught, it inspired and it motivated. This was true when we roamed the savanna and migrated to every corner of the earth, and it is true now that we plan missions to Mars and beyond. As story-telling is an ingrained part of organizational culture, each team activity becomes a story. It has a beginning, a middle and an end, where threats, problems, solutions and heroes create memorable life. The appeal and power of stories is an indispensable tool in the leader's arsenal.

An inherent downside of motivation is that in many cases, it is considered a form of manipulation. Team members know that it is not an intervention in relation to the course of action as it does not involve structural changes or resources and, in addition, it will end at some time. In essence, it is 'air' that works on the ego of the individual and tries to make up for something that is missing or lacking (team maturity, resources, etc.). This might not be enough to fill the gap and leaders will then have to take a more pragmatic approach to fill what is missing. In addition, motivation is based on feelings, not choices or obligations, and in that sense it cannot be as strong as they are. For example, we don't need motivation to watch our favourite TV show, while we do need it in order to stay an extra hour at work.

An alternative to motivation that in the view of many is more effective is commitment. The difference is that commitment is based on understanding the values of and what is actually important to the individual team members. It reflects respect for the identity of individuals and empowers them as it reflects a personal choice. People prefer to have a sense of control over their own destiny rather than been suggested.

In order for leaders to alleviate the negative influences of motivation, a possible alternative might be to engage in the creation of a working environment (both physical and social) that allows team members to build a life of their own. This could be achieved by getting a critical mass of participants engaged in the process to reduce barriers to entry and spending the time to provide continuous 360-degree feedback on performance. At the same time, support should be evident at all levels of engagement, even if some team members are not present at the beginning. Actions could focus on fostering team interaction, support for peer-to-peer networking and even engaging outsider stakeholders. These actions will allow team members to take ownership of their participation in the team, trust their fellow team members and eventually commit to the goals and objectives of the team.

Coaching: As a modern (motivational for many) tool in the leadership practice, coaching has been seen as a way of enabling others to build and act on their strengths. It is usually considered in relation to motivation as it enables engagement, and it is based on building strong and trustworthy relationships that in return benefit the organization through strong team cohesiveness and increased productivity. Coaching makes team members clear about the leader's intentions and expectations, makes them feel valued and cared for, increases performance, and energizes and assists them in reaching their full potential. Followers have a major role to play in the process of building relationships and their role in coaching comprises personal responsibilities and organizational responsibilities. They are required to keep track of their promises to themselves and the actions they have implemented, to be open and frank with the coach, to provide objective feedback, to focus on the issue of the conversation, and to be methodical, action-oriented and honest.

From the theoretical point of view, a number of frameworks have been developed to account for coaching, with Goals, Reality, Options and Way Forward (GROW) being a popular one. This suggests that coaching can be used for motivating, team building, monitoring task performance, planning, reviewing, delegating and decision making, among others. Another approach is the action-centred framework and is particularly useful in addressing individual, team and task needs. Common features found in almost all theoretical approaches include the consideration of coaching as a systematic process designed to facilitate development and growth in awareness and responsibility, that is customized to the individual subject and that encourages coaches to assume charge and be accountable for their actions. Regarding the coach, there is agreement in theories that effective coaching is based on the establishment of trust, listening, questioning and setting realistic and clearly stated goals that are aligned with the capabilities of the individual who is being coached.

Along with their similarities, theoretical approaches differ in many ways, such as the need for the coach to have domain-specific expertise or knowledge of the area of interest of the individual being coached, the degree to which a coach can influence an individual's values and to what extent a coach is a facilitator or guide. In addition, there is debate as to whether the focus of coaching should be growth or performance, its appropriateness for addressing feelings or actions, its short-term or long-term nature, and the type of awareness it should raise (about feelings or situations).

An important point to clarify here is that coaching is not mentoring, although the differences between the two might appear subtle. One interpretation might be that mentoring is a form of suggestion, where the mentor advises and guides the subject to reach their full potential, while coaching is a form of discovery, where the coach simply helps the subject discover the right decision and reach their full potential. Alternatively, we can see coaching as focusing more on growing the individual who is coached, while mentoring focuses on the individual learning. Slipping into mentoring is one the issues that coaches need to be aware of, especially when they have expertise in the domain of those being coached. It is helpful to remember here that coaching is not about telling someone what to do, but rather to help them discover what they really want to do given the circumstances they face. In addition, coaching is usually structured and scheduled on a regular basis by time-limited interventions, while mentoring is ongoing and can last for a long period of time, is informal and is usually performed when the individual being mentored has a need for advice, guidance or support. The time differentiation exists because coaching mainly focuses on specific work/activity issues or development areas, while mentoring takes a broader view of the future/personal development of a person. If this sounds like therapy, it is because it shares aspects with therapy such as sharing one's innermost beliefs and values, and requires personalized and individualized attention. This is the reason why matching the one who is to be coached with the right coach is of outmost importance in order for coaching to work.

Another misunderstanding regarding coaching is that many relate it to training. The latter is a professional skills-based activity that is under the control of the trainer, while the former is a goal-setting and problem-solving approach that is under the control of the learner. The aim of training is the acquisition of new knowledge and skills by groups that will help in a specific task, while coaching, when used formally, aims at improving the critical thinking and decision-making ability of individuals to help improve their performance and behaviour. In general, coaching should be seen as assisting a learner to improve their interpersonal skills, become better listeners, balance priorities, focus their attention and broaden their horizons.

As a skill, coaching raises the question of whether it can be learned. In order to be effective as coaches, leaders need to possess high emotional intelligence so that they can relate and understand people. They also need to be able to reflect with accuracy in order to confirm their understanding, show empathy and provide feedback in a clear, relevant and non-evaluative way. They also need to have strong listening and questioning skills, to ask for clarifications and to be good at building rapport and providing feedback.

One of the challenges coaches face is acknowledging their own prejudices and biases so that they won't impose or project them onto those they coach. Biases come in many forms – cognitive, cultural, emotional, etc. They develop over the years as we associate emotions with patterns of behaviour and observations we experience. This is a valuable process as it allows us to make assumptions based on prior experience and judgements. Unfortunately, it breaks down when we receive partial information that seems familiar when in essence it is not. In these cases, we end up triggering the wrong emotions to the information pattern in front of us, resulting in inappropriate behaviour and bad decisions. Domain and expertise biases, for example, can lead coaches to make recommendations, switching in this way into mentoring.

The difficulty with biases comes from the fact that they operate in the subconscious, so they creep up into our conscious without warning. They might lead us to attach emotional importance to information that does not warrant it and to subsequently perceive the patterns we want to see and not what reality presents to us. Another bias that influences decision making is our familiarity with a person and/or an environment. The bonds we build can affect our judgement and the way we act, making it difficult at times to let go and move on to something new. Memory can also become a bad advisor as it might associate a present situation with a past one when we have overlooked or undervalued important details that point in a different situation. This effect is aggravated if strong emotions were attached to past experiences and brought these to the forefront of our memory.

The reason we have focused a little more on biases here is because they affect the quality of coaching that a leader can deliver and are one of primary reasons why someone is seeking a coach. In real life (without coaching, that is), we become aware of biases when we see the results of our bad reactions and behaviour. The issue becomes worse when there is lack of monitor and control (Figure 6.5) in our decision-making process. Certain conditions can promote errors in judgement, whether these relate to our life choices or career. In essence, our emotions act based on past experience without revisiting our initial assessment and overshadowing the possibility of error. This happens almost instantaneously and is helpful in crisis (fight or flight) situations, but could be disastrous in ambiguous situations and volatile environments where alternatives need to be considered.

Coaching can be quite effective in raising awareness about biases and can provide insight about ourselves and our situation. At the individual level, it is a great way for leaders to help their subordinates develop their full potential. It is also a good way for leaders to guide individuals in becoming leaders and to ensure that a capable successor will take over when they go. At the organizational level and in addition to the benefits for the individual employee, it can assist in team member engagement and commitment as it displays genuine care and interest in the individual. Challenges for organizations when considering coaching include the demands it places on time commitment and the resources required to enlist qualified coaches. When internal resources are used, caution is required as it can be difficult to genuinely coach direct subordinates as within the relationship the 'hierarchy is projected from below', resulting in constraints in the conversations that are intended to help the subordinate achieve personal mastery.

Learning: One of the characteristics of the waterfall model of Figure 6.5 that wasn't addressed as much as its emphasis on the image intended is 'Learning'. This is so critical that without it, anything will be useless in terms of the value that an experience can contribute to future success. This is based on the reality that everyone fails, especially the leaders (given the multitude of decisions they make). The difference between individuals usually comes down to how well they learn from their failures. Statistically speaking, if one does not repeat the same mistake twice, they are bound to reach a level of perfection in what they are doing, hopefully within the lifespan of the role they have been assigned and provided they are afforded another chance.

Experiences lead to learning that eventually becomes knowledge that we use to modify our behaviour in anticipation of future outcomes. Eventually knowledge reaches the sphere of metacognition, which is thinking about thinking. This stage is where we can make conscious interventions on what we know and how to best use it. For practical purposes, learning can be seen as an interrogation process coupled with repetition to reinforce the synaptic potential in our brain's neurons regarding a situation that faces us. Figure 6.9 (left image) depicts the practice of interrogating reality as perceived through the signals our senses send and our intelligence processes. The interrogation 'diamond' (also seen in Figure 5.17) allows for the exploration of the sensory information (the rectangular plane of 'When', 'Where', 'Who', and 'What') to deduce the process ('How') and establish a cause and effect ('Why') relationship of what we perceive. This sense-making process will presumably create a subjective reality that will hopefully closely reflect the actual reality (the right side of Figure 6.9).

From the theoretical point of view, the perspective we have towards learning is our epistemological stance. This guides our perceived relationship, with the knowledge

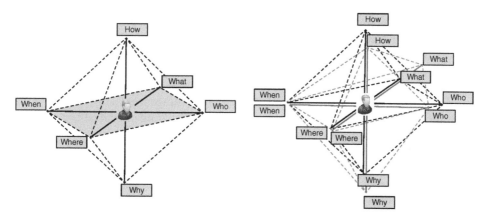

Figure 6.9 The interrogation diamond

we are discovering being either internal (we shape it and are part of it) or external (it exists without our interpretation). Our views in this respect will frame our interaction with what we are learning and will depend on our view of what is real. For example, our approach will be objective if we see knowledge as being governed by the laws of nature, or subjective if we see knowledge as something that is interpreted by individuals. Eventually, it all comes down to what we believe is true and what is real.

In the leadership domain, in which we are interested here, a constructionist approach is probably the most popular way of approaching learning. Knowledge, according to this epistemological stance, is produced or invented in social processes as individuals interact through language and construct an agreed-upon reality. Since leadership exists in social contexts (here we exclude leadership in animals), a constructionist approach that considers agreement on what leadership is will better address the interpretation of the phenomenon and the models like that developed in the previous chapter.

In organizational settings, learning can change focus according to whether it is targeted towards the individual, a process or system, a culture, the management of knowledge or for continuous improvement. Individuals learn through training and development activities on how to resolve problematic situations. This learning helps organizations to strengthen their knowledge and develop their knowledge management systems. Learning organizations, as a popular form of metaphor, are those that can organize, understand and manage their experience by developing a culture where individuals continually contribute and leverage their collective learning to improve organizational performance as they themselves grow and mature as professionals. In this way, knowledge is constantly created, absorbed and disseminated, enabling organizations to transform in response to external stimuli and sustain their competitive edge.

In order for effective and purposeful learning to occur, individuals need to be able to focus their attention and efforts, to develop and exercise patience, to be willing to see and accept reality, and to commit to a continuous improvement and re-evaluation of their personal vision. The latter provides individuals with a sense of purpose that guides them in the pursuit of their goals and personal values, which shape their behaviour and commitment to develop themselves. It is also boosted by motivation and the training they have received throughout their lives.

Learning is also assisted by cognitive tools (mental models) individuals use to describe the cause and effect of the phenomena they observe and the interactions they have. These tools include assumptions, representations and constraints that support individuals' understanding of situations and guide their actions. They help individuals to organize, plan and resolve issues, as well as supporting the acquisition of skills.

In addition to demonstrating and sharing mental models, leaders can assist the process of learning by developing knowledge capture and dissemination plans, while promoting a team and organizational culture that is transparent and conducive to collaboration and the sharing of information. Team learning is crucial for improving team performance. It can be amplified in committed teams with clear goals by a supportive organizational culture, leadership support, development and training. In team settings, other elements that support learning include the development and adoption of a shared vision and a systems approach to investigating thinking. A shared vision bonds a team in pursuing a shared future, while systems thinking enables a holistic approach to situations, allowing team members to see the deeper patterns and details of all the factors that affect a situation.

With respect to leadership in team settings, one form of learning (distinguished from training-induced learning) involves the detection and correction of error. Normally, in such cases people look for alternative strategies to take corrective action on the parameters that define the situation. This form of learning is called single-loop learning to distinguish it from double-loop learning, where one questions the validity of the parameters and variables that define the boundaries of the problematic situation. This type of learning may eventually lead to an alteration of the governing variables or the introduction of new ones, resulting in this way in a shift in the way in which resolution strategies and consequences are framed. This latter form of learning aims at changing the rules in terms of how problems are viewed and traditional techniques are used, and allows for the questioning of the framing and learning system that underlies the actual goal and strategies. A significant feature of this type of learning is that instead of trying to impose a 'template' solution to a situation (as in single-loop learning), it tries to apply a template to the situation and in this way it modifies and expands the template in order to address the new situation.

The aim for leaders and their teams in organizational settings should be to increase their capacity for double-loop learning so that they can efficiently respond to the challenges posed by their operational environment. While the process of learning (single- and double-loop) can be internal and personal to each individual, it can easily apply to organizational entities, from complete organizations to the teams we are studying here. Given an organization's (or a team's) structure and characteristics, and its position within its operating environment, double-loop learning can be through a multitude of levels (Figure 6.10). Solutions to the challenges that an organization faces could exist in its environment as well as within the organization itself. Interventions and information from higher levels can assist in effective resolutions of issues at lower levels, in this way enabling learning at lower levels. From the top levels to the lower levels and eventually the individual members, information and problem framing is transmitted for the effective application to problem solving. Regardless of

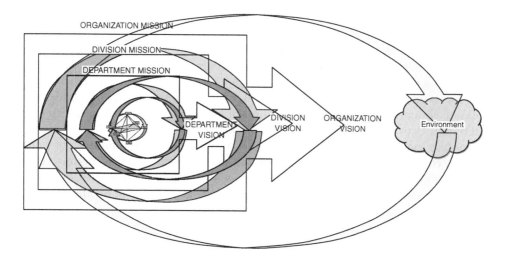

Figure 6.10 Single- and double-loop learning at various organizational levels

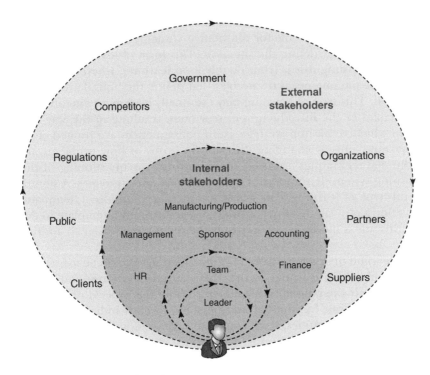

Figure 6.11 Multi-loop learning

the outcome (success or failure), the lessons learned can be transmitted and diffused following the bottom-up route. In this way, knowledge creation at the lower levels can feed learning at the higher levels. Eventually, through its products and services, the organization as a learning entity contributes to 'teaching' the environment. All the various entities in the process grow as a result of effective learning. The double-loop process, if effective, will eventually aim to ensure that successes are repeated and that failures are eliminated.

A multi-loop view of learning from an individual's perspective is given in Figure 6.11. Learning is viewed in this way as a continuous feedback and reflection process that dissipates the effects of learning from bigger pools to the individual and vice versa. This process ensures that information is valid, control is distributed, and entities are informed, committed and empowered to make free choices that will maximize the ideal responses to internal and external challenges.

A modern perspective in organizational learning is that of communities of practice. This concept is based on the notion that people come together because they find value in their interaction. In the knowledge domain, individuals (for example, the members of a team) form communities to exchange knowledge for the purpose of improving. Communities of value form when people have some things in common (like goals), but not everything (like skills). In this way, synergies maximize value for the community and each of the members individually. In order for such communities to exist and grow, three conditions are necessary: there should be domain specificity to define a set of issues or knowledge gaps, a group of individuals who care about the domain, and practice. The latter refers to sharing so that value is added to the domain either in the form of traditional domain knowledge or the latest advances. Coming together allows individuals to complement and develop their expertise in order to advance complex problem solving. For this process to be effective, a barrier to entry is imposed in the form of baseline knowledge/skills for someone to be accepted and identified as member of the community.

A special characteristic that separates communities of practice from other organizational forms is that their figureheads act more as coordinators than leaders. Their role is mainly to act as enablers that bring members together to produce solutions and define direction. The formation of these communities is mostly circumstantial, such as when individuals come together under pressure in order to solve a problem. Their interaction slowly forms the commonality of shared history. The persisting commonality in itself will create a need for further specialization and role differentiation as the members attempt to complement their expertise and maximize their synergies. This process further enhances the identity of individuals within the community, which results in community cohesiveness and prestige. Treating teams like communities of practice, in addition to enabling the efficient flow of learning among the team members, is a good way for leaders to build team identity and commitment, coupled with the pride and satisfaction of being part of the team.

A point of caution to note in relation to everything we discussed about learning is that we should not equate learning and knowledge with wisdom or maturity. The latter two are gained through our experiences in life and include the additional element of good judgement instead of merely clarity of facts and truth. If we were to account for the source of wisdom, then intuition and the individual's self should come to mind. An additional element identified by many (which we will encounter later on) that we might want to consider here is character. This defines our identity and marks our behaviour as distinct individuals in our social groups.

Ethics: Human interactions (like those that occur in the teams discussed here) always raise the issue of ethics. The word originates from 'ethos', which translates as customs, conduct or character. In its plural form, which we will use here, ethics refers to the beliefs and aspirations that represent the spirit of ideals and proper behaviour for a team member. In this sense, it is similar to morals, which reflect the beliefs of individuals about what is right or wrong. Morals are influenced by the individual's personal values and ethics are used to convert values into action. They are customized perceptions of right and wrong that differ from one person to another. This individualization often makes ethics look like a minefield. The moment you set up ethical standards (mines), someone who is new to them (and thus steps on a mine) is bound to explode.

The reason why ethics is considered here to be a tool is because of the diversity of interpretations and practices that various national and organizational cultures consider as ethical. What is ethical in Saudi Arabia, for example, might not be ethical in the US or China. National cultures and norms pose challenges for leaders in charge of multinational teams or when their teams interact with stakeholders from other regions and/or industries. With respect to leadership, ethics is important as it acts as a proxy to 'trust', which is further associated with predictability and safety. People tend to trust ethical leaders simply because they are predictable with respect to their adherence to acceptable norms, so beyond the philosophical aspects of being ethical, there are more far-reaching practical consequences of engaging in ethical behaviour.

In addition to the cultural implications on ethics, there are a variety of factors that separate one leader from another in terms of their ethics and morality. Leaders can vary in relation to their ethical behaviour as a result of their moral identities. Traits like sensitivity, compassion and honesty create a self-perception that is reflected in the leader's beliefs and moral stance. This becomes a self-regulating mechanism for leaders that is rooted in their sense of what is right and wrong. When expressed as behaviour, it sets the tone for what others should expect from leaders and what type of behaviour the leaders consider to be ethical in others.

The very mention of 'self' here should alert anyone to the subjective nature that ethical and moral standards can have. Some leaders (who have low moral grounds and are self-centred, greedy, narcissistic, etc.) might seek to maximize their personal returns at the expense of others rather than distributing earnings equally or proportionally among all stakeholders. Under certain conditions, this behaviour can even be displayed by those who would normally be regarded as 'good' people. As a result of pressure and fear, rationalization might be at play, leading people to focus on the intent instead of the action itself. One might say that they are breaking the law in order to help others in need. Another might say they hurt others by obeying the law/orders in their line of duty. In the former, a leader might continue doing something wrong, such as compromising safety standards, simply because nobody voiced objections or concerns, while in the latter, leaders lose their sense of reality and feel entitled to more than they deserve. Apart from the 'intentional' factors of unethical behaviour, we can also exhibit unintentional factors like motivated blindness. This is when we see what we want to see and ignore information that might contradict what we try to establish. This can result in conflicts of interest or the need to cover up for a mistake we have made.

In addition to everything we have mentioned here, let's not forget that the leaders in their capacity as role models of ethical behaviour set the example for others to follow. When considering how ethical behaviour can be displayed and enforced, and how leaders can create an ethical environment, we need to realize that it is not as easy as saying 'I want us to be ethical' or 'here is the code of ethics that we follow'. These are empty words as they might mean something different to everyone and, in addition, it might be viewed that we are trying to enforce our standards on others. Good or bad behaviour can be infectious and, as a result, others in the organization might be 'inspired' to behave unethically. If this continues, it is easy to see that the collapse of the organization (like the empires of the past) will soon follow.

The core ethical values that form the basis for ethical decision making and that guide actions include fairness, honesty, responsibility and respect. By treating all stakeholders that are involved in the pursuit of a goal fairly, we ensure that no impression is given of there being winners and losers and that no preferences or privileges are afforded to certain groups or individuals that discriminate them from the rest. There is of course the expectation that all actions in business should aim to increase shareholder value, but abiding by this principle should be done with the outmost care and sensitivity. For example, firing a portion of the workforce to cut costs might be a legitimate practice and might be necessary for the survival of the organization, but it should at least be done with transparency and respect for those who are adversely affected and should come as no surprise. Making sure that all intentions and effort have been devoted in that direction says much about the character of a leader and the organization they represent.

Being honest will lead to being seen as trustworthy and will allow people in the individual's environment to count on that individual's reactions and responses. In this way, they can be assured of the individual's future behaviour. In the same category, we find integrity as a quality of ethical leaders. Integrity means that one's actions are in alignment with one's words. In addition, it suggests that the individual uses rational principles in decision making and in this way it further contributes to the feeling that such individuals pose little threat. Another factor in relation to honesty is respect. Being respectful incorporates aspects of morality and also implies honesty. Showing respect also suggests that the inner worth of an individual is appreciated and is treated as an equal with kindness and courtesy.

From an organizational point of view, ethical behaviour is expressed through codes of ethics and ethical standards. The former has been popularized by professional associations and groups, while the latter are usually selected and adopted by each organization according to their specific culture and environment. Usually, ethical standards can be seen as organizational requirements that are mandatory and as aspirations that employees are expected to strive to uphold. By mandatory here we mean proper behaviour that does not deceive, including but not limited to making misleading or false statements and/or withholding or providing information out of context. Aspirations include anything that aims at being collaborative and supportive, such as providing accurate information in a timely manner.

In situations where teams come together for a limited amount of time, the adoption of ethical standards might need to be negotiated and clearly communicated to everyone involved. This is a requirement for anyone wishing to be part of a team where there is no cultural or professional uniformity. Personal standards in such cases will either have to be 'compromised' or amended to enable the team to function and achieve its goals. This of course can be considered an ethical violation as it raises the question of how 'standard' are the standards if they can be modified to suit the situation. Here is an example; presenting gifts in exchange for getting what you want might be considered respectful and appropriate in one culture, while in another it might be considered bribery. Adopting the ethical standards of the culture we interact with might be very good for our transactions, but very bad for our beliefs and integrity. Where one draws the line is really a personal decision, no matter how anyone wants to present it to the outside world. If we were to quote history, most revolutions were unethical until they succeeded and most religions were heresies until they were established.

A similar situation to diverse teams with varieties of ethical standards is when outsourcing is involved. Moving production, for example, to a country with low wages and benefits, low environmental and safety standards, corruption and a weak legal system that does not protect against child labour and animal rights, etc. might be a very attractive way of reducing costs and increasing competitive advantage long enough before anyone realizes the abuse that it entails, but it is nevertheless considered unfair treatment and unethical. When big corporations get involved, the situations can become messier as multiple levels of outsourcers are involved. While an organization might be able to control the ethical practices of its direct outsourcers, it might not be possible to control where these outsourcers outsource work unless something alerts it that wrongdoing is taking place. Trying to catch up with issues as soon as they surface and being proactive and performing due diligence might be the best way for leaders to protect their ethical standards and the team/organization they represent.

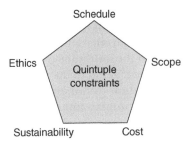

Figure 6.12 Constraints for goal/project execution

A concept closely related to ethics that we will briefly touch upon here is sustainability or, to put it another way, ethics for the environment. By 'environment', here we mean both the social and the physical environment in which a team or an organization operates. The foundation of doing what is right for the general public and our future societies is based on equity between social balance, economic prosperity and protection of the environment. These three elements are also expressed as 'people, planet, profit', i.e., PPP (the triple Ps) or the triple bottom line (TBL). In addition to the triple Ps principle, sustainability requires a time (short- and long-term) and a location (local and global) orientation to ensure the coverage of every aspect of its reach. In terms of organizational and team behaviour, it is based on personal values and ethics as well as transparency and accountability. With respect to accomplishing the team's goals and objectives, sustainability is often seen alongside main goal/project constraints (Figure 6.12). Leaders need to ensure that the scope of sustainable goal management includes project management policies, actions and relationships that are undertaken or formed in response to concerns relating to the natural environment and to social and economic issues.

While the value of sustainability as a concept and practice is undoubtedly important and can greatly benefit organizations in the long term, it can be challenged by situational factors like economic crises and the competitiveness of the global market, which values revenue maximization and survival at any cost. In such an operational environment, decision making with highly dubious ethical foundations can become the dominant mode of operation and safety is often compromised in favour of low-cost solutions and speedy execution. This situation might influence leaders in considering sustainability to be a public relations obstacle to growth. This factor can be especially strong for underdeveloped societies that fall into the 'sustainability trap' (their resources are not enough to justify further investments that would make them sustainable).

In responding to moral and ethical challenges with respect to their teams, their organizations and their environment, leaders can move their 'Ethics Centre of Gravity' either towards the 'dark' or the 'light' side of moral behaviour. The former involves forcing one's will on others, while the latter achieves order by capitalizing on the synergies of everyone's talent and contribution. While the former is easier and faster to enforce, the latter is more enduring as it is based on acceptance and respect of each individual who willingly and enthusiastically contributes to the common goal. Although the dark–light side theme is universal and almost the norm in most movies (for example, *Star Wars*) and real life, we still haven't learned that the easy and fast way of achieving something is usually not the most enduring and rewarding one.

Measuring: In a similar way to how individuals aware of their fragility perform health checks to establish their physical condition, leaders need to be able to perform checks to establish the health of their organizations. The case for metrics can be seen in many of the business clichés that have been used, such as 'if it can't be measured, it can't be controlled', 'if you measure it, then you are forced to do something about it' and 'nothing can be understood unless it is measured'. Measurements are necessary as they are the first indicators that something different from the norm is going on. Change is inevitable and having our plans work out exactly as they were intended to is an unrealistic expectation. The monitoring and controlling phase in the life-cycle of a goal is there to reflect this reality. To assist them in this practice, leaders need to be able to compare performance and results to what they intended these to be. This is where the measurement process comes into play as it allows for comparisons in terms of metrics of various aspects of a situation. Measuring something allows two parties to form a common understanding about what is measured. Between two business entities, the measurement might be part of how they measure success.

Metrics can include, among others, observations, values, categories, order (something is bigger than something else), statistics, samples, expert judgement and more complex forms, like simulations and decision analysis models. Ideal metrics should reflect a need for measuring something and their purpose needs to be clear as to what is measured, how it is measured, its margin of error and how the results are interpreted. In addition, the information provided should reflect the true status of the measured item, be acceptable to all parties involved, reflect the potential for success of failure and be practical in terms of suggesting a direction of action. Another way to provide a quick reference to the quality of metrics is by ensuring they are specific, measurable, attainable, realising and timely (SMART).

Overall, metrics spread throughout the organization, measuring the competencies of employees and their output at every stage from product or service design, development and distribution (Figure 6.13). The market provides feedback about the product's or service's performance. This feedback guides the future direction of the organization (its vision) and in essence provides a metric for the organizational mission effectiveness. Organizations in response can modify their mission to improve the competencies and effectiveness of their operations in order to better align with delivering what the market needs. The process repeats itself endlessly in response to changes in the environment and challenges from the competition.

Metrics can be categorized broadly as results indicators (RIs) when they provide information about what has been accomplished and key performance indicators (KPIs) when they can provide information that can drastically improve performance towards the adopted objectives. The distinction between the two is also of strategic importance as RIs focus on the current status of what they measure (organization), while KPIs are meant to focus on how future outcomes can be achieved. Considering RIs under the general term 'metrics' (to differentiate them from KPIs, which are more specialized), we can have a variety of categorizations, with the simplest one being quantitative (those that can be expressed numerically) and qualitative (those that can be ordinal or nominal. The latter can also be seen as a numerical progression (ordinal), like when we assign numbers to months, or categorization (nominal), like when we assign numbers to groups. More purposeful categorizations can include

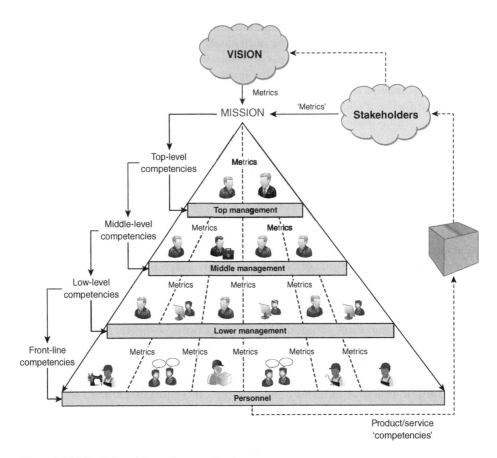

Figure 6.13 Metric breakdown in organizations

categories like quantitative, practical (dedicated to improving efficiency), directional (dichotomous in nature, for example, risk is increasing or decreasing), actionable (requiring change like investing more resources), financial (like ROI and profit margin), milestone (like task completion) and/or end result (product success).

Regardless of the category, there is a plethora of metrics used by organizations. Some of them can indicate progress towards a desirable outcome and thus be categorized as KPIs. Typical metrics that can also be adopted as KPIs include cost, schedule variance, performance indexes, resource utilization and customer loyalty. Adopting KPIs (Figure 6.13) can be either a top-down process or a bottom-up process.

A top-down approach usually relies on some sort of state-of-the-art earned value analysis to identify the performance problems and follows up with the activities that are critical and responsible for alerting about the problem. A bottom-up approach will usually rely on some well-known risk analysis to identify highly sensitive activities at the operational level and, using them, to deduce the negative impact they might have on organizational performance. The ideal approach for an organization really depends on what will maximize the acceptance of the adopted metrics from the various levels of management and front-line employees. If the process is imposed by the top, it can create a lot of resistance, in addition to the fact that it might not reflect the realities at the bottom. If it is imposed to ensure front-line effectiveness (from the bottom), it might not be able to capture the environmental changes that a strategic top-down approach could capture, thus risking the long-term survival of the organization. Ideally, we might see the development of KPIs as an agreement between the two extremes, where both present and future needs are addressed.

The need to consider the higher-level (strategic) view of organizations in metric development led to the establishment of supplemental practices to RIs and KPIs. When we are interested in measuring performance against business objectives, the balanced scorecard (BSC) is a popular method used by organizations. Lately, it has also become popular in the development of strategy itself. It is based on the premise that measurements (especially financial ones) only report on past decisions and if we are to have a realistic representation of the current objectives, a more balanced set of measures is required. BSCs promote the examination of performance from four specific and interrelated organizational perspectives. A financial perspective is required to address the interest of those who control and have a state in the financial wellbeing of the organization. This in turn relates to an interrelated customer and internal business perspective. The former identifies the perceptions of customers with respect to the organization's products, services, relations and value-added, while the latter identifies the expectations of employees and trading partners of the organization in terms

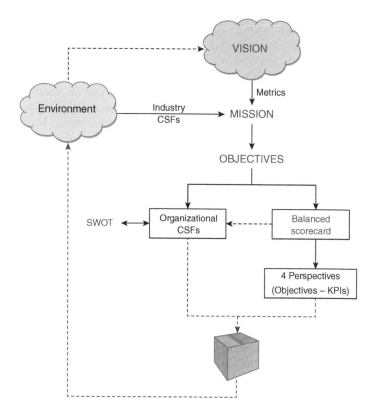

Figure 6.14 Metric adoption

of areas of excellence. Finally, a fourth item, the innovation and learning perspective, which interrelates to the previous two, closes the loop. This reflects the improvements and future value that the organization needs to achieve to ensure stakeholder satisfaction. For each perspective, objectives and their respective measures (KPIs) need to be identified to ensure that these have been adequacy addressed and monitored.

Having established (using the BSC or another method) what information will be used to measure performance, we can focus on what needs to be done to achieve them. This is where another measuring technique, the critical success factors (CSFs), come into play. These are usually broad categories (and thus not necessarily measurable) and their analysis is useful when we need to identify what needs to be done or changed in order to achieve the desired objectives, as they could point to any new information and/or system needs. CSFs are ideally applied to a limited number of areas that are considered critical for the successful performance of a team or organization. They highlight critical areas of activity that require constant attention and monitoring of performance to ensure success. If we consider that 'Metric' has been replaced with CSF in Figure 6.14 and consider the entry point in the displayed loop to be the external stakeholder/industry, we have the normal flow of defining CSFs from the industry to the top level of executives and so on. One exception here with respect to the flow is that because of the strategic nature of CSFs, they are rarely used for the bottom line. Examples of CSFs include access to resources, timely delivery, adherence to quality, customer satisfaction, etc. They can vary from one case to another, but when combined with the BSC, they provide a way of obtaining agreement on the priorities that need to be addressed in achieving the set objectives. While CSFs are popular for formulating strategies, they can also be used to establish agreement between two parties as to what is important with respect to a given objective. This could also include the characteristics of a product or service.

CSFs analysis (occasionally also known as 'key issue analysis') can be used in different ways according to the situation at hand, but a popular use is for the purpose of interpreting objectives in terms of the action required to achieve them. It can be used to examine external stakeholders, like the market and overall industry, or internally by leaders in order to prioritize activities for their attention in terms of their importance relative to the leaders' goals. The process of establishing CSFs begins with the identification of objectives. Normally, each objective will be reflected by its own CSFs, but as the process moves forward, CSFs might need to be consolidated across objectives since many of them will recur. The next step will be to prioritize them in terms of importance and practicality, and finally identifying the information that will need to be collected to evaluate their status. The process of adopting CSFs can bring an organization together as it requires involvement and commitment from leaders, ensures a consensus on what is important and critical for the success of the organization/team, and provides guidance as to what information is needed for decision making. Despite its advantages, we need to be cautious here, as the inappropriate use of CSFs can cause frustration and rejection. A typical problem with CSFs is the confusion between what is important and what is critical. These terms are often perceived as meaning the same thing and, as a result, the process of identifying CSFs might lead to including almost everything that the organization does. To ensure that they retain their practicality, CSFs need to be used in a formal and structured way in order to distinguish them from pure information collection practices and to ensure that people understand and are prepared in advance for their use.

While CSFs and KPIs can measure performance and suggest directions for action, organizations need to be able to compare their performance with that of others in the field. Benchmarking (setting a mark on a bench linguistically) can be used in this respect as it signifies a reference point in determining one's positions. In business, it serves to indicate a standard achieved or set (like a model organization) against which something else (another organization) is measured. It involves comparing actual or planned practices, such as processes and operations, to those of comparable organizations in order to identify best practices, generate ideas for improvement and provide a basis for measuring performance. The entities compared during benchmarking can be internal or external. Benchmarking allows for analogies from entities in a different application area to be made.

A lot of confusion often results from interchangeably using the words 'benchmarking' and 'benchmarks'. Apart from their grammatical difference (one is a verb while the other is a noun), benchmarking is used nowadays in a strategic perspective to indicate a continuous process of improvements and an ongoing search for best practices in order to improve organizational performance. Benchmarks, in contrast, are the specific measurements that gauge performance against a standard that has often been achieved by another entity. It is distinguishable from operating statistics as these provide incomplete comparisons by drawing attention to performance gaps without any evidence or explanation for their existence. On the contrary, benchmarks will reveal specific differences in operations, systems and procedures or differences in the way in which performance is tracked and measured. Both items are actionable and will provide insights about what the next steps should be. Benchmarks are ideal for managing change as they can provide early signs that something is wrong, either in terms of being a performance deficiency compared to others or a lost opportunity.

A general categorization of benchmarking includes three categories: process, performance and strategic. Process benchmarking is used to compare discrete processes (usually core processes) and operations (recruiting, strategic planning, project execution, etc.) and it is one of the most effective such practices as they are displayed by the leaders in the field. Performance benchmarking allows for comparisons between the products and services of an organization with others that pose a competitive threat to them. Items considered in these comparisons may include product price and quality, service delivery speed, reliability and other performance characteristics. Some ways to perform such benchmarks include analysing operations data, performing direct service or product comparisons and reverse engineering, among others. Finally, strategic benchmarking involves the identification of winning strategies as they were performed by successful organizations in various industry fields. Unlike process benchmarking, where the benefits are usually observed early on, strategic benchmarking affect the long-term strategies that an organization will adopt and in this respect the results of such initiatives take longer to accrue.

While the advantages of metrics and benchmarking in providing opportunities for continuous improvement are undeniable, we need to be cautious about how we select and interpret them. Selecting them without planning for alternative action based on what they might produce is without any practical significance. As Albert Einstein allegedly put it, 'not everything that counts can be counted, and not everything that can be counted counts'. When the metrics pick up deviations from the desired position and performance, action needs to be incorporated after reflecting on the measurements to allow for a new way forward that will bring the organization back on track. In addition to the challenges imposed by selecting appropriate metrics, we need to be aware of a multitude of other factors that could affect the proper adoption of metrics and even result in a deterioration in organizational performance.

Metrics by their very nature trigger comparisons, which on a human level might result in anger and disappointment because not everyone can be above the average or the minimum set for performance. This can be bad enough because it blinds us to other possibilities and stalls productivity. However, in harsh economic conditions and in competitive environments, the situation might be even worse as metrics that relate to employee satisfaction might be overlooked in favour of project performance. Prioritizing metrics might be one way to alleviate the situation, but in doing so the metrics might lose their power, as some might be seen as more important than others, leading to the marginalization of those regarded as being low priority. Employee satisfaction often tends to be one such marginalized metric.

At other times, metrics might be considered too detailed and time-consuming, requiring valuable effort and resources to sustain them. When this is coupled with the reality that metrics are not synchronous and always measure the past, or at least with respect to operations, we can see why their adoption can be problematic if it is not done correctly. The right balance between the quantity and the quality of metrics is required as too few metrics might fail to capture the whole picture, while too many might deplete resources whilst providing redundant and useless information. The former case might provide leaders with inadequate information or be difficult to interpret, while the latter might confuse them with too much, hiding the critical elements that might require urgent attention.

Possible solutions for overcoming some of the above scenarios and issues might include ensuring that metrics are self-validating, which can be accomplished by carefully planning and arranging the metrics, simplifying and making the metrics clear to understand and capture by all team members and systems. In that direction it will help if we can provide appropriate training and educate everyone involved and affected by the process. In addition, it helps if we establish a metrics library that describes the metrics in detail and contains examples and a comparable history of captured metrics and techniques, reducing the number of useless metrics and focusing on the core essential and strategically important metrics and, above all, instilling a culture of honesty and trust in the organization that encourages team members to be open and transparent in relation to progress and risks.

In concluding the discussion on measuring, we need to keep in mind that not everything can be measured, at least to a level and detail that will realistically represent its status. For example, efficiency, effectiveness, uncertainty, risk and innovation might be difficult to measure. In order for measuring to have a lasting effect, it should be closely tied to a change. Above all, it should not be seen as a static process, but as a dynamic one, as Figures 6.12 and 6.13 show. As time passes and the environment poses new challenges, metrics and the measurement process need to be adapted to reflect the new realities if they are to provide meaningful and timely information.

Negotiating: Every human interaction can be seen as a form of negotiation where we might trade something of value like money, effort, attention, a product or a service, to name but a few, for something that we need, like other products or services, someone else's effort, money or attention. Although it might sound strange, even love is a form of exchange, whether it is in the form of excitement, fulfilment, inspiration, safety, security or care, among others. This makes negotiation a universal practice that from the leaders' perspective is also a core skill in order for them to play their role.

Normally, negotiation processes are considered to be a blend of various disciplines ranging from game theory, psychology, political science, communications, law, sociology and anthropology. They involve a trade-off between gains and losses due to the negotiators' positions. Some of these are planned, while others can catch those involved by surprise. Questions that require consideration include: what are my priorities? How far can I go? Why is the other side following a certain strategy? Would I do the same if I was them? Are they honest and truthful? How do they understand commitment? Should I start the bidding first? Should I be aggressive? Should we spend more time getting to know each other? Should I walk away? Should I make more concessions? The answers we come up with to these questions will shape our strategy and will lead to the success or failure of negotiations. Strategy and behaviour become expressions of each other and establishing one can determine the other.

During a negotiation process, leaders function as optimizers, trying to identify the best solutions between their own needs, the other side's needs and what is available to both sides. Based on their perception of the environment in which negotiations are taking place, they need to plan their strategy and adapt their tactics minute by minute and according to what the stakes are. The target is to maximize short-term and long-term gains, keeping in mind that the outcome will impact themselves as professionals and the organization they represent.

Leaders who engage in negotiation processes can be viewed as knowledge systems that are influenced and shaped by different environmental factors as they mature as individuals and professionals. Starting with the basic ingredient of each human being in the form of the DNA each one of us inherits, we are raised in family environments that operate in societies that are nothing more than microcosms within nations, regions and the world at large. Each environmental layer (as we also saw in the previous chapter) encloses and exerts primary influence on those it encloses and, to a lesser degree, its outside layers. In other words, as we are influenced by the world, we also influence the world, at least in our own vicinity. For a person, this is expressed in the form of education and experience while interacting with others.

As Figure 6.15 (which is similar to Figure 5.20) shows, messages we send and receive go through layers of influence that can be affected by our heritage (whether genetic, social or cultural) and the environment in which we operate. If that isn't enough, it gets worse when we consider the same for the person we are negotiating with. It's a kind of filtering that any negotiator needs to be aware of if they are to code their message to clearly reach another party. Decoding the messages on the receiver side is also vital unless the other party is aware and trained enough to code their message so that it doesn't get polluted by the different influence layers.

One way of seeing the negotiation process is through a framework which will ensure that all the parameters of a negotiation issue and the positions of the interested parties are understood and projected clearly. Figure 6.16 presents one such framework where the negotiation process is shown as a sequence of steps that we consciously or unconsciously take in reaching our goal. Making it visible is meant to help in making us aware of what is going on and how we can make the most of it. As Figure 6.15 outlines, a negotiation is about looking for the characteristics of a situation, making sense of it, planning an action and executing it. We start with the intelligence phase, where

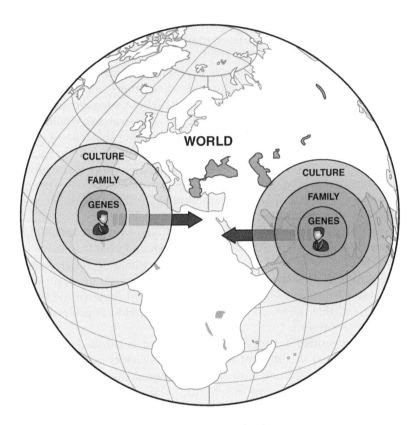

Figure 6.15 Influence layers during communication

we try to find as much information as possible on the issue at hand and the parties involved. We then try to make sense of what we have found in the perception phase and, based on that, we build our negotiations strategy. Finally, we execute the strategy by communicating our intentions and our proposals.

The transitions between phases can vary in terms of speed and while sometimes it may appear that we jump phases, we do actually go through them. For example, even when we have all the information in advance, it is unlikely that we will formulate a strategy unless we reassure ourselves that the facts are those we have and nothing more (meaning that we go through to the *intelligence* phase) and that we understand and interpret their meaning correctly (meaning we then pass on to the *perception* phase). Similarly, it is unlikely that we will communicate something without first ensuring that it is aligned with our intended strategy: having said that, we should keep in mind that just because we follow such a process, it does not mean that individual elements are rational. Optimization of skills is a completely different issue and relates to our abilities, our experience and the situation at hand. As one would have probably figured out by now, nothing is really set in stone. Understanding, flexibility and good judgement will help negotiators choose their approach and strategy specific to the issues they are facing.

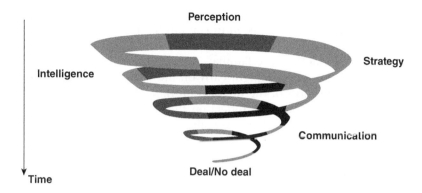

Figure 6.16 Evolution of the negotiation phases in time

Figure 6.17 Negotiation dominated by the communications phase

As we act to solve the problem, we transcend the spiral of *intelligence, perception, strategy* and *communication* (Figure 6.16) until we reach an agreement or abandon the negotiation. It goes without saying that the length of each phase is not constant (Figure 6.17). It is obvious that we need to spend more time on the *intelligence* phase at the beginning of the negotiation when we are not familiar with the issue at hand instead of at the end, by which time we will have formulated a clear understanding of the issues and the variables that affect them due to our previous exchanges with our counterparts. *Perception* again is one of the phases that we would expect to decrease over time as the interaction and information exchange moves on with our counterpart, hopefully gaining a better understanding of the issues and process as time passes. On the other hand, the *communication* phase and, to a lesser degree, the *strategy* phase should be expected to dominate the negotiation as time goes on. We experience rapid exchanges of information in order to clarify issues and reach an agreement.

As we reach the end of the negotiation process, the loops in the framework become shorter, following rapid exchanges of information in order to clarify issues and reach an agreement, until we make the final decision to commit to an agreement or walk away without a deal. For certain types of negotiation, like those that we encounter frequently or with cases with which we are familiar, we might spend very little time on *intelligence, perception* and *strategy,* and might early on move on to the *communication* phase, where we will spend most of the negotiation time. This is a natural and expected move, but we should occasionally reflect on the suitability of our applied strategies even in routine negotiations, since exceptions might appear that require additional consideration.

Nowadays, with many negotiations taking place online, we have information technology as an additional element that affects negotiations. Technology can affect communications and increase the capabilities of negotiators by making it easy to acquire information, to provide support with negotiation decision support systems and to expand stakeholder participation, especially now that the popularity and impact of social media has grown. E-negotiations can be seen as the subset of negotiations that rely exclusively on technology. Their major advantage is their ability to record every detail of the communication process, including intentions, outcomes and information exchanged. This can provide a better understanding of the negotiation process and behaviour, and can enable analysis and evaluation of strategies that would be impossible in face-to-face negotiations. In addition, the resulting time lag from the asynchronous communication exchange has been shown to make negotiators pay more attention to the substantive content of messages, has reduced the emotional stress brought about by conflicting positions and has made it easier to overcome socioeconomic differences.

However, the challenges that someone is faced with when negotiating online can frequently outweigh the benefits. The lack of face and body cues is very difficult for many to overcome. The online medium is also considered cold and biased towards non-native English speakers that don't have the fluency of expressing themselves in English. The fact that you might be typing from left to right while someone else reads from right to left or top to bottom might seem trivial, but it can cause profound differences in how things are expressed and interpreted. Perceptions of time are another cause of misinterpretations and misunderstanding. Imagine you speak a language where there is no future tense or the verb 'to be' does not exist. These are realities that exist between languages and even between variations of the same language like English.

In spite of the challenges that have arisen and will continue to arise, negotiators will still need knowledge, judgement and expertise. All that is needed nowadays is adaptation to the new realities. This is not a matter of choice – it is a survival requirement. Prior to engaging in negotiations online, it is important to consider whether it is 'tasks' or people that will be affected by decisions. This is important since tasks are impersonal and can benefit from the structure and permanence of the online medium, while decisions about people need the expressive power of human beings with their verbal and non-verbal cues to fully express and represent a situation. When deciding on the communication mode to use when negotiating on an issue, it is important to accommodate the needs, skills and communication preferences of all parties as much as possible and to choose the most practical and most efficient option.

6.4.3 Virtual teams

The way in which teams work has changed dramatically over the last few decades, which is more like an unprecedented evolutionary jump. People working together in real time from different parts of the globe became the reality of virtual teams and distributed or dispersed teams. The former category refers to teams with high levels of interdependence and cooperation of members independent of location, while the latter category refers to loosely coupled teams that operate in different locations. In this section we will treat these as the same, at least from the leadership point of view, as they both represent a physical separation or distance between the leader and the followers. Another related term here is 'transient' teams, which might be applied to both virtual and distributed teams. It refers to teams with a short life-span and sometimes we also refer to them as a task force.

Organizations like Apple and Intel have product development and manufacturing teams scattered throughout the world engaged in hundreds of projects every year in different groups and with different leaders. Managing such global projects can be demanding for a project manager, in part due to the multitude of organizational and local cultures involved and in part due to the challenge of interacting and communicating via the internet across time zones and physical locations. From a leader's perspective, we can visualize the case of leading virtual teams by considering a classical symphony orchestra composed of the traditional four groups of instruments: woodwinds (flutes, oboes, clarinets and bassoons), brass (horns and trumpets), percussion (timpani) and strings (violins I and II, violas, cellos and double basses), but with one notable exception. Each group is situated in a different part of the world, as are you as the conductor. You are expected to coordinate your work over the internet and record a symphony in real time. The magnitude of the challenges faced in such endeavours is a good indicator of the difficulties and challenges that virtual teams face.

From an organizational point of view, imagine that multiple symphonies are in production concurrently. In such a world, the organizational structure becomes a key factor in the way in which virtual and distributed teams are organized. Matrix forms become easier to operate than functional forms simply because they can allow team members to correspond virtual and physical presence to matrix and functional forms. This allows them to report to the project manager (wherever this individual is located) for the project deliverables and to their on-the-ground manager for their functional group. The picture resembles more outsourcing situations where a centralized command and control delegates responsibilities to partners around the globe. Compartmentalizing work into complete deliverables per site is indeed a miniaturized way of outsourcing. The difference is that both the command and control unit and the outsourcers belong to the same organization, at least for the duration of the project.

The benefits of employing virtual teams are the exploitation of local talent on an as-needed basis, fast responsiveness to market and customer needs, and cost reduction. The latter is due to the temporary nature of the employment and the fact that organizations don't have to pay for facilities, travel, benefits and support for such employees. In essence, virtual team members are more like subcontractors that work on a specific project. In addition to these benefits, virtual teams are not limited by distance or time as they can function around the clock and from anywhere in the world.

While the aforementioned benefits are from an organizational point of view, there are plenty of benefits from the employee point of view. First of all, virtual employees do not have to commute and have maximum convenience, as they work from the comfort of their home or from where they want their office to be. This results in a tremendous amount of savings in terms of both money and time. In addition, employees own their working schedule, they become independent and can keep in touch more efficiently and effectively as they have fewer distractions and are in their preferred work environment. Overall, it is a less stressful situation away from organizational politics and friction, which results in a better work/life balance.

Of course, nothing good comes for free, so in order for the benefits of virtual teams to materialize, certain barriers and challenges need to be overcome. Difficulties in communication arise due to imbalances in technology expertise and availability. Not everyone is comfortable collaborating online, especially on complex tasks and not all individuals and parts of the world have the necessary technology infrastructure to support the fast internet speeds required for transmitting rich content information. Separation, whether real or perceived, is a major challenge for trust building and forming relationships. In addition, the few face-to-face interactions involved in virtual working might make team members vulnerable to process losses and performance problems as commitment and engagement is left to the individual. While it is usual for employees to participate in multiple teams/projects at a time in normal settings, in the virtual domain, working towards team cohesiveness is highly dependent on technology. In the cases where virtual teams are distributed among different organizational and subcontractor teams that are dispersed, additional challenges include the site configuration in the locations where subgroups operate, the culture and operating styles of the various groups and the imbalance in terms of contribution and control where there is an uneven distribution of team members. The diversity of cultural backgrounds and competencies involved may lead to misunderstandings and conflict.

A special challenge for virtual team leaders is conflict resolution. Employee conflict can get out of hand in virtual teams as anyone can log-off at any time, leaving the leader and co-workers with no means of communicating with that person. An importance aspect of conflict is whether it is interpersonal or task-related. The former is more difficult to resolve as it can lead to avoidance like the one we mentioned previously. Task conflict usually results from internal competition for limited resources and checks and balances, and is somewhat easier to deal with. It can even be considered a healthy and constructive form of conflict as it can lead to improved operational performance. Regardless of the type of conflict, the virtual environment can prove to be both helpful and difficult at the same time. The good news is that the separation between co-workers reduces the chances of relationship conflict as team members usually focus on the task and less on interpersonal issues and office politics. The bad news is that separation prevents the build-up of empathy that usually relieves tension and task-related conflict can often quickly become relationship conflict (for example, nasty email exchanges).

The challenge for leaders in virtual conflict is to prevent task-related issues from turning into personal issues. Solutions like task reassignment, issue ownership or the development of 'common' virtual areas for releasing tension might be appropriate. For example, a commonly shared discussion forum can help virtual team members pitch their ideas and gather support and feedback for them from other colleagues, while helping them to let off steam without being stigmatized or resented. In addition to allowing for transparent and honest communication, the discussion forum could potentially serve as a natural repository for new and old team members to go and find information and explore the rationale for the adoption of practices. These forums can effectively act as means of conflict resolution and decision support systems. Complementing them with regular real-time communication (preferably audio and video) will also help prevent conflict situations and release tension when conflict builds up.

In addition to the organizational challenges, there are also personal challenges for individuals working remotely. An individual needs to be well organized and disciplined as they need to develop their own working schedule and stick to it. Although there are no disturbances caused by co-workers, there could be plenty of disturbances from their family and domestic life in general around them that diverts their attention. 'Working in your pyjamas' might sound like a luxury, but it does relate to leisure in our brains and to overcome it requires a change in our mindset. Individuals also need to be managers of themselves to ensure proper monitoring of and control over their performance. Last but not least, while technology has brought us closer to each other in terms of status updates, it has moved us further apart in terms of human/emotional contact. As humans, we value our individuality and existence in terms of how it relates to others. Being connected to someone through a machine is not the same as having someone physically present, where we can see and feel the impact we have on them. As a result, working from home can get very lonely and those working in this environment need to strategically plan their social time to counter this influence.

The core element for the interaction and collaboration of virtual team members from both the organizational and the individual's perspective is 'virtual' communication or communication over distance. Separation/distance can be seen as objective distance when the separation can be measured in units of length (for example, kilometres) or as subjective distance which refers to an individual's perception of distance. We will focus here on an established objective separation and how to translate it into a minimal perceived separation. This can be approached by considering a technology orientation and/or a systems orientation. The former considers the degree of 'virtuality' from the length, frequency and quality perspective of the virtual/electronic communication and is complemented by the frequency of face-to-face interactions. The latter views technology as only one element in the immediate team interactions, with additional factors like team cohesion and the mediums of communication (video, audio, text, collaborative platforms, etc.) also contributing to team effectiveness.

To address the challenges of virtual and dispersed teams, leaders need to strive for the formation and adoption of desired norms and values among team members. Planning and control become critical in such situations and leaders need to be actively involved in breaking the work down into greater detail (even atomizing some elements), defining clear responsibilities, and setting out clear communication and reporting rules and practices. Frequently promoting team norms and practices while engaging individual team members and task leaders will help in the perception of a collaborative environment with task interdependence where team members feel connected to each other.

In virtual environments, where praise and the building of relationships is not as easy as it is in face-to-face work environments, task accomplishment becomes a core value. Individual team members rely heavily on the sense of accomplishment as a motivating factor in addition to the other benefits mentioned earlier. The value of accomplishment as a universal cultural value and a component of self-concept is demonstrated by competence in the execution of work and suggests personal success, which is considered essential to the experience of meaning. In that respect, values, especially in virtual settings, become essential and function as interests that motivate behaviour and commitment in a particular direction, along with providing criteria for and justifications of behaviour. Leaders can assist the adoption of values through socialization and individualized attention to each group member.

The special attributes and skills that leaders of virtual teams need to have include, among others, technical expertise and an understanding of the communication medium and the challenges it poses in the transmission of information and emotions, as well as task orientation for a clear definition of task boundaries, reporting and feedback procedures. In the area of soft skills, cultural sensitivity and understanding of local norms and practices is imperative, as well as the ability to build relationships and motivate team members. Of added value is past experience in international settings and hopefully in virtual teams as a member and/or leader.

6.5 Measuring leadership

After taking a brief snapshot of how leadership is practised, one might wonder how we can tell when leadership is successful for sustainable development and growth and not merely for the short term, where this can easily be confused with management. Evaluating leadership might seem like a challenge from a theoretical point of view, as different perspectives can influence our understanding of leadership according to our point of view. The closer we get, the more details are revealed, but the further away we move from generalizations that persist and characterize the phenomenon. However, in practice, evaluating leadership is done continually and for every individual and organization. Organizations are always on the lookout for practices which ensure that their leaders add value and sustain a competitive advantage. Measuring the effectiveness of leadership behaviour requires, to a great extent, quantification of the benefits to organizational performance as a result of the behaviour. Providing tangible evidence in this form can justify the advantages of adopting a specific type of leadership behaviour.

In evaluating leadership, we can consider characteristics, attributes and skills in the operational and situational context of its application. It is important to bear in mind here that attributes refer to the positive or negative evaluative statements about leaders, while characteristics refer to the ways in which attributes are expressed. For example, while leaders have power as an attribute due to their position, when they express it abusively, it becomes their characteristic. Another way to separate the two is to see attributes as professional credentials, while characteristics relate more to effectiveness in execution. In practice, we often tend to group attributes and skills into categories. This is practical in screening individuals for leadership positions and for training and development, since they can be easily targeted and measured, but we need to be cautious that in such cases we will only be able to measure what the instruments we use measure within their reliability and validity limits. In practice, many of the important leadership characteristics like persistence, creativity and empathy are hard, if not impossible, to measure.

Some of the characteristics of leadership have been grouped into areas of competencies. As such, we have intellectual competencies, usually measured as intelligence quotient (IQ), and include, among others, critical analysis capabilities and judgement, imagination and the ability to form strategies and express a vision. Another area of competencies includes emotional ones like motivation, self-awareness, emotional resilience, sensitivity, conscientiousness, intuitiveness and influence, which are usually measured as emotional quotient (EQ). Finally a well-known category of competencies is managerial competencies, which includes managing resources, empowerment, achievement, engagement, communications and development, usually measured as managerial quotient (MQ). Mentioning specific tools that exist today for measuring the aforementioned competencies is beyond the scope of this book. The interested reader can easily locate many of them through a simple Google search, but should pay special attention to exactly what they measure and how accurate they are.

Another important point when evaluating leaders is to avoid being misled by the 'halo effect' that leaders' past experience might play in overshadowing important attributes. Just because a leader was successful in one situation in the past doesn't mean that they will also be successful in similar situations or different ones in the future, as the environment would have definitely changed, while no two organizations or teams are ever the same. In fact, while critical, situational factors are often overlooked due to the stereotypes, myths and truths about leaders that recruiters maintain.

There is quite a literature regarding such myths, so the select few mentioned here are only meant to provide a 'light' coverage of the topic. Leaders are often presented as team players and extroverts. The truth might be less clear-cut than that, as most exceptional leaders are independent thinkers who assemble diverse teams. Being an extrovert or an introvert is actually irrelevant to good leadership and only relates to the way in which one releases energy and recharges to avoid burnout. Another myth is that great leaders provide hands-on coaching and are closely involved in mentoring others. The truth is that great leaders select strong team members so that they can fully delegate tasks to them, allowing them to learn though experience and mistakes. Often, great leaders are confused with politicians with raw ambition and great oratory and public speaking skills. This again is far from the truth, as many display modesty and could be awkward and shy in public settings. In one-to-one situations, though, they can be highly competitive and dynamic. A final myth that is worth mentioning here is that great leaders should fit the organization. The truth is that if they fit the organization, there will be no change that would lead to growth. Leaders should have diverse backgrounds in order to be able to adapt and adjust when the environment changes.

7   Future dimensions

With the advent of information technology and the globalization of almost every aspect of human life, modern societies and their organization have grown from isolated and mostly uniform social groups that functioned within geographically distinct areas to operating and interacting with diverse groups and entities from all over the world. This breach of boundaries and the interconnectedness of the physical and the newly discovered virtual worlds has also affected leadership as a phenomenon and practice. A project and team orientation of work in modern organizations was necessary to allow for frequent adjustment to the constantly changing social and market environments.

A way of viewing the practice of leadership in organizations as leadership of work teams was discussed in the previous chapter. Critical characteristics of teams that affect the way in which we view organizations and leadership include their goal orientation and their transient nature. Someone could be the leader in one team and the follower in another. This diffusion of roles was there in the past, but it became more prominent in modern organizations as the turnaround of both leaders and followers intensified due the multiple fronts on which an organization needed to engage. Decision-making responsibility had to spread from the organizational head to the organizational extremities simply because organizations needed to react quickly to a multitude of global and local threats at the same time. Having semi-autonomous units that can function as self-managed work teams is ideal in such environments.

Leadership in such scenarios had to evolve and spread throughout the organization (Figure 7.1). Teams nowadays are multigenerational (even up to four generations can work side by side), mixed gender and race, spanning multiple nationalities, experiences, expertise and even distributed around the globe. Integrating teams and ensuring they perform as expected becomes a priority, and managerial functions like coaching and managing relations become infused into the leader's role. While some of these functions were also necessary in the past, nowadays the ways of providing support and direction require more collaboration, transparency, openness and buy-in to a shared vision to ensure the commitment of team members.

Selecting the right leaders for teams might be challenging for organizations as the operational environments are fluid and unpredictable, so planning for one situation while facing another is not unusual. Focusing on skills might not be the best way to choose leaders as there are so many skills that could be considered that it would make it challenging to prioritize them and devote time to their development. In today's environment in which the workforce is highly mobile, building skills and developing traits is left to a great extent to the individual. Organizations can easily choose from what is already out there instead of investing in developing their staff, which at any

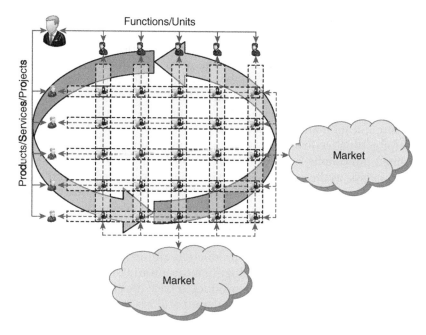

Figure 7.1 Leadership spread throughout the organization

time can leave to join the competition, taking their skills with them. As a result, leaders who transition from one organization to another, motivating and providing the right incentives, become much more efficient and cost- and time-effective in most situations than by following any other approach.

7.1 Disruption and crisis

The biggest threat identified is the one that cannot be identified as a threat because there is no theory or practice that can be applied to prepare one for something that hasn't appeared yet. In business terms, this simply means that in addition to those issues that leaders had to worry about in the past, like new rivals with better or cheaper products or services, nowadays competitors might appear from areas that have not previously been classified as competitive. Classic examples include Amazon and Travelocity, which, as digital invaders, changed the face of their respective industries. In such situations, there are no clear boundaries between industries and business types, and being the first is not just an aspiration, it is the difference between survival and extinction. In addition to industry convergence, there are a multitude of factors like working from 'anywhere', the spread of consumer power, alternative finance and financing mechanisms, and the sharing economy.

New terms and practices appear continually to address the changing needs of the organizational environment and to capture the essence of what is going on and what needs to be done. The need for innovative solutions and decision support systems and practices is vital for leaders who want to be effective in their role. *Ideation* is becoming popular as a concept that helps in that direction, as it encapsulates creativity and imagination. Generating collaboration through the organization is more important than ever. While there are many methods through which one can generate collaboration, a popular and modern alternative that we will mention here is design thinking.

As a conceptual innovation that stormed the business world *design thinking* is an alternative way of seeing a problem with respect to process innovation. It involves the development of artifacts that solve problems. At its core, the focus is on the concerns, interests and values of the customer. An additional building principle includes multi-faceted teams with expertise from diverse fields, including engineering, sociology, the humanities, communication and ethnography. Finally, prototyping is assumed to be the fastest way for getting feedback, learning and improvement.

The underlined philosophy in all of the previous is simple: one size does not fit all, especially nowadays, as the operational environments are diversified and change constantly. Today's problem space is evolving so fast that teams require maximum collaboration to come up with solutions to the unique problems that the market throws at them. Design teams draw participation for multiple organizational divisions, ensuring in this way the commitment of wider organizational sections. This allows the teams to move from design to production and to customers faster than ever. In industries like information technology that can afford fast prototyping cycles, this process has even evolved into specific product/service life-cycles like *agile*. Such methodologies resulted in developing error-tolerant artifacts that perfectly matched user needs.

Another concept similar to design thinking that is very popular in the leader's dictionary in *innovation*. This concerns the adoption of new practices by a community of people (employees in most cases) that usually target products/services and processes. The key word here is *adoption*, which is a proxy for commitment. Adoption might even take years to materialize, if it ever does, as the vast majority of start-ups prove, because it doesn't work like an invention that happens in a flash and can be accelerated with perspectives like design thinking. For example, many people praise companies like Apple for their innovativeness, but they forget the hard work and years that it took the company to overcome the challenges it faced in order to reach that stage. Innovative artifacts do not appear suddenly out of thin air; their components and even the complete artifact might have already existed in some form. What makes the difference is the ability of the organization to draw individuals with interest and skills around its artifacts, building a core of committed adopters who invest their time and effort in expanding the capabilities of artifacts to reach greater audiences and expand the communities yet further. Tablets, for example, existed before the iPad, but it was the design and the added capability of a plethora of apps that made the iPad a success. Apple had its first tablet, the Apple Newton, in 1987, long before it launched the iPad in 2010, and so did Microsoft in 2002 when it released its Windows XP Tablet PC. None of these devices managed to do what the iPad did, but they have all contributed to clearing the 'minefield' of issues and have identified the best practices for the innovation that created the iPad.

This is because innovation is often confused with the more spectacular but rarer form of innovation, *disruptive innovation*. This radical form of innovation reconfigures the competitive landscape so drastically that new forms of communities are created around the practices it introduces. Uber is such an example, as was Amazon in the past. While these types of innovations are usually related to an artifact (product or service), the truth behind their success is entrepreneurship.

When it comes to disruptive innovation, technology is the mediator of almost everything that has radicalized the marketplace. Technologies that will persist and will enable further innovations include cloud computing, the Internet of Things (IoT), cognitive computing, advanced manufacturing technologies (3D printing is one such example), new energy sources and solutions that are environmentally friendly and more efficient, and bioengineering for the development of better crops, foods, medicines and medical devices. Cloud computing can afford higher processing speeds and service agility, while requiring lower capital expenditure and operating costs, allowing organizations to collaborate better and make more efficient and productive use of their core resources. Similarly, the IoT promises to allow for the better utilization of assets and for personalized offerings by enhancing services and converting products into services, while cognitive computing will provide better insights into customer behaviour and intentions, allowing organizations to better engage them and predict their needs. Other than the aforementioned advances that information technology can offer, manufacturing efficiencies and cost savings will come from advanced manufacturing technologies that will also allow for easy experimentation and mass customization. With everything that can potentially change, leaders need to understand what is going on and be able to identify new trends and develop their responses to them. In practical terms, leaders need to be continually educating themselves, learning new skills, brainstorming, using analytics (both predictive and prescriptive), and engaging in scenario building, simulations and crowdsourcing. Using everything in their technology arsenal is something leaders will have to continually do.

To enable innovativeness to thrive in their organizations, leaders will have to develop a culture that will support adaptation and allow creativity to grow. Meeting such a challenge requires an attitude change towards lifelong learning, alertness and creative conduct. Of added value to an innovative culture is its ability to assimilate ideas and practices that have worked for the best in the field easily and without any hesitation. This might seem insignificant, but the truth is that many organizations and leaders suffer from the originality syndrome, which prevents them from borrowing and imitating ideas that made others great. In a sense, importing someone else's best practices is seen as cheating or stealing, and is associated with shame and an inability on behalf of the leader to be seen as creative and visionary. However, the true name of this practice is not shameless stealing, but simply benchmarking (as we saw in the previous chapter). Another term that can be used in such cases that more accurately reflects the importance of the practice is *innovative adaptation*. This is a much sought-after competency if organizations are to quickly adapt to the challenges that their environment (competitors mainly) throw at them. All organizational levels must be ready to encourage and embrace as a simple reality the fact that one cannot beat everyone all the time in the creativity and originality game.

Organizational cultures can overcome the barriers to borrowing in a systemic way by integrating actions, policies, stories, etc. in a cohesive narrative that can be followed by anyone. The repetition of these elements eventually creates a reality that is passed from one generation to the next and creates a true learning organization. In addition to enabling the borrowing component in their organizational cultures, leaders can develop value-driven cultures that embrace information sharing, empowerment, teamwork and learning. They can achieve this by first role-modelling a behaviour that embraces change and enthusiasm towards problem solving and opportunity creation, and then ensuring that the right people are in the right positions.

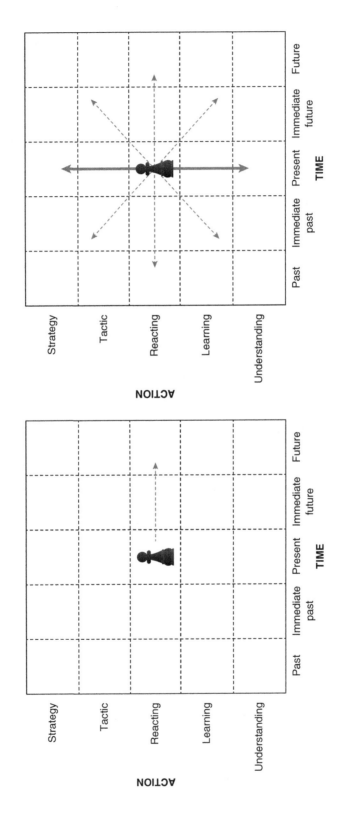

Figure 7.2 Employees in leadership roles

From the leaders' perspective, it is vital to know how to prepare for such an environment so that they can effectively deal with threats and also take advantage of the opportunities they offer. Traditionally, leaders would focus on improving or expanding their range of products and services or improving their supply chain, among other things, but today their competitors might be invisible until they are too strong for the leaders to deal with. Threats can come from existing players (like Amazon, which tries to sell everything, or Google trying to sell groceries) or from newcomers like Uber and Airbnb, which while initially small can become equally dangerous. These newcomers carry no organizational inertia from heavy infrastructure and organizational culture that took years to build. They are small, agile and smart, and in some cases they don't even have an infrastructure simply because they use other's assets.

To deal with these new realities, leaders require a panoramic view of the 'battlefield' where even the smallest disturbances can quickly be spotted, accounted for and reacted to. Given the breadth of the 'battlefield', networks and alliances become vital and, as a result, leadership needs to be distributed to where the action is instead of following the conventional hierarchical structures. Sharing resources and allowing others who are more familiar with the new game and are better equipped to deal with it and to take the lead will allow both the leader's organization and its allies to grow together. In addition to acting on an organization's behalf, allies also serve as key sources for intelligence as they can provide their own perspective of the battlefield. If the ally is new, jointly conducting small projects together will allow the two organizations to build trust and familiarize themselves with the way in which the other party works.

This distributed leadership philosophy in modern organizations will need to extend all the way to their frontline 'troops', empowering their employees more and more so that they can effectively respond to change by creating solutions and implementing decisions. Employees need to act as leaders instead of just 'pawns' (Figure 7.2).

In addition to contributing significantly to solutions, empowered employees can even resolve problems in their infancy as they have freedom of action to respond to threats and can provide local intelligence early on about external stakeholders like partners and customers. Combining this insight with the various points of view of organizational allies (mentioned earlier) allows leaders to capitalize on the collective understanding of the market-field and form ideas about the trends and technologies that will shape the future. This early warning intelligence network allows all the members of the ecosystem to prepare and compete more effectively. Of course, ecosystems are sensitive entities and can be greatly endangered by their weakest members (dinosaurs are a testimony to this), so effort must be extended to ensure that each 'species' within the organization (partners, employees, etc.) is capable of functioning at its peak.

7.2 Culture and diversity

The value of people as assets is undeniable in modern organizations. With the advent of technology that accelerated the disruption process mentioned above, talent became a core organizational value. It is usually referred to as *social capital* and represents the cumulative performance potential of an organization's workforce as it interacts to deliver the organization's products or services. Its full expression is closely associated with *empowerment* as it allows people the freedom to use their talents individually or collectively to make decisions and affect their work. When the character of these interactions is strong and based on mutual respect and appreciation, it leads to the engagement and commitment of individuals and teams, which eventually results in efficient and effective problem solving and innovation.

Usually observed types of organizational cultures with respect to performance include passive/defensive, aggressive/defensive and constructive. In passive/defensive cultures, employees are defensive in their working relationships, avoiding conflict and confrontations, and seeking approval before they take action out of fear of reprisals, while in aggressive/defensive cultures, employees are confrontational and protective of their positions and status. These two types of working culture are usually not associated with high-performance organizations as the interactions amongst employees are less constructive and they also tend to be less motivated than in constructive cultures where employees are more collaborative, share and feel appreciated, and are committed to the organization's vision and purpose.

While we have already examined organizational cultures in Chapter 5, it is worth breaking down the circles of influence on individuals, focusing here on the individual's characteristics (Figure 7.3) that contribute to workforce diversity. A key contributor to organizational culture is the personalities of the individual employees that influence their behaviour when they interact with each other. One popular typology (the Big Five) breaks down personality into five factors/dimensions – neuroticism, conscientiousness, extraversion, agreeableness and openness:

- *Neuroticism* as a domain comprises the facets of anxiety, hostility, depression, self-consciousness, vulnerability and impulsiveness, so in many cases it is also identified as negative emotionality or nervousness. Behaviourally, it contrasts emotional stability and even-temperedness. The 'positive' aspect of it manifests itself when people accept the good and bad in their life patiently and without complaint or bragging. At its high end, it is expressed in the form of poor coping skills and reactions to misfortunes and life's challenges, while at its low end, we find individuals with greater relationship satisfaction and those feeling committed to work.
- *Conscientiousness* refers to socially prescribed impulse control that is expressed in task- and goal-directed behaviour, such as thinking before acting, delaying gratification, following norms and rules, and planning, organizing and prioritizing tasks. Behavioural examples of this type of person include those who arrive early or on time for appointments, study hard in order to be at the top of their class and look for perfection in their work. At the low end, we find people who behave recklessly, those who abuse their bodies (through substance abuse, poor eating and exercise habits) and those with attention deficit/hyperactive disorders.
- *Extraversion* includes the facets of sociability, talkativeness, cheerfulness and optimism that jointly compose the higher-order dimension of 'positive affect'. People who possess this trait enjoy change and excitement in their lives, and in general have a positive emotional predisposition about outcomes in activities in which they engage. The opposite is an introvert, who in general displays a negative valence mood about events and outcomes – also termed 'negative affect'. The degree of introverting represents one's level of subjective distress and dissatisfaction. High negative affect reflects a wide range of negative mood states, including

fear, anger, sadness, guilt, contempt, disgust and self-dissatisfaction. In contrast, high positive affect results in expressing enthusiasm, joy, energy, mental alertness and confidence.

• *Agreeableness* is best conceptualized as summarizing specific tendencies and behaviours, such as being kind, considerate, likable, cooperative and helpful. Individual differences in agreeableness might be reflected as expressions of intimacy, union and solidarity in groups, where they can work as part of a motivational system. Biobehavioural research also suggests a link between child development and agreeableness as an inhibitor of negative effects. At the high end, agreeableness indicates better performance in work groups, while at the low end, it shows someone with interpersonal problems.

• *Openness* to experience/intellect includes facets of originality, complexity, aesthetics and values to a person's mental and experiential life. Openness is shown to be the trait that accounts for most individual differences in personality. Individuals with a high level of this trait are those who take the time to learn something new because of their joy for learning and look for stimulating activities to break up their routine. Artistic expressions and tendencies are attributed to openness, as are long-term education and research. At the low end, we find conservative attitudes and preferences in relation to politics, social behaviour and life in general.

Another contributor to organizational culture is the national culture of employees. Research identified general characteristics of such cultures that lie along different

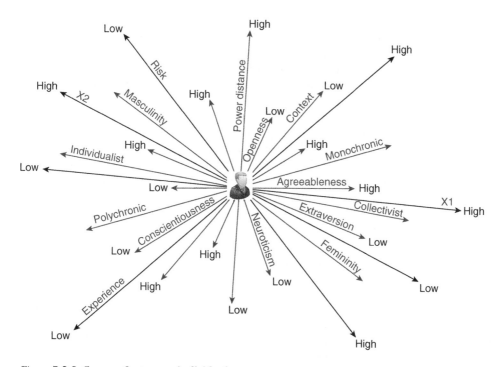

Figure 7.3 Influence factors on individuals

dimensions. A classical breakdown of national cultures types includes the following five dimensions (see Figure 7.3):

- *Individualist/collectivist*: this refers to the degree by which the common values and beliefs of the community emphasize the needs of the individual instead of the needs of the group. In an individualistic culture, there is an emphasis on personal needs and goals, regardless of whether they negotiate for themselves or for the group. In a collectivist culture, the goals of the individuals are aligned with the other members of the group and, when negotiating, they will consider the impact of their actions on the group, and any personal gain should not be perceived as a threat to group norms.
- *Power-distance*: this is a measure of the perception of, and attitude towards, authority and power. A characteristic of high power-distance cultures is a strong sense of hierarchy with set rules of communications and decision making between different levels of the hierarchy. In lower power-distance cultures, although social status differences exist, people are less receptive to the differences, and power and social status are considered equal in negotiations.
- *Masculinity/femininity*: this refers to the importance of masculine characteristics like achievement and material orientation in the culture versus feminine characteristics like the quality of life of people and the relationships between them.
- *Monochronic/polychronic*: this describes the degree of structure we impose on our lives in relation to time. In unstructured/polychronic cultures, people tend to involve themselves in parallel activities with many more people, while in very structured/monochronic cultures, people tend to focus on one activity at a time and only involve people related to this activity. While polychronic cultures may seem chaotic, it is actually that culture's outlook on life that is different. In essence, polychronic cultures live for the present, while monochronic cultures live for the future. In literature, polychronic cultures are referred to as having a non-linear perception of time, while monochronic cultures have a more linear perception of time.
- *Context*: this is a measure of the richness that is expected in communication messages in order to form appropriate perceptions. In high context cultures, the context of a message is interpreted within the context of its transmission as shaped by its environment. This includes the physical environment and the social environment with its power relationships and roles, in addition to the economic and political environment in which communication takes place. High context cultures require more than textual information in order to fully process messages, meaning that social cues like facial expressions and body language play a significant part in forming perceptions. In low context cultures, the content of a textual message carries most of the information required to form an accurate perception.

In addition to the personality and cultural (national) influences on an individual's behaviour, there are situational factors (see Figure 7.3) like the nature of the problem or situation that an individual might be facing, the risk involved, the amount of training required to address the challenge, the stakeholders' interests and influence, etc. Superimposing the circle of influence from Chapter 5 onto Figure 7.3, we can see the relationship between the personality, culture and situational factors as the sources of influence upon a decision maker. As individuals mature, their internal components

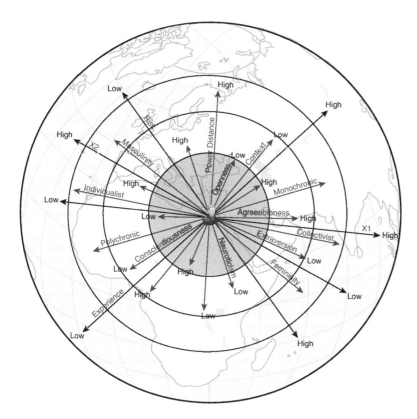

Figure 7.4 Predominant behavioural factors at an instance in time

become more solidified and difficult to change (for example, personality forms early on in childhood). Knowing this can be very useful for leaders as they can focus on what they can control and change, whilst being aware of their 'shortcomings' ('challenges' is probably a more politically correct term).

Knowing how individuals are affected by their environment helps us understand how they contribute to their organizational cultures. Today, the traditional composition of organizational cultures is heavily challenged by an unprecedented level of diversity in the workforce. With respect to gender, there are more women than ever before, now comprising almost 50 per cent of the workforce, and many of them are young and have children. This percentage is bound to increase in executive positions as their value and worth gradually gains acceptance. In terms of age, the increase in the retirement age and harsher economic conditions have driven even retired people to seek work to supplement their income, which results in a multigenerational workforce with occasionally up to four generations working side by side. Racial and ethnic differences also seem to be of less importance as migration levels are greater than ever and the demand for talent knows no boundaries.

In addition to these factors (as we will also see later on), the workforce experiences a new type of employee unlike anyone else: the virtual employee. Anyone with access to the internet can contribute to product and service development and to any other organizational function (the exceptions being manufacturing and production) that does not require physical presence. These employees can offer organizations cost savings and access to talent, but they pose significant challenges, like integration and engagement with the existing workforce.

Although these changing workforce demographics contribute to organizational diversity, they do not guarantee that their potential is captured to the advantage of the organization. In fact, in many situations, organizational cultures don't seem to be able to adjust to the new realities, as they are not inclusive enough to handle diversity. These types of organizational cultures fail to realize that talent has no age, gender, race, religion or ethnicity and that if they don't capture it, there will be others that will do so. This might not be the case for virtual employees, as many of the differences that contribute to diversity disappear in the online world. In addition to talent, a diverse workforce can provide insights into a more widespread customer base, contribute new ideas and viewpoints, and offer solutions to highly complex problems that arise from today's turbulent and uncertain operational environments.

Despite the efforts of leaders enforcing the culture they perceive as appropriate for their organizations, they might fail for a variety of reasons. Allowing too much complacency is a common error, as it does not contribute to a sense of urgency and will almost certainly delay workforce integration. Failing to create buy-in, at least from a core group or from the leadership team, that will work in overcoming organizational inertia and opposition is another reason why culture change initiatives might fail. This is also the reason why the removal of obstacles (whether perceived or actual) might fail. Cohesive core teams that are committed and enthusiastic are alert enough to appreciate and anticipate obstacles early enough for them to be removed and to prevent employees from slipping back into old habits.

To overcome the aforementioned causes of failure, leaders can invest in communicating the power of vision that guides the culture change. Employees will follow someone they believe will lead them to a better place, so leaders have to sell them a vision that will result in feasible and realistic benefits. A successfully communicated vision about a required culture change will align and inspire the actions of employees in terms of working towards the change. Another helpful tactic is to create short-term wins. This helps to create the feeling that half the battle is won and that the change is feasible. Culture transformations take years to achieve and employees might become dispirited if they do not see some concrete signs of progress. However, caution should be exercised, as declaring victory too soon will lose credibility when challenges arise – which is almost inevitable.

Addressing the challenges of assimilating and managing diversity, leaders might be required to demonstrate their commitment to protect it and cultivate an environment where it can thrive as a main contributor to organizational growth. In order for diversity to work to an organization's advantage, it would have to be seen as a strategic imperative completely independent of any legal and moral obligation, otherwise it will just be a compliance issue and an obstacle to growth.

7.3 Entrepreneurial leadership

Operating in a competitive and changing environment is difficult for some, but it could be quite familiar for others. This special breed of individuals includes entrepreneurs who function in unchartered territory, sometimes creating something out

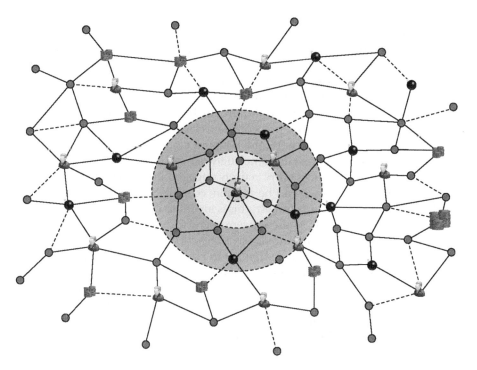

Figure 7.5 The business world from the perspective of the entrepreneur

of nothing and in an environment where one would think there was nothing more to create. The steps required for the development of an entrepreneur have been extensively analysed and presented in numerous research publications and, in summary, we can say they involve the following: opportunity identification; outsourcing of resources for the formation of a business and exploitation of an opportunity. Entrepreneurs are members of their societies and the world at large, and in that sense they live and interact with individuals, organizations and the market. If we visualize the world of the business as composed of different entities that include people, resources and opportunities (Figure 7.5), we can form a network of nodes and connections that at each point in time can represent the position and status (internal capital) of an individual in relation to this abstract world/market representation.

Some of the nodes could represent personal attributes such as intelligence, courage, persistence, will and drive, while others could represent resources that entrepreneurs can utilize, such as money, experience and their network of family members, friends, professional acquaintances and even organizations. To organize the environment into categories, consenting regions around the entrepreneur are used as an approximation of their internal and inherent characteristics and values (the innermost circle – no internal structure is shown due to limited size), their close family and friends circle that they regularly interact with (the middle circle) and their expanded network of acquaintances and resources they have established in their life up to that point (the outermost circle). Outside these regions lies the vastly unexplored region of global resources and connections that to some extent may be visible to the entrepreneur but not yet attained.

In this representation, success (coins in the image) and failure (black bombs) are also included as nodes in the entrepreneurial space. Obviously one could add many more different types of symbols and connectors that could represent every possible aspect and entity that might exist in the world of an entrepreneur, but for the purposes of the analysis here, the elements chosen are adequate for now. Connections between nodes will be used to easily display influence and dependencies either formed (solid lines) or in progress/potential (dotted lines) and will in general form the sphere of influence of the individual. Again, the different attributes of the lines (such as thickness and colour) could be used to represent finer classifications for the connectors, but for our simplified version used here, the adopted ones will suffice.

The extent of the entrepreneur's influence network can be seen as the space within the possible networks that connect every actively engaged individual and resource of the business world we live in or could be influenced physically and conceptually by the individual entrepreneur. Conceptually, this is meant to indicate that nodes can be created or removed dynamically as the entrepreneur formulates ideas and relationships between other entities and resources. An alternative visual representation would be to think of it as a wetland that one attempts to cross by throwing stepping stones in the water to form pathways to dry spots until one reaches one's destination. In that type of representation, an opportunity is any path that connects the entrepreneur to success, which is nothing other than wealth creation according to the definition adopted in this book. Apparently there can be many or no opportunities based on the availability of paths, but intuitively we can see that the denser the network,

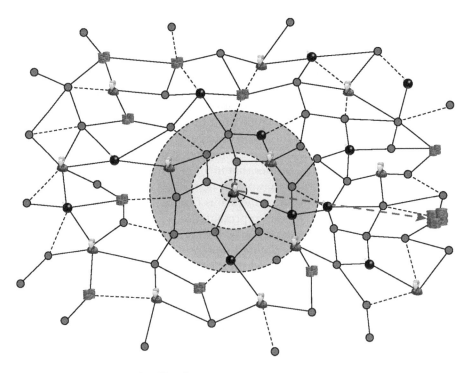

Figure 7.6 Opportunity identification

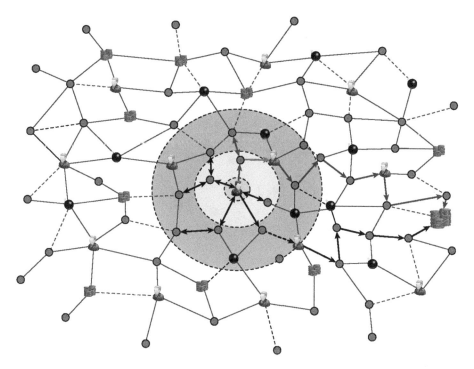

Figure 7.7 The pathway to success

the stronger the possibility of paths that could lead to success. In fact, the denser network would most likely ensure that multiple opportunities are available and within the reach of the entrepreneur.

Let's assume for our purposes that Figure 7.6 depicts the identification of an opportunity by an entrepreneur outside their sphere of influence. Having spotted the opportunity, the entrepreneur now begins to visualize possible pathways (or stepping stones) they might follow to reach it. Visualizing a solid destination route (the arrows in Figure 7.7) is vital for success as the wrong paths could lead to dead ends or, even worse, failure. In fact, there could be more than one path to reach the destination, but eventually the entrepreneur will decide on the one that appears most efficient in terms of the resources it involves, the people it connects and the distance it covers.

Identifying the stepping stones should be seen as a dynamic process that evolves over time. At each stepping stone, the entrepreneur would have to visualize the potential pathways for the remaining part of the route and to choose the optimum ones they believe will get them to their destination. Often they will need to backtrack and follow alternative routes, while at other times they might even need to build new stepping stones to reach their destination. Eventually one of these pathways will appeal to them for some reason or another and will become their choice of action.

This is where things get interesting, as the entrepreneur in essence solves problems along the way, exploring the space around them and establishing shortcuts (Figure 7.8) that will allow them to grasp the opportunity faster and more efficiently. This is the

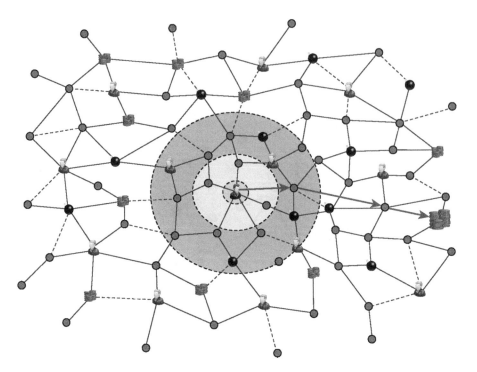

Figure 7.8 Building shortcuts to success

actual process of building their organization until finally they have developed a profitable product or service. Eventually a direct link to success (Figure 7.9) is established. At that point, the creation process is complete and will give way to managing the entities that comprise the venture and streamlining its operations.

While the situation shown in Figure 7.9 establishes a successful entrepreneur, it is the process that proves entrepreneurial attitudes and, as such, there will at times be failures, while at other times ideas will remain as a concept on the drawing board. In fact, one could say that for most people, it will remain just a dream that formed at some time or another and never managed to materialize. This could be due to a lack of a strong vision or resources (both physical and spiritual), or even an inadequate extended network that could provide a pathway to success. Regardless of the reasons, failures will be there. But for the successful entrepreneur, these will be more like opportunities for learning than irreversible obstacles in the way of their passion for success.

If we were to view the exploitation process over time, it would look like pieces (entities and resources) coming together one after another, forming the firm up to the point of the first production and delivery of the product or service that the opportunity represented (Figure 7.10). Through the timeline, the potential for profit moves up and down as we get closer to the final goal and according to the achievements, missteps and breakthroughs that the entrepreneurial team faced and overcame in its path. Recalling the diamond probe we introduced at the beginning of the chapter,

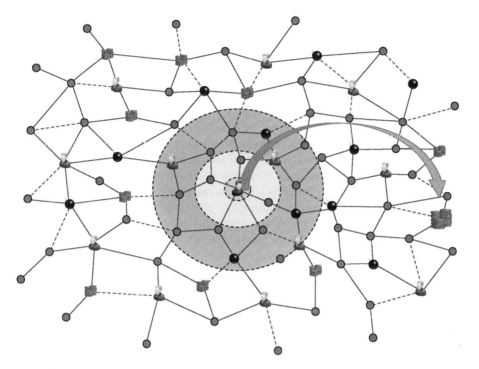

Figure 7.9 Maturing into success

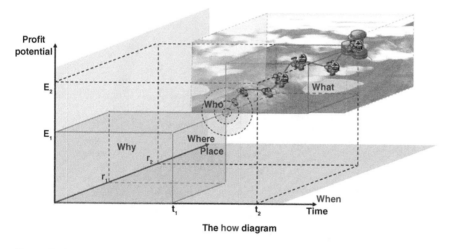

Figure 7.10 The evolution of the exploitation process

the entrepreneurial timeline in Figure 7.10 is a description of 'What' takes place (orthogonal parallelepiped) in a time/'When' (horizontal axis) and place/'Where' (horizontal axis). 'Who' refers to the entities involved in the process, while 'Why' is the past of the entrepreneur that led them to the point in time when the exploitation of the opportunity process began.

Bringing everything together, we can summarize the answers to the aspects of Figure 7.10:

- 'When': entrepreneurs are constantly searching for opportunities. Given their availability and market conditions, a potential opportunity will come into focus and become the exploitation target.
- 'Where': this is directly linked to 'When' and refers to the geographical and virtual places where all the action took place.
- 'Who': starting with the entrepreneur who just decided to exploit an opportunity and an initial core of human and physical resources they believe are required for the realization of the venture, we move along the time and space dimensions building the entrepreneurial team. Customers are virtual in the process and are physically attached to the venture as it begins operating in the market.
- 'What': while many actions are common, like the build-up of the team, ensuring financial support and dealing with the legal and operational aspects of the new venture, some might be product- or service-specific.
- 'How': the decision-making process – everything we have mentioned up to now in this chapter.
- 'Why': the motivations and rationale behind intentions and actions that lead to decisions.

Moving from entrepreneurship to multipreneurship, we need to assemble everything we have presented so far and, considering the theoretical findings present in the research literature, build a possible model of entrepreneurship. Combining

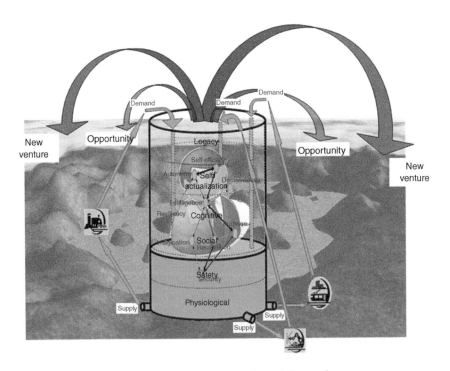

Figure 7.11 Converting opportunities into supply and demand streams

the various concepts we brought together in explaining entrepreneurship, we can extrapolate their features and derive the visualization of leaders as entrepreneurs in Figure 7.11. As the image shows, we see the exploration and exploitation process that is enabled by the network of qualities, attributes and external entities of leaders/entrepreneurs and, through the principles of supply and demand, enables the exchange of internal capital that leads to a steady surplus for the entrepreneur. The attraction to diversification seem to be intrinsic in the personality of the entrepreneurial leader and its display as they mature, changing from what appeared as a push effect initially to its pure state as a pull effect. The engagement in diversification also implies that entrepreneurs have high levels of tolerance in terms of enduring the difficulties of setting up a firm and can effectively leverage their past accomplishments.

Entrepreneurial drives

The drives behind the choice to become self-employed and venturing into entrepreneurship/leadership can be different for each individual and can be affected by personality traits and the environment in which the individual lives and operates (Figure 7.12). In general, we tend to have two categories of factors that drive entrepreneurship: the positive ('pull' factors) and the negative ('push' factors). One can be attracted/pulled to an activity or forced/pushed to engage out of necessity. Well-known factors that attract someone to entrepreneurship include the need to be independent and in control, to secure an income, the potential to exploit a market opportunity for profit, tradition, the joy of creating something new and even an attempt to seek excitement. Factors that 'push' someone towards entrepreneurial behaviour include unemployment, the need to secure a viable income and a lack of flexibility and alternatives, among others. Tradition (inheriting a family business) is another factor that, depending on the person and the situation, can make the engagement either attractive or necessary.

Three main drivers have been identified that cover to varying degrees the growth initiatives in every case of entrepreneurial leadership: *security, fulfilment* and *excitement.* Security is evident in low-level entrepreneurs and essentially, in their case, diversification aims at sustaining one's income during fluctuations of the micro-business

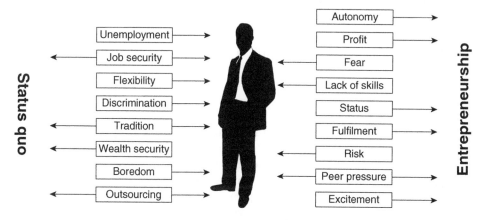

Figure 7.12 Pull and push entrepreneurial drives

environment. In the same way as a restaurant with a single item on the menu has less chance of success, an entrepreneur focusing on one type of business is solely dependent on the behaviour of the market segment that their product or service targets. Staying focused on one industry exposes an entrepreneur to competition from existing and new entrants, changing customer needs and preferences, and the political, social and economic environment that influences that market. Low-level entrepreneurship is dominant in many poor countries around the world and in economies with high unemployment rates. Although in these cases entrepreneurship is triggered by the need to ensure survival more than anything else, one cannot ignore the growth and excitement factors at least in their more basic forms.

At the higher level of entrepreneurship, although growing through diversification might count as an attempt to secure one's welfare level and fortune (an indication of mature entrepreneurs), the drive for fulfilment is dominant. Entrepreneurs and conglomerate organizations are drawn by a vision to reach the highest levels of success in the business world. They achieve this by forming strong entities that cross national boundaries and cultures. Forming a business empire is similar in terms of motivation and drive to the expansion tendencies of the great historical empires – it's just that the field happens to be a different one. The market as the terrain of business and economic activity has a different nature from the geographical terrain into which the old empires were seeking to expand. The terrain is now shaped by consumers and its hills and valleys represent their capabilities to buy and consume.

Fulfilment comes from a sense of destiny and it appears to be prevalent in high-profile entrepreneurs, in many cases going back a generation. It creates a sense of continuity between the past, present and future, and acts as a primal drive pushing entrepreneurs ahead. It is clearly reflected in the aspirations and spirit of their family and the lessons and inspiration they drew from their parents. It gives them the satisfaction that they have performed their duty, the origins of which can be traced to their parents and the role models of their childhood and early adulthood.

Excitement, on the other hand, is expressed in two ways in their level. One includes the excitement involved in creating a new business, while the other refers to the excitement of producing a certain product or service (which is the case for technology entrepreneurs). Creating a new business is like any form of creation that is naturally satisfying in itself. Rewards are easy to see and feel; they engage other people and they expand the physical and emotional space. However, creating a product or service where none existed before is a different feeling and involves the excitement of the discoverer and pioneer. This is a primal kind of excitement, which is purely emotional and levitating, and involves the thrill of adventure and exploration.

Entrepreneurial skills

A typical question that arises in academic research is whether repeat entrepreneurial performance is due to innate talent or the accumulation of entrepreneurial experience. This debate is apparently in relation to market context rather than anything else as the more one is engaging in a particular market, the more experience one acquires, the easier it will be to deal with familiar problems specific to the nature of the particular market. In our case of entrepreneurs, though, the market specifics are of little influence since the individuals venture into diverse markets and so one would expect that a different element needs to be involved. The primary candidate for that role is talent. The question is: talent in what?

Looking at the skills that successful entrepreneurs have might provide part of the answer. Skills that are considered essential include, among others, the ability to network with other individuals, financial and government establishments; an understanding of how organizations function and perform; and a good understanding of the generic market mechanisms with the consumers and their communities. Other skills, such as understanding financial statements and negotiating deals, might also be essential.

Of great importance is the fit between the business venture and personality of the entrepreneur. It is evident from their backgrounds and styles that the business ideas of entrepreneurs seem to match their personalities. For example, if we were to read the childhood and early adulthood of the high-profile entrepreneurs like Elon Musk and then be presented with a list of business types, it is highly likely that we would match the entrepreneurs with their real businesses correctly. Although this might sound obvious here, in real life, mismatches are a major reason for why failures occur. This proves the point that knowing who you are and going after the things you like are vital for achieving success in life.

An entrepreneurial skill that occasionally shows up in the literature and that one would expect to see in entrepreneurs is empathy. As part of emotional intelligence, empathy is a characteristic that great leaders display; high-profile entrepreneurs are, in many respects, great leaders, so one would naturally expect that they will be high on empathy. This is also expected primarily because the sense of knowing the customer and providing accordingly is often expressed through an understanding of the customer's position as a human being with needs and wants. While this does exist in entrepreneurs and is especially expressed during a firm's genesis, later on it is expressed more on an intellectual or market-driven level rather than on the personal level that has been theorized to exist. It is true that entrepreneurs build things and provide services that satisfy the needs of people, but this is purely on the basis of receiving a return in exchange, which is something that people with high empathy generally do not expect.

An undeniable skill for entrepreneurs is expertise in executing their plans. Entrepreneurs tend to be exceptional at this and in that respect they are excellent project managers. The main difference from that group is the personal stand they take towards risk, as a project manager tends to be on the risk-adverse side of things. Firm formation always involves risk and entrepreneurs seem to feel quite comfortable taking risks. While normal entrepreneurs seem to have gone through the risk-taking phase and to have settled after their firm reached maturity, multipreneurs are comfortable with (and even at times 'drawn to') risk and view it as a natural part of the business formation process. Risk is higher at the start-up phase and reduces as a firm reaches maturity. The type of risk is also different during the various stages of firm growth. At the beginning and in the aftermath of the exploration phase, the entrepreneurial team is young and the venture idea has not yet crystallized, resulting in an internal/organizational form of risk that team dynamics create. Later on, when the firm reaches maturity, the nature of the risk becomes more external as organizational performance is more affected by the social and market environment in which it operates. Multipreneurs are quite comfortable with the crisis management type of risk and, as such, they outperform others in the first category of risk at the start-up phase. This enables them to engage in diverse ventures again and again. For the second/ external type of risk, they seem to delegate control to subordinates who they leave in charge of their established firms and intervene only in the face of crisis.

A side-effect of risk-taking that is often ignored by theorists and practitioners, especially those involved in policy making, is the high probability of failure (see Figure 7.13). By their very nature, multipreneurs engage in diverge ventures that involve different industries and, as such, this is like starting from the beginning, at least with respect to learning the specifics of an industry. One can easily see that run-ning an airline is different from running a restaurant or developing a microwave. Multipreneurs are bound to fail, but this certainty appears normal to them and they see it in a completely different light – as a learning experience. Of course, as a child perfectly knows by instinct, falling is the only way to learn how to walk, and in that sense falling is not a failure, but is part of learning how to stand up. Multipreneurs seem to have retained that aspect of learning and they are quite tolerant to failure.

The entrepreneurial leader model

Replacing 'venture' with 'goal' we can develop an appropriate model for an entre-preneurial leader. Combining the arsenal of skills we described before and fuelled by their motivation drivers, entrepreneurial leaders engage in their primary activities – opportunity identification and risk-taking. Intuition and a calculative methodology are their allies in this process. The rewards from risk-taking and the return on invest-ment they enjoy as a result allow such leaders to break away from stagnation and continue on their entrepreneurial path. This process brings with it the possibility of failure in forthcoming goals. This is where entrepreneurial leaders excel by manag-ing to engage their support network and dissipating the risk across their connections. However, the difference between them and the average leader is that they don't really do that in an attempt to minimize risk to themselves, but mainly to ensure that it is minimized with respect to the endeavour. For that reason, they make sure they have the support of a strong and committed team, as well as placing an unparalleled value on execution. Strong teams for entrepreneurial leaders are more like strong alliances that are respected and valued. As such, entrepreneurial leaders are not afraid to share their earnings with those who have helped them build their organizations, whether these are team members, other businessmen, politicians or supporters. In doing so, they ensure their future support, an investment they will cash in on in the form of success in new goals.

Having ensured the successful flow of value from one goal, entrepreneurial lead-ers turn their attention to new opportunities. If they discover promising ones, they engage in forming new goals to exploit them. Some of these will fail, but some will be successful and will become part of the profile of the entrepreneurial leader. At this stage, as we saw in the previous chapters, the entrepreneurial leader effectively closes the circle of supply and demand that related to the opportunity (Figure 7.13). The situation will repeat itself for as long as the 'glass of self-actualization' has room to fill and time doesn't run out.

Internally, we can say that there is a conversion process, where the benefits of the effective supply and demand circles of the established goals are converted into new

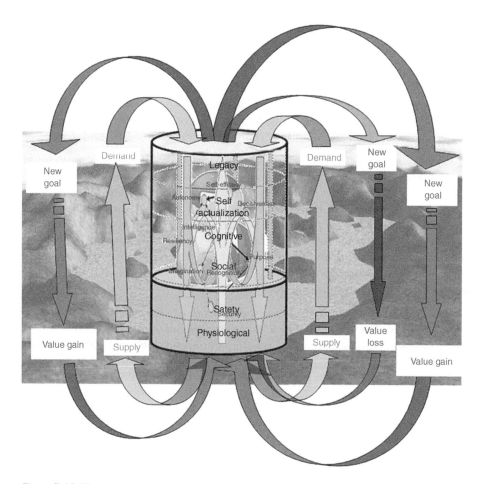

Figure 7.13 The entrepreneurial leader model

goal streams. Some of them will succeed and in this way will be converted to efficient supply and demand circles, while others will fail, weakening the established supply and demand cycles. The advantage for entrepreneurial leaders is that they can convert failure into learning that strengthens their internal network of skills and attributes, and can be used to raise the probability of success in future opportunity exploitation cycles.

7.4 Leadership life hacks?

Most searches for leadership on the internet nowadays produce results that give a 'how to' list of how one can become a great leader. Unfortunately, leadership is not like cooking, where following a sequence of steps in a recipe results in delicious food, provided one has the basic skills for cooking. While 'how to' lists can occasionally serve an inspirational purpose, they do express some well-known and commonly accepted realities. Having resisted the temptation to devise such a list in this book up to now, it is nevertheless important to sum up some key points that should have become apparent by this stage. The below points should be seen as subjective and a sample, and not as an ultimate and exhaustive collection of what could be:

Leadership is a lot (really a lot) of hard work. Leaders need to keep themselves updated with the latest developments in their field and nowadays, due to the disruptive nature of the market, the latest developments in others fields too. This requires a lifelong commitment to studying, supplemented by a lifelong commitment to acquiring new skills as simple as thumb texting on a mobile phone to applying complicated financial calculations and planning complicated processes and strategies.

Self-esteem is more important than self-confidence. People usually find it easier to build their self-confidence than their self-esteem and, conflating one with the other, may end up with a long list of abilities and achievements. Rather than facing up to their imperfections and failures, they hide them behind their certificates and prizes. However, a long list of abilities and achievements is neither sufficient nor necessary for healthy self-esteem. While people keep on working on their list in the hope that it might one day be long enough, they try to fill the emptiness inside them with status, income, possessions, relationships, sex and so on. Achievements and intelligence are no substitute for wisdom.

Dialogue adds more value than discussions and certainly more than debates. Dialogue shapes points of view by mutually reaching a common ground that could be closer to that of one of the participants. In dialogue, one submits one's best thinking, expecting that other people's reflections will help improve it rather than threaten it. In dialogue, one listens to understand, to make meaning and to find common ground. Discussions are less aggressive processes for discovering the truth than debates, where one aggressively defends assumptions as truth in order to ensure victory. They don't achieve solutions as effectively as dialogue does, as the focus is on the flaws and differences of positions.

From time to time, conduct a personal SWOT and PEST analyses. The world has been loaded with information that, in most instances, is noise. Leaders need to be able to distinguish the signal from the noise in the information flood around them. This requires the ability to concentrate and focus on demand so that they can screen the information they receive for the gold nuggets of quality that are necessary for solving the problem or issue they are facing. When this isn't enough, they need to be able to exercise their influence and engage their network of collaborators and affiliates to receive the added knowledge and expertise they miss.

Change is the norm. The future will definitely pose challenges, but for today's leaders. change in all forms is a reality. Change might include different geographical locations where a leader might have to engage, changes in job description, changes in outcomes like moving from success to failure and bouncing back, and changes of perspective, among others. In order to survive in such an environment, leaders need to be alert of present trends, to anticipate future ones, and to develop an adaptive mindset to easily assimilate the realities of situations while exercising critical thinking and insight.

Appreciate questions more than answers. In a world that doesn't change, answers are gold, but in a world that changes, existing answers will not work for new problems.

Questions that help to focus attention and effort on the direction to follow in order to find solutions are more valuable. Questions invite a different and more powerful form of participation. It's no longer just about spreading the word and persuading others – it's about inviting others to explore a new domain and to help generate new ideas and insights. Leaders can become mobilizers, helping to draw in new people and creating environments where people can connect and explore an evolving agenda of questions. The most powerful networks would take the form of creation spaces that support the formation of tightly knit teams and then connect these teams in a broader space where they can seek out help from each other.

Copy and paste and paraphrase (ideas and best practices). There is no need to re-invent the wheel. The competition is not about originality of ideas and leadership practices – it is about the organization's growth in accordance to its vision and mission. Paraphrasing is critical here as what might work in one situation for one organization might need a certain amount of adaptation in order to work for another.

The normal distribution rules but does not dominate. This is meant to mean that while cultures are different, people are different, etc., there are differences in behaviour and character within social and professional groups. This is also the truth about everything around us. Not everyone is smart and there is always someone smarter and more capable than us. If you are dealing with a conservative culture, it doesn't mean that the person you are talking to is conservative. If you are dealing with a culture where discipline is valued, it doesn't mean that the person you are working with is disciplined. In other words, stereotypes reflect the opinion or perceptions of 68 per cent of the population (if that is even true); there will still be a significant percentage of the population that doesn't fit the stereotype (Figure 7.14).

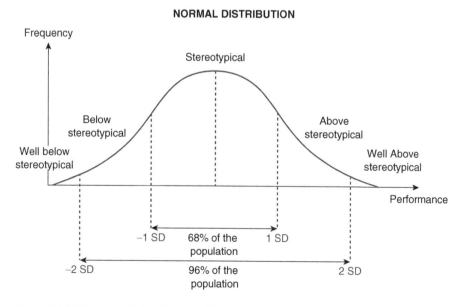

Figure 7.14 The normal distribution of stereotypes

All decisions are influenced by emotions. We are chemically based decision support systems, so the elementary/atomic blocks of our constitution are chemicals. Prominent among these are the neurotransmitters that regulate the communication between neurons in our brain and hormones that regulate our bodies. If any of these categories doesn't work properly, we won't be able to be successful in terms of our decision making. Both systems are interrelated as they affect each other, but one way to distinguish between the two is that neurotransmitters mediate the flow of information between neurons, while hormones mediate communication from out brain to our body cells. Excluding our genetic predisposition, which we currently cannot control, we need to be cautious of the effects of poor diet, stress and addictions (substance abuse and/or compulsive behaviour) that can affect the levels of neurotransmitters and hormones and, as a result, our mental capability to properly process information communicated to our brain and body.

Being a good leader doesn't mean you will continue to be a good leader. Anyone can be a leader in the right circumstances with the right upbringing, the right mentoring, the right coaching, the right personality, the right training, the right education, the right skills, the right intelligence, the right wisdom, etc.

If you are not discouraged yet about the leader's job description, go back to the first life hack, otherwise exit (humour sustains sanity even in the worst situations).

Bibliography

Alimo-Metcalfe, B., & Alban-Metcalfe, J. (2005). Leadership: Time for a new direction? *Leadership, 1*(1), 51–71.

Anantatmula, V. S. (2010). Project manager leadership role in improving project performance. *Engineering Management Journal, 22*(1), 13–22.

Ashmos, D. P., & Duchon, D. (2000). Spirituality at work: A conceptualization and measure. *Journal of Management Inquiry, 9*(2), 134–145.

Avolio, B. J., Bass, B. M., & Jung, D. I. (1999). Re-examining the components of transformational and transactional leadership using the Multifactor Leadership. *Journal of Occupational and Organizational Psychology, 72*(4), 441–462.

Bass, B. M. (1991). From transactional to transformational leadership: Learning to share the vision. *Organizational Dynamics, 18*(3), 19–31.

Bass, B. M. (1997). Does the transactional–transformational leadership paradigm transcend organizational and national boundaries? *American Psychologist, 52*(2), 130.

Bass, B. M. (1999). Two decades of research and development in transformational leadership. *European Journal of Work and Organizational Psychology, 8*(1), 9–32.

Bolden, R., & Gosling, J. (2006). Leadership competencies: Time to change the tune? *Leadership, 2*(2), 147–163.

Chemers, M., & Skrzypek, G. (1972). Experimental test of the contingency model of leadership effectiveness. *Journal of Personality and Social Psychology, 24,* 172–177.

Crevani, L., Lindgren, M., & Packendorff, J. (2007). Shared leadership: A post-heroic perspective on leadership as a collective construction. *International Journal of Leadership Studies, 3*(1), 40–67.

'The Curse of the Superstar CEO' (n.d.). Retrieved 9 October 2014, from http://hbr.org/2002/09/the-curse-of-the-superstar-ceo/ar/1. Ferreira, P. G. S., Lima, E. P. de, & da Costa, S. E. G. (2012). Perception of virtual team's performance: A multinational exercise. *International Journal of Production Economics, 140*(1), 416–430.

Fiedler, F. E., & Garcia, J. E. (1987), *New approaches to effective leadership effectiveness: Cognitive resources and organizational performance.* New York: Wiley.

Fiore, S. M., & Salas, E. (2002). The role of shared cognition in enabling shared leadership and team adaptability. In C. L. Pearce & J. A. Conger (Eds.), *Shared leadership: Reframing the hows and whys of leadership* (pp. 103–122). London: Sage

Fisher, D. H., & Fowler, S. B. (1995). Reimagining moral leadership in business. *Business Ethics Quarterly, 5*(1), 29–42.

Halkias, D., Santora, J., Harkiolakis, N., & Thurman, P. (2017). *Leadership and change management: A cross-cultural perspective.* Abingdon: Routledge.

Harkiolakis, N. (2014). *Multipreneurship: Diversification in times of crisis.* Farnham: Gower.

Harkiolakis, N., Halkias D., & Abadir, S. (2012). *E-negotiations in cross-cultural business settings.* Farnham: Gower.

House, R. J., & Mitchell, T. R. (1975). *Path-goal theory of leadership.* DTIC Document.

Kayworth, T. R., & Leidner, D. E. (2002). Leadership effectiveness in global virtual teams. *Journal of Management Information Systems, 18*(3), 7–40.

Kellerman, B. (2004). Thinking about . . . leadership: Warts and all. *Harvard Business Review, 82*(1), 40–45.

Langowitz, N. S., & Allen, I. E. (2010). Small business leadership: Does being the founder matter? *Journal of Small Business & Entrepreneurship, 23*(1), 53–63.

Levasseur, R. E. (2004). People skills: Change management tools – The modern leadership model. *Interfaces, 34*(2), 147–148.

Lin, C., Standing, C., & Liu, Y.-C. (2008). A model to develop effective virtual teams. *Decision Support Systems, 45*(4), 1031–1045.

Lindgren, M., & Packendorff, J. (2009). Project leadership revisited: Towards distributed leadership perspectives in project research. *International Journal of Project Organisation and Management, 1*(3), 285–308.

Liu, A., Fellows, R., & Fang, Z. (2003). The power paradigm of project leadership. *Construction Management and Economics, 21*(8), 819–829.

Lord, R. G., De Vader, C. L., & Alliger, G. M. (1986). A meta-analysis of the relation between personality traits and leadership perceptions: An application of validity generalization procedures. *Journal of Applied Psychology, 71*(3), 402–410.

Luthans, F., Norman, S. M., & Hughes, L. (2006). Authentic leadership: A new approach for a new time. In R. J. Burke & C. L. Cooper (Eds.), *Inspiring Leaders* (pp. 84–104). Abingdon: Routledge.

Malhotra, A., Majchrzak, A., & Rosen, B. (2007). Leading virtual teams. *Academy of Management Perspectives, 21*(1), 60–70.

Miller, B. (2000). Spirituality for business leadership. *Journal of Management Inquiry, 9*(2), 132.

Ollila, S. (2000). Creativity and innovativeness through reflective project leadership. *Creativity and Innovation Management, 9*(3), 195–200.

Payne, S. (2010). Leadership and spirituality: Business in the USA. *International Journal of Leadership in Public Services, 6*(2), 68–72.

Pieterse, A. N., Knippenberg, D. van, & Dierendonck, D. van. (2012). Cultural diversity and team performance: The role of team member goal orientation. *Academy of Management Journal.* doi:10.5465/amj.2010.0992

Prince, E. T. (2008). Business acumen: A critical concern of modern leadership development: Global trends accelerate the move away from traditional approaches. *Human Resource Management International Digest, 16*(6), 6–9.

Quan, J. (2008). Evaluating e-business leadership and its link to firm performance. *Journal of Global Information Management, 16*(2), 81–90.

Rae, D., Price, L., Bosworth, G., & Parkinson, P. (2012). Business inspiration: Small business leadership in recovery? *Industry and Higher Education, 26*(6), 473–489.

Raelin, J. (2011). From leadership-as-practice to leaderful practice. *Leadership, 7*(2), 195–211.

Ruggieri, S. (2009). Leadership in virtual teams: A comparison of transformational and transactional leaders. *Social Behavior and Personality: An International Journal, 37*(8), 1017–1021.

Shachaf, P. (2008). Cultural diversity and information and communication technology impacts on global virtual teams: An exploratory study. *Information & Management, 45*(2), 131–142.

Shamir, B., House, R. J., & Arthur, M. B. (1993). The motivational effects of charismatic leadership: A self-concept based theory. *Organization Science, 4*(4), 577–594.

Shenhar, A. J. (2004). Strategic Project Leadership: Toward a strategic approach to project management. *R&D Management, 34*(5), 569–578.

Smith, G. R. (1999). Project leadership: Why project management alone doesn't work. *Hospital Materiel Management Quarterly, 21*(1), 88–92.

Sorenson, R. L. (2000). The contribution of leadership style and practices to family and business success. *Family Business Review, 13*(3), 183–200.

Spillane, J. P. (2005). Distributed leadership. In *The educational forum* (Vol. 69, pp. 143–150). Abingdon: Taylor & Francis.

Sveningsson, S., & Larsson, M. (2006a). Fantasies of leadership: Identity work. *Leadership, 2*(2), 203–224.

Wikimedia Commons. 'Alexander Mosaic from House of the Faun, Pompeii', https://commons.wikimedia.org/wiki/File:Alexander_(Battle_of_Issus)_Mosaic.jpg. Accessed 26 September 2016.

Yoo, Y., & Alavi, M. (2004). Emergent leadership in virtual teams: What do emergent leaders do? *Information and Organization, 14*(1), 27–58.

Zaccaro, S. J., & Klimoski, R. (2002). The interface of leadership and team processes. *Group & Organization Management, 27*(1), 4–13.

Zigurs, I. (2003). Leadership in virtual teams: Oxymoron or opportunity? *Organizational Dynamics, 31*(4), 339–351.

Index

For Product Safety Concerns and Information please contact our EU
representative GPSR@taylorandfrancis.com Taylor & Francis Verlag GmbH,
Kaufingerstraße 24, 80331 München, Germany

Printed and bound by CPI Group (UK) Ltd, Croydon, CR0 4YY

01/05/2025

01858389-0008